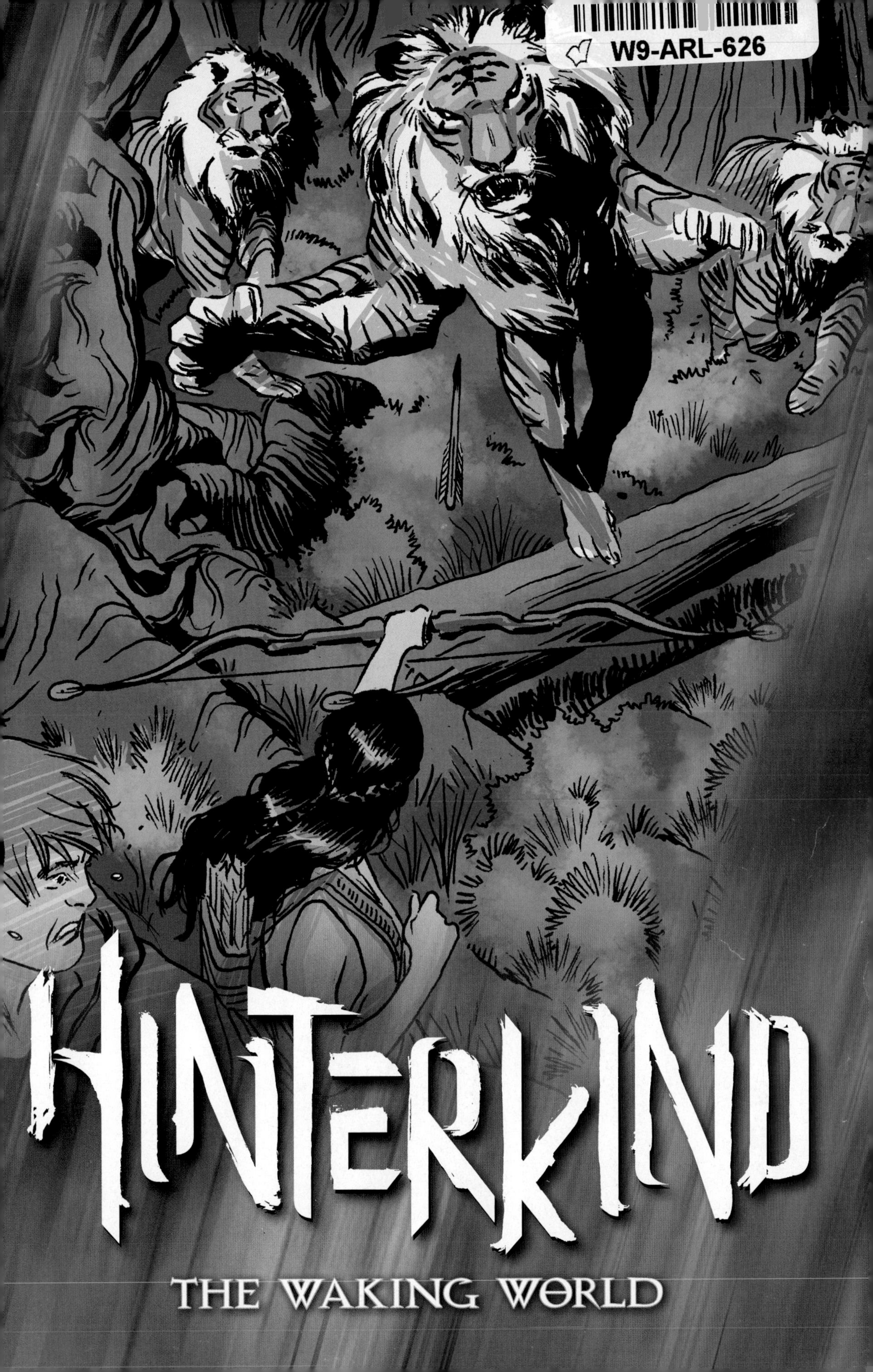

HINTERKIND

THE WAKING WORLD

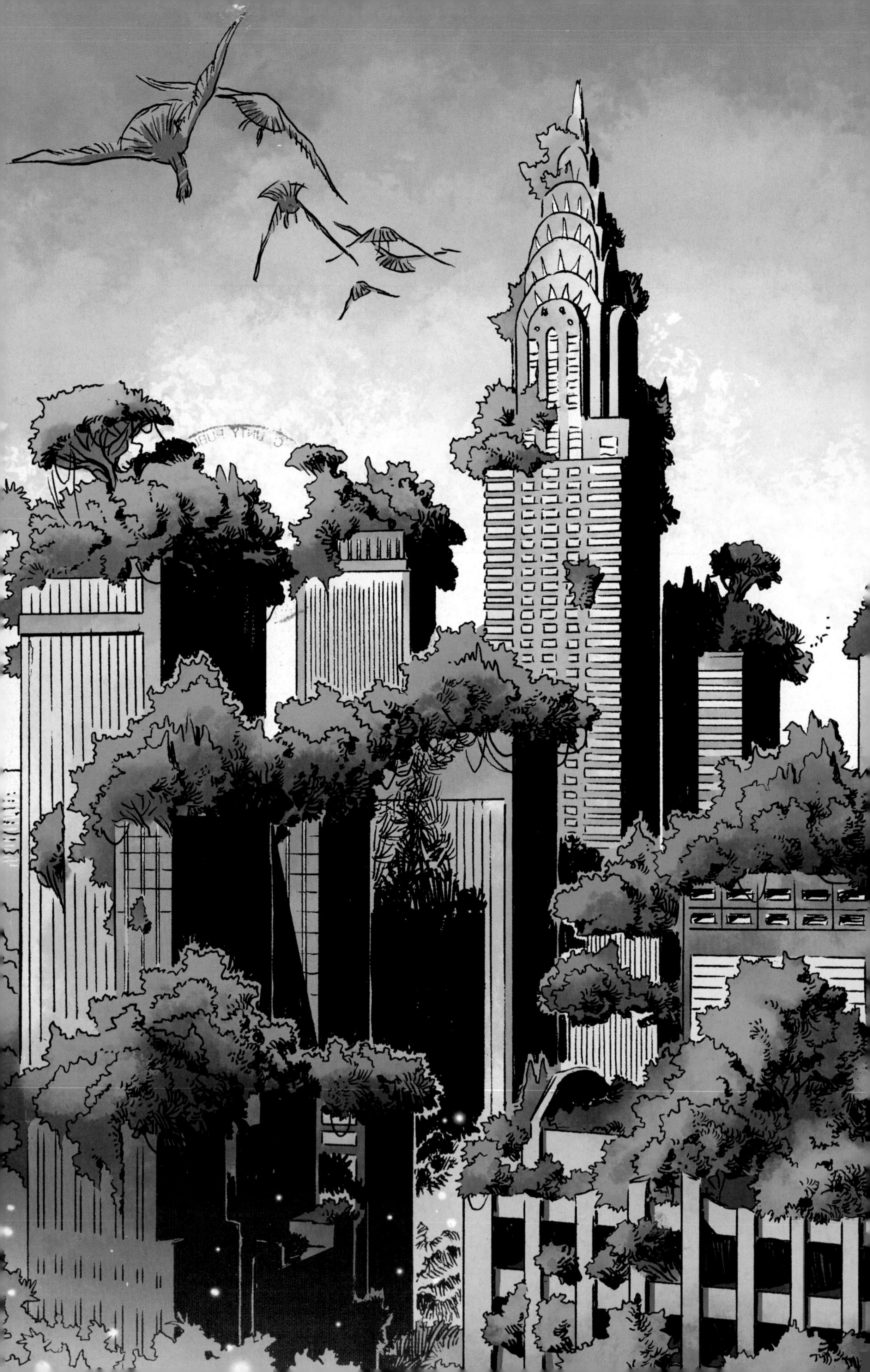

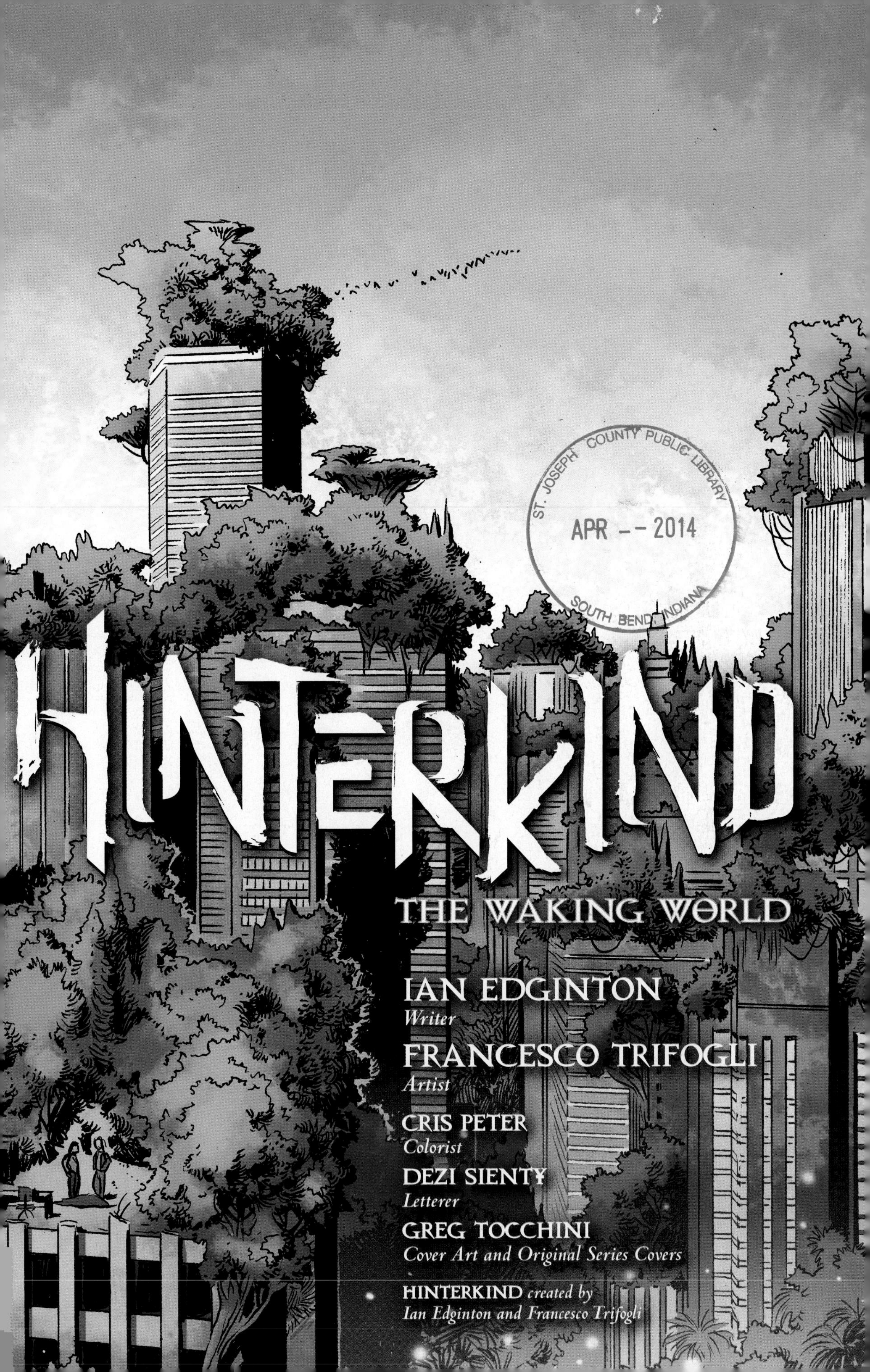

HINTERKIND

THE WAKING WORLD

IAN EDGINTON
Writer

FRANCESCO TRIFOGLI
Artist

CRIS PETER
Colorist

DEZI SIENTY
Letterer

GREG TOCCHINI
Cover Art and Original Series Covers

HINTERKIND *created by*
Ian Edginton and Francesco Trifogli

WILL DENNIS EDITOR – ORIGINAL SERIES
GREGORY LOCKARD ASSOCIATE EDITOR – ORIGINAL SERIES
SARA MILLER ASSISTANT EDITOR – ORIGINAL SERIES
SCOTT NYBAKKEN EDITOR
ROBBIN BROSTERMAN DESIGN DIRECTOR – BOOKS
CURTIS KING JR. PUBLICATION DESIGN

SHELLY BOND EXECUTIVE EDITOR – VERTIGO
HANK KANALZ SENIOR VP – VERTIGO AND INTEGRATED PUBLISHING

DIANE NELSON PRESIDENT
DAN DIDIO AND JIM LEE CO-PUBLISHERS
GEOFF JOHNS CHIEF CREATIVE OFFICER
JOHN ROOD EXECUTIVE VP – SALES,
          MARKETING AND BUSINESS DEVELOPMENT
AMY GENKINS SENIOR VP – BUSINESS AND LEGAL AFFAIRS
NAIRI GARDINER SENIOR VP – FINANCE
JEFF BOISON VP – PUBLISHING PLANNING
MARK CHIARELLO VP – ART DIRECTION AND DESIGN
JOHN CUNNINGHAM VP – MARKETING
TERRI CUNNINGHAM VP – EDITORIAL ADMINISTRATION
ALISON GILL SENIOR VP – MANUFACTURING AND OPERATIONS
JAY KOGAN VP – BUSINESS AND LEGAL AFFAIRS, PUBLISHING
JACK MAHAN VP – BUSINESS AFFAIRS, TALENT
NICK NAPOLITANO VP – MANUFACTURING ADMINISTRATION
SUE POHJA VP – BOOK SALES
COURTNEY SIMMONS SENIOR VP – PUBLICITY
BOB WAYNE SENIOR VP – SALES

DC COMICS, 1700 BROADWAY, NEW YORK, NY 10019
A WARNER BROS. ENTERTAINMENT COMPANY
PRINTED IN THE USA. FIRST PRINTING.
ISBN: 978-1-4012-4518-4

Library of Congress Cataloging-in-Publication Data

Edginton, Ian, author.
  Hinterkind. The Waking World / Ian Edginton ; illustrated by Francesco Trifogli.
    pages cm
  ISBN 978-1-4012-4518-4 (paperback)
  1. Graphic novels. I. Trifogli, Francesco, illustrator. II. Title.
  PN6737.E34H56 2014
  741.5'942—dc23
                          2013049813

SUSTAINABLE
FORESTRY
INITIATIVE

Certified Chain of Custody
At Least 20% Certified Forest Content
www.sfiprogram.org
SFI-01042
APPLIES TO TEXT STOCK ONLY

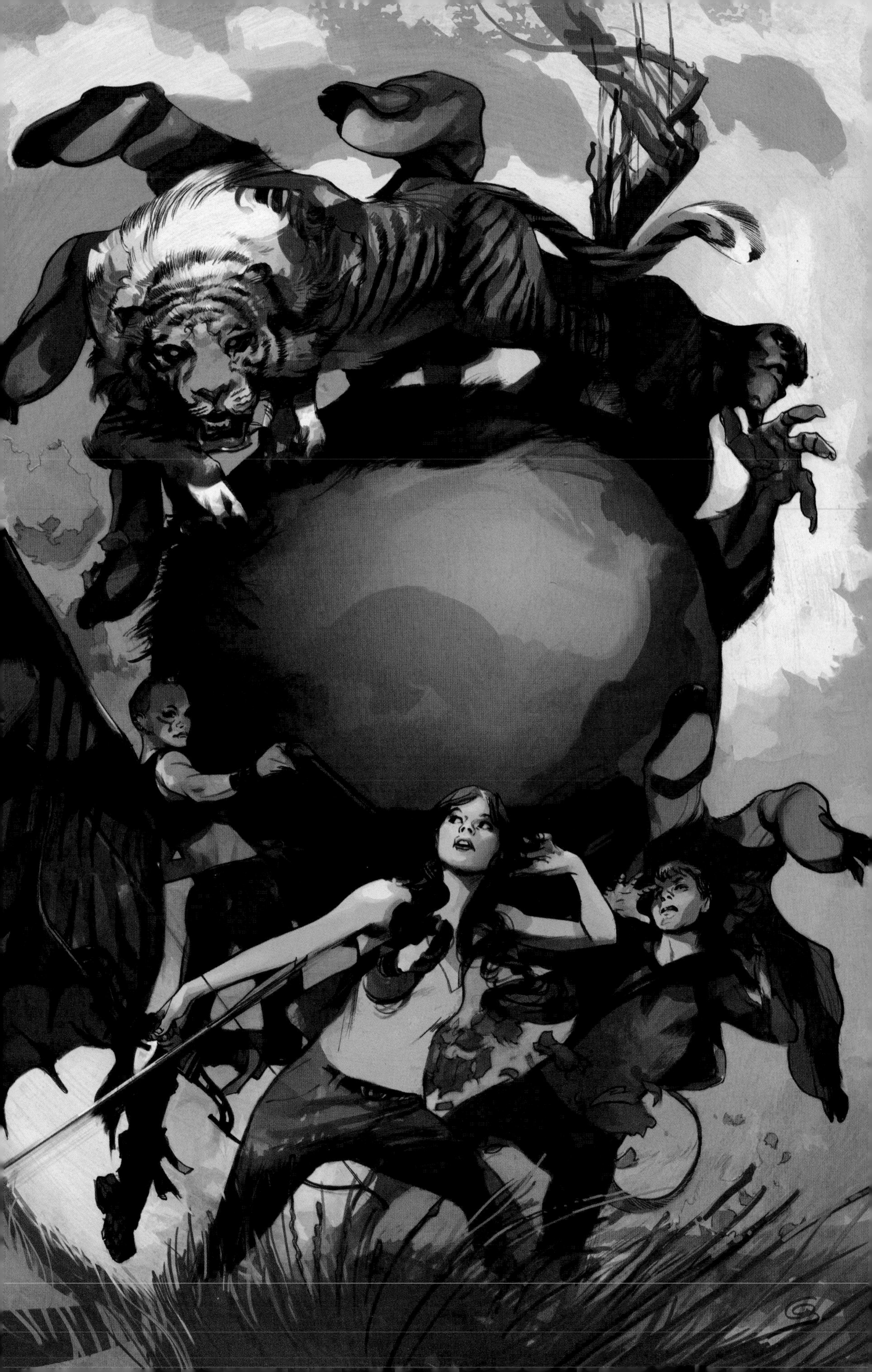

Variant cover art for issue #1 by Jae Lee. Color by June Chung.

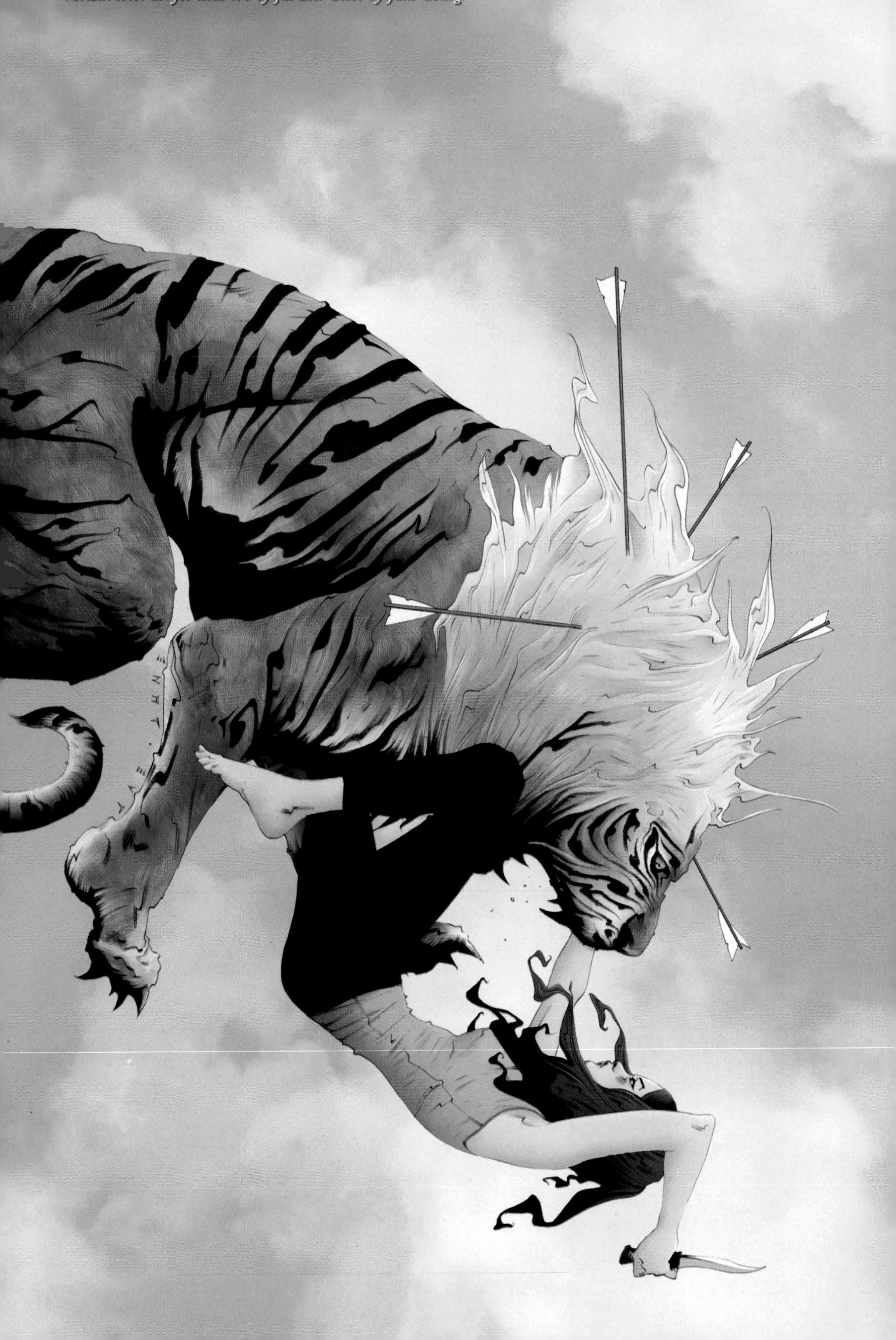

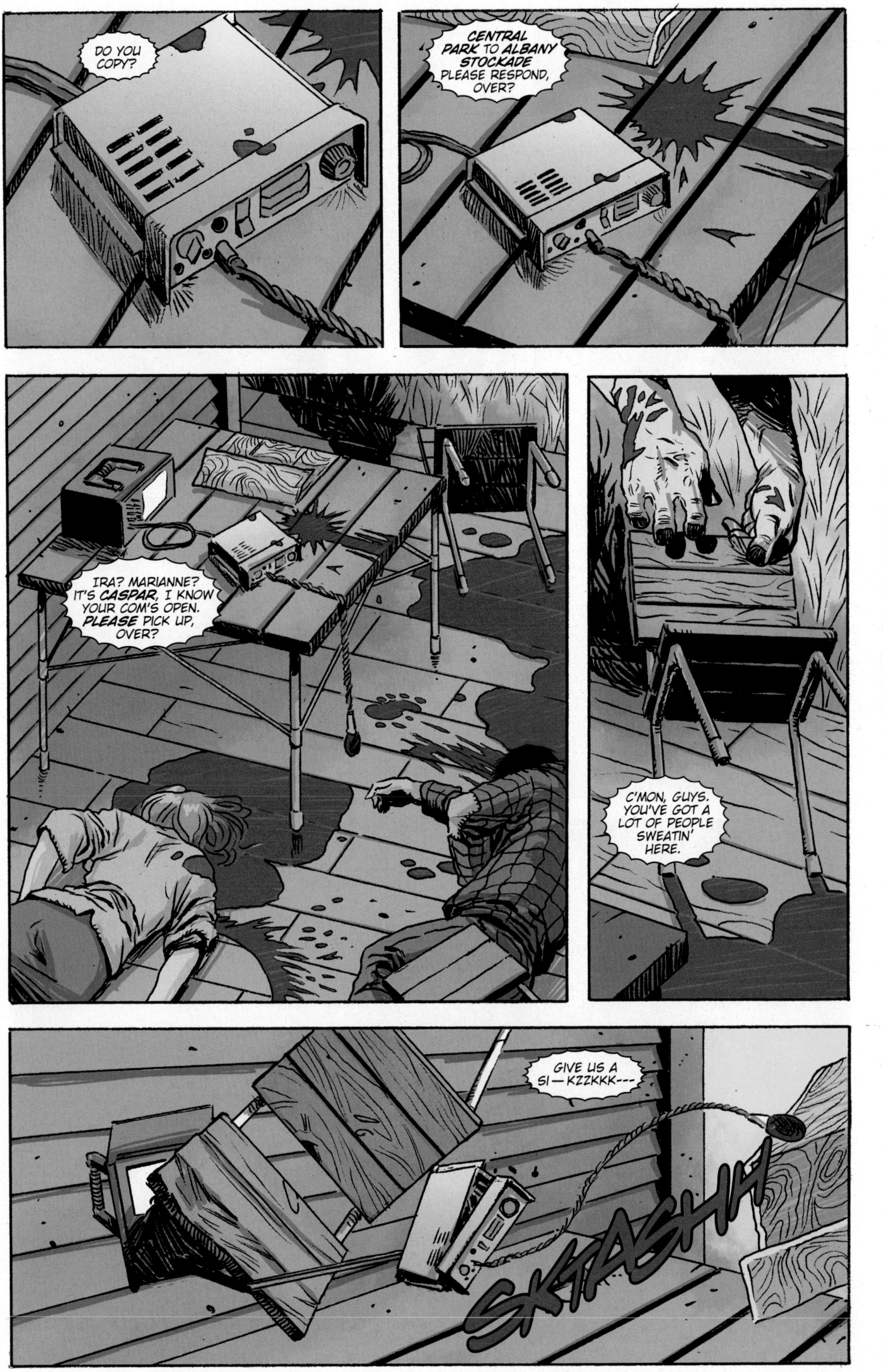
DO YOU COPY?
CENTRAL PARK TO ALBANY STOCKADE PLEASE RESPOND, OVER?
IRA? MARIANNE? IT'S CASPAR, I KNOW YOUR COM'S OPEN. PLEASE PICK UP, OVER?
C'MON, GUYS. YOU'VE GOT A LOT OF PEOPLE SWEATIN' HERE.
GIVE US A SI— KZZKKK---
SKTASHH

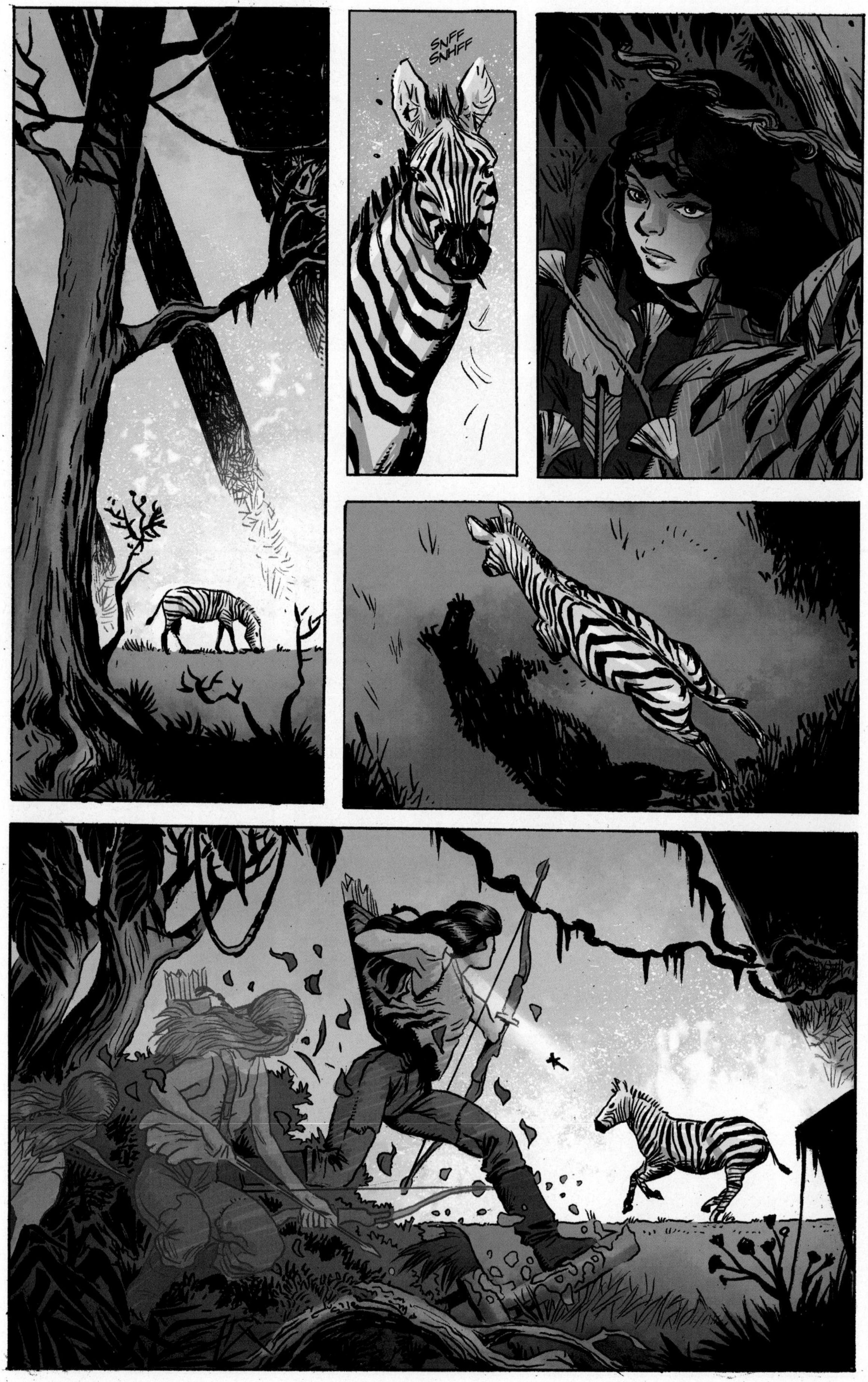
SNFF
SNHFF

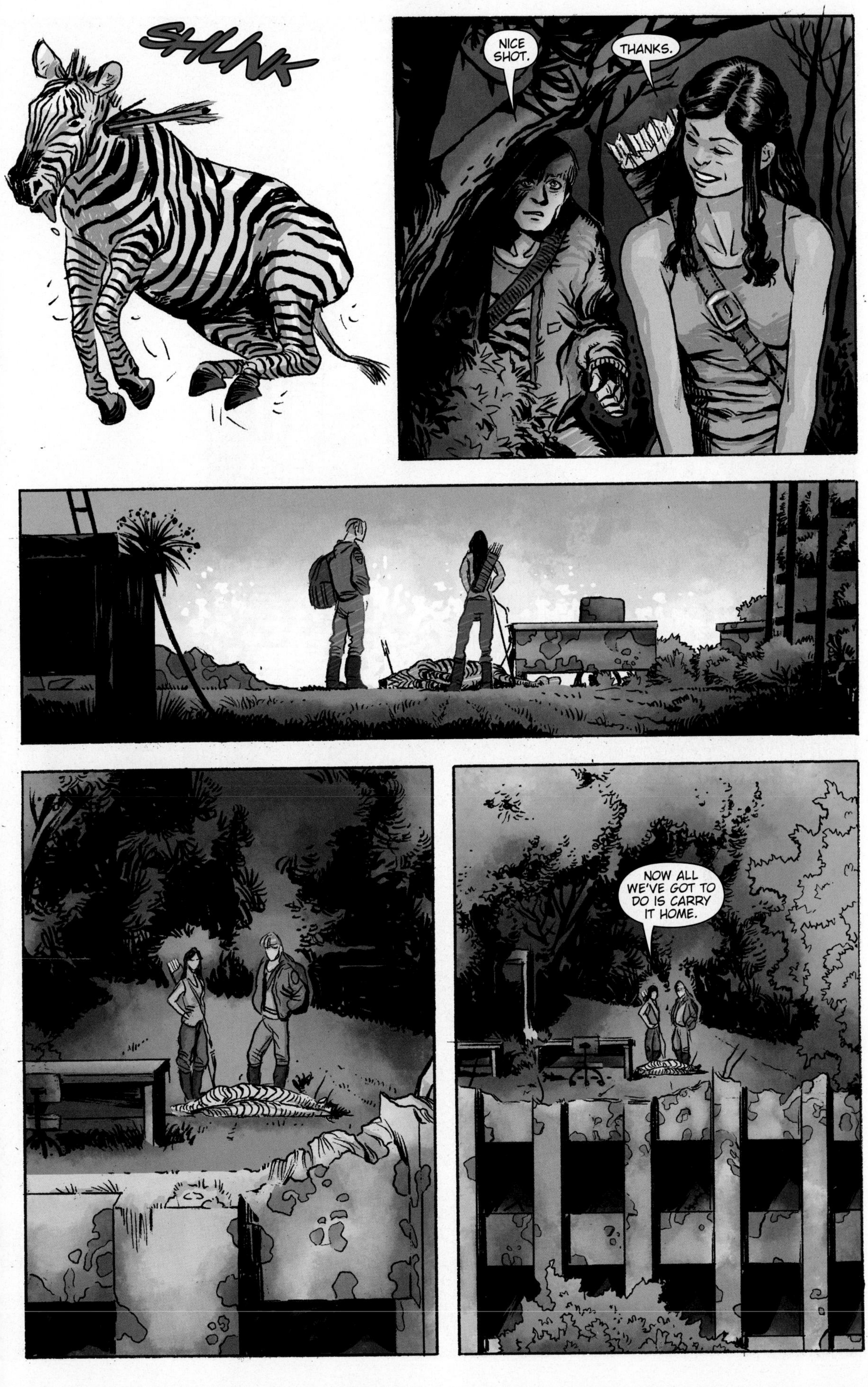
SHUNK
NICE SHOT.
THANKS.
NOW ALL WE'VE GOT TO DO IS CARRY IT HOME.

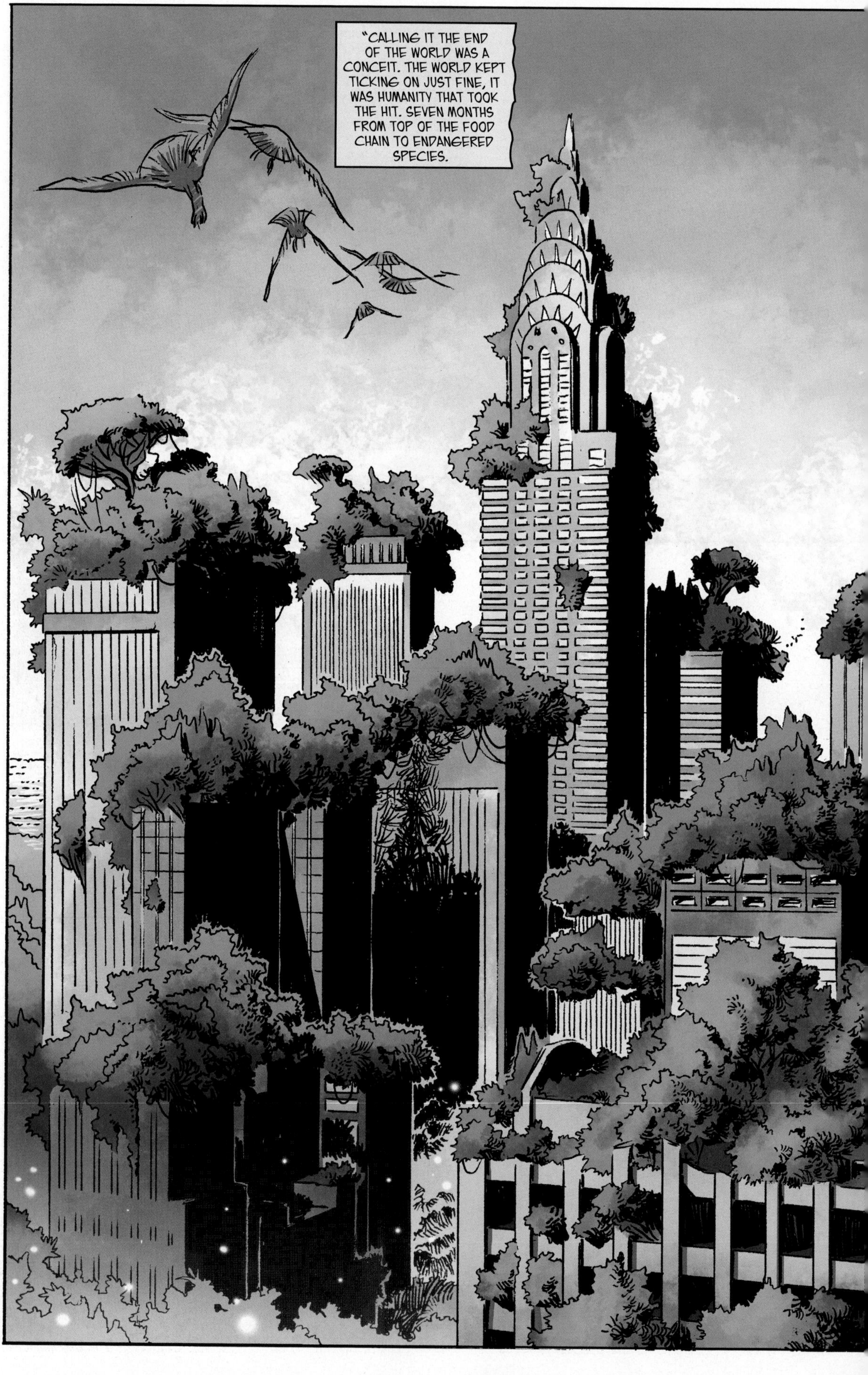
"CALLING IT THE END OF THE WORLD WAS A CONCEIT. THE WORLD KEPT TICKING ON JUST FINE, IT WAS HUMANITY THAT TOOK THE HIT. SEVEN MONTHS FROM TOP OF THE FOOD CHAIN TO ENDANGERED SPECIES.

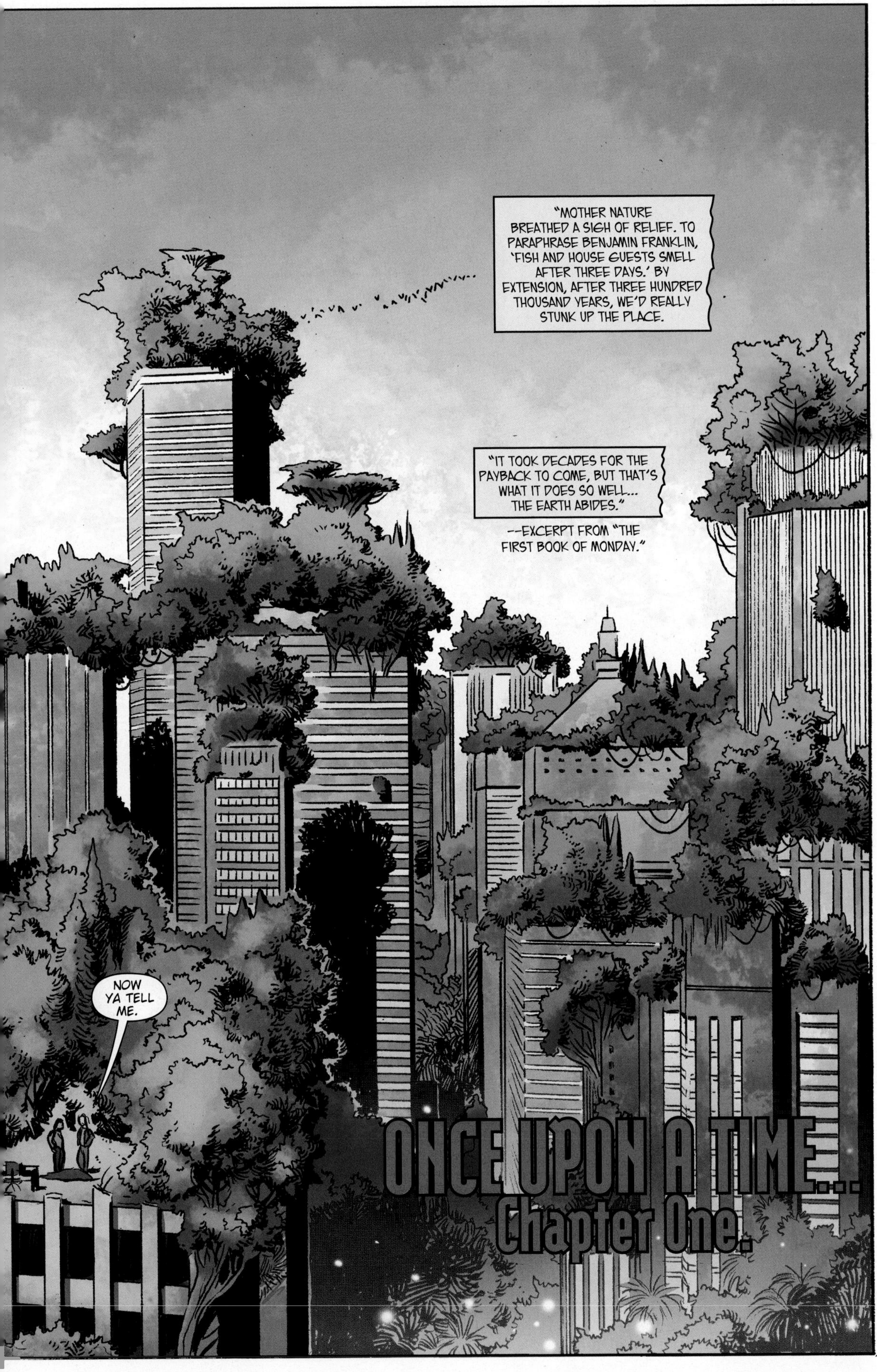
"MOTHER NATURE BREATHED A SIGH OF RELIEF. TO PARAPHRASE BENJAMIN FRANKLIN, 'FISH AND HOUSE GUESTS SMELL AFTER THREE DAYS.' BY EXTENSION, AFTER THREE HUNDRED THOUSAND YEARS, WE'D REALLY STUNK UP THE PLACE.
"IT TOOK DECADES FOR THE PAYBACK TO COME, BUT THAT'S WHAT IT DOES SO WELL... THE EARTH ABIDES."
--EXCERPT FROM "THE FIRST BOOK OF MONDAY."
NOW YA TELL ME.
ONCE UPON A TIME...
Chapter One.

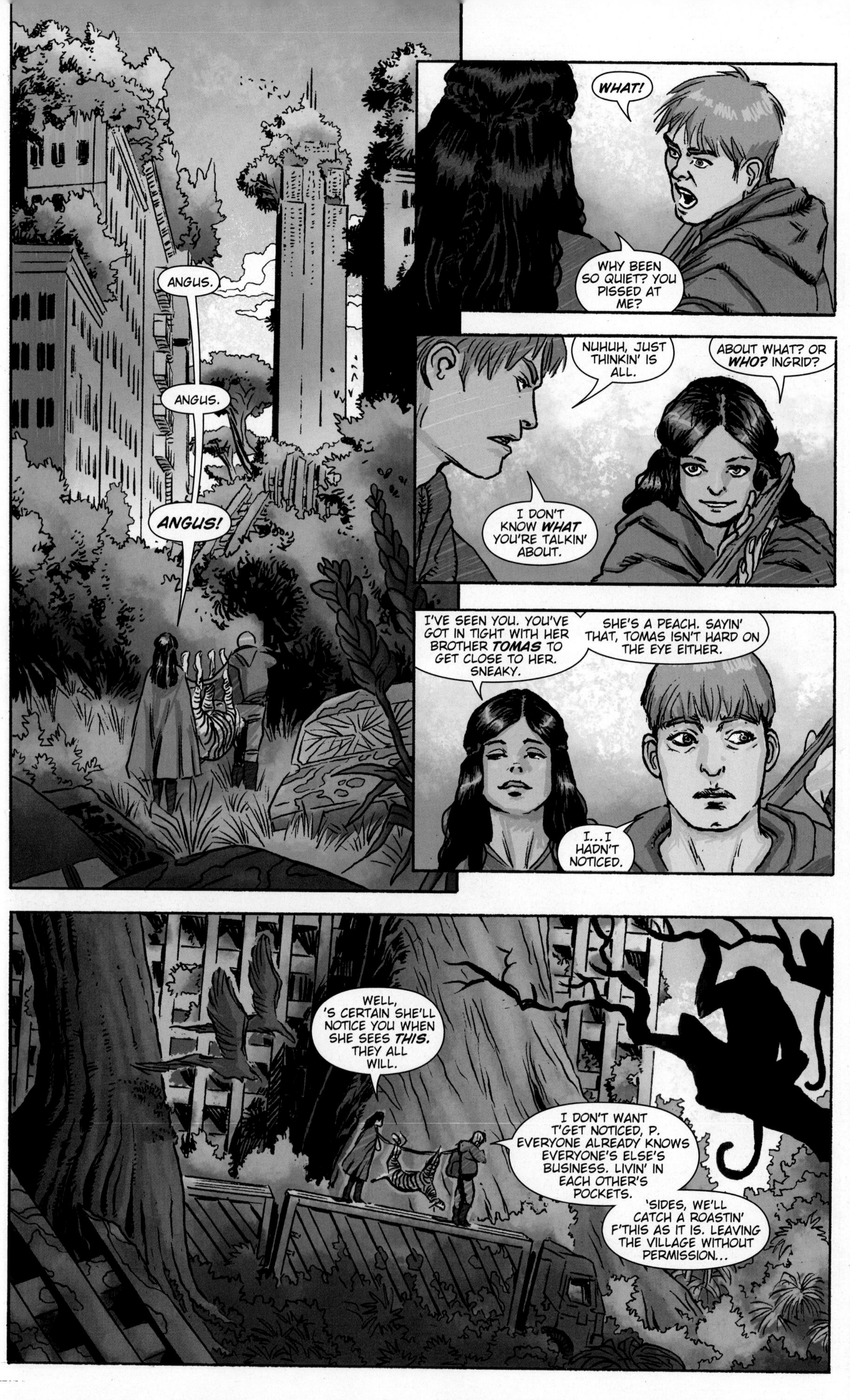
ANGUS.
ANGUS.
ANGUS!
WHAT!
WHY BEEN SO QUIET? YOU PISSED AT ME?
NUHUH, JUST THINKIN' IS ALL.
ABOUT WHAT? OR WHO? INGRID?
I DON'T KNOW WHAT YOU'RE TALKIN' ABOUT.
I'VE SEEN YOU. YOU'VE GOT IN TIGHT WITH HER BROTHER TOMAS TO GET CLOSE TO HER. SNEAKY.
SHE'S A PEACH. SAYIN' THAT, TOMAS ISN'T HARD ON THE EYE EITHER.
I...I HADN'T NOTICED.
WELL, 'S CERTAIN SHE'LL NOTICE YOU WHEN SHE SEES THIS. THEY ALL WILL.
I DON'T WANT T'GET NOTICED, P. EVERYONE ALREADY KNOWS EVERYONE'S ELSE'S BUSINESS. LIVIN' IN EACH OTHER'S POCKETS.
'SIDES, WE'LL CATCH A ROASTIN' F'THIS AS IT IS. LEAVING THE VILLAGE WITHOUT PERMISSION...

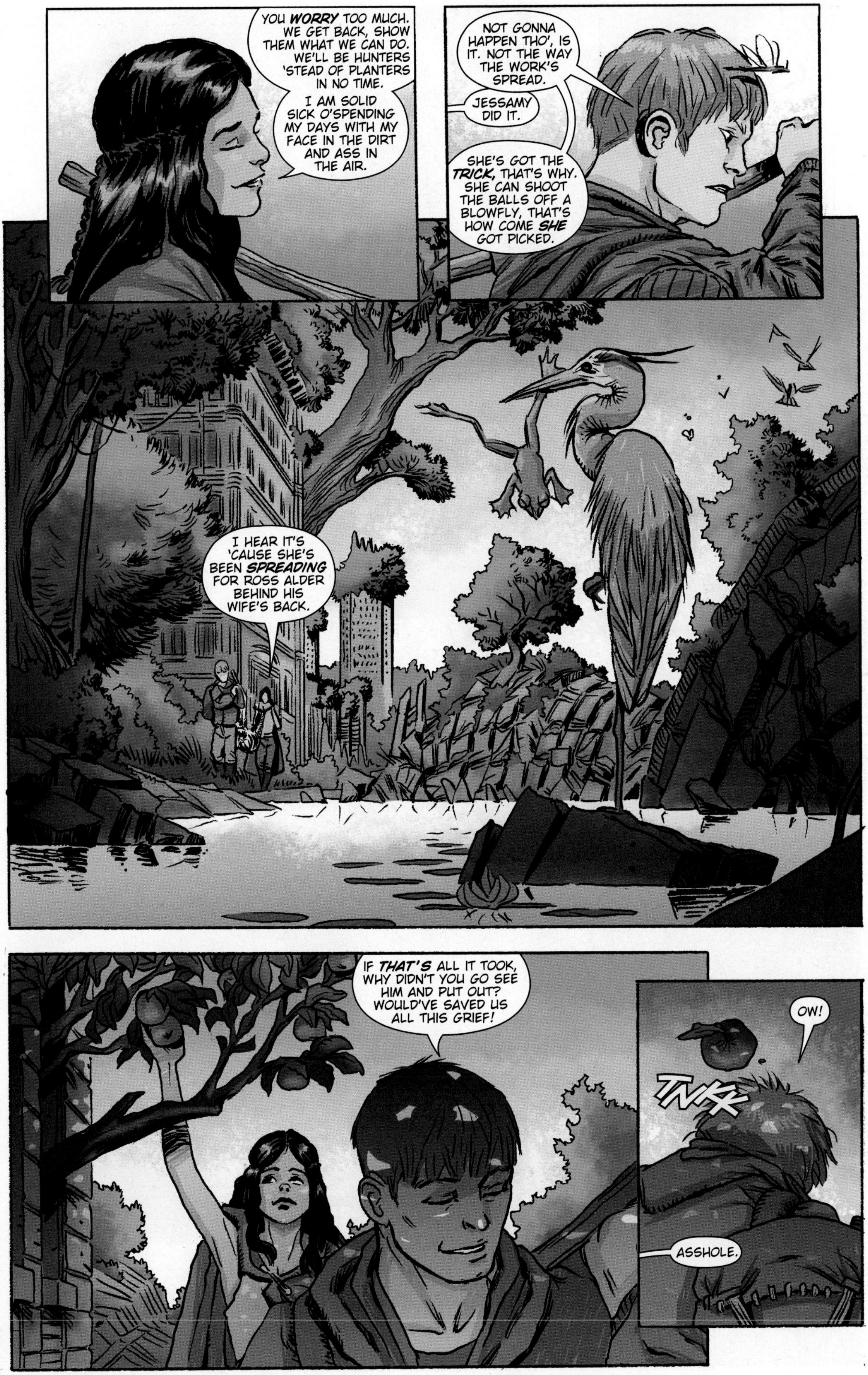
YOU WORRY TOO MUCH. WE GET BACK, SHOW THEM WHAT WE CAN DO. WE'LL BE HUNTERS 'STEAD OF PLANTERS IN NO TIME.
I AM SOLID SICK O'SPENDING MY DAYS WITH MY FACE IN THE DIRT AND ASS IN THE AIR.
NOT GONNA HAPPEN THO', IS IT. NOT THE WAY THE WORK'S SPREAD.
JESSAMY DID IT.
SHE'S GOT THE TRICK, THAT'S WHY. SHE CAN SHOOT THE BALLS OFF A BLOWFLY, THAT'S HOW COME SHE GOT PICKED.
I HEAR IT'S 'CAUSE SHE'S BEEN SPREADING FOR ROSS ALDER BEHIND HIS WIFE'S BACK.
IF THAT'S ALL IT TOOK, WHY DIDN'T YOU GO SEE HIM AND PUT OUT? WOULD'VE SAVED US ALL THIS GRIEF!
OW!
TNKK
ASSHOLE.

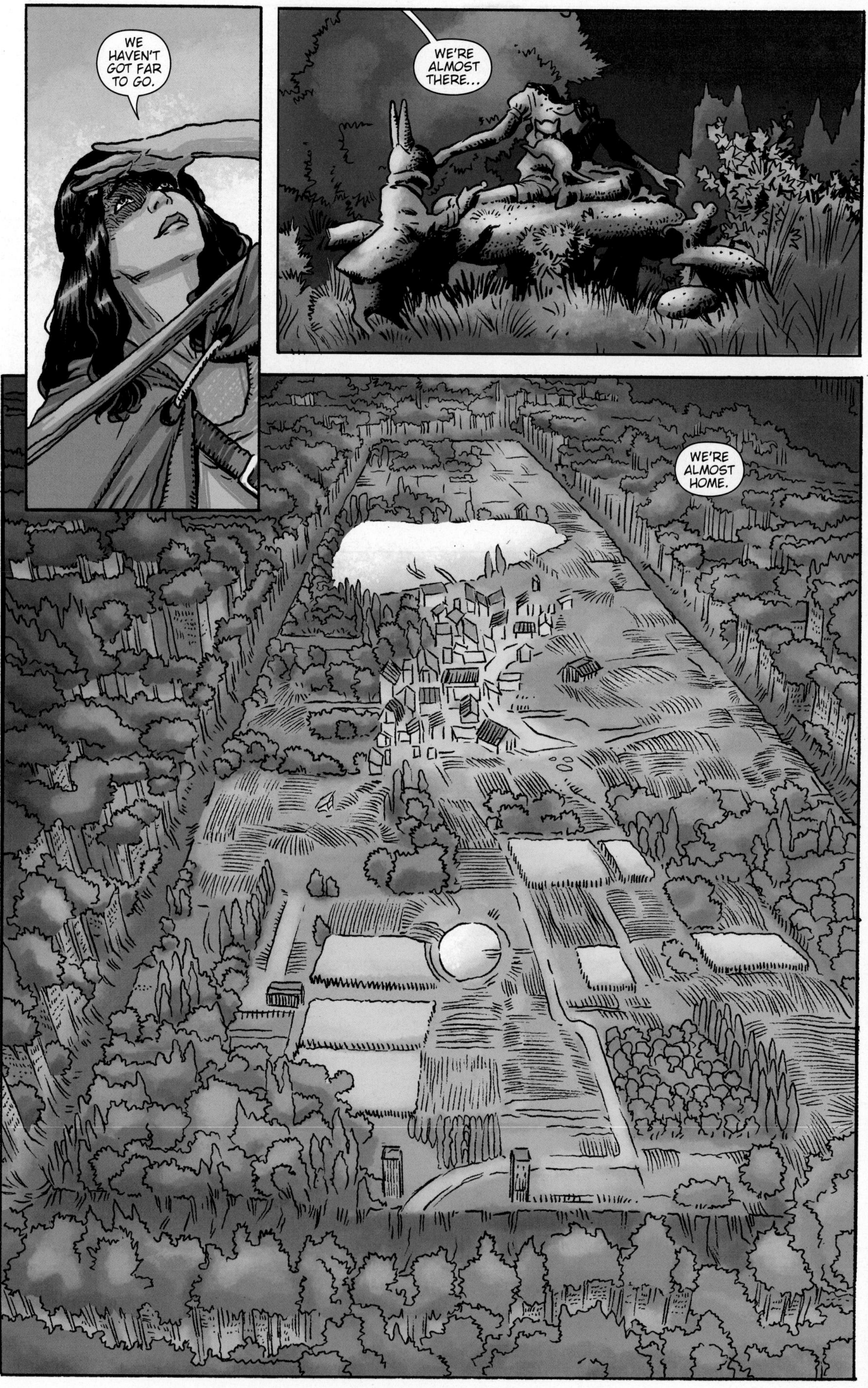
WE HAVEN'T GOT FAR TO GO.
WE'RE ALMOST THERE...
WE'RE ALMOST HOME.

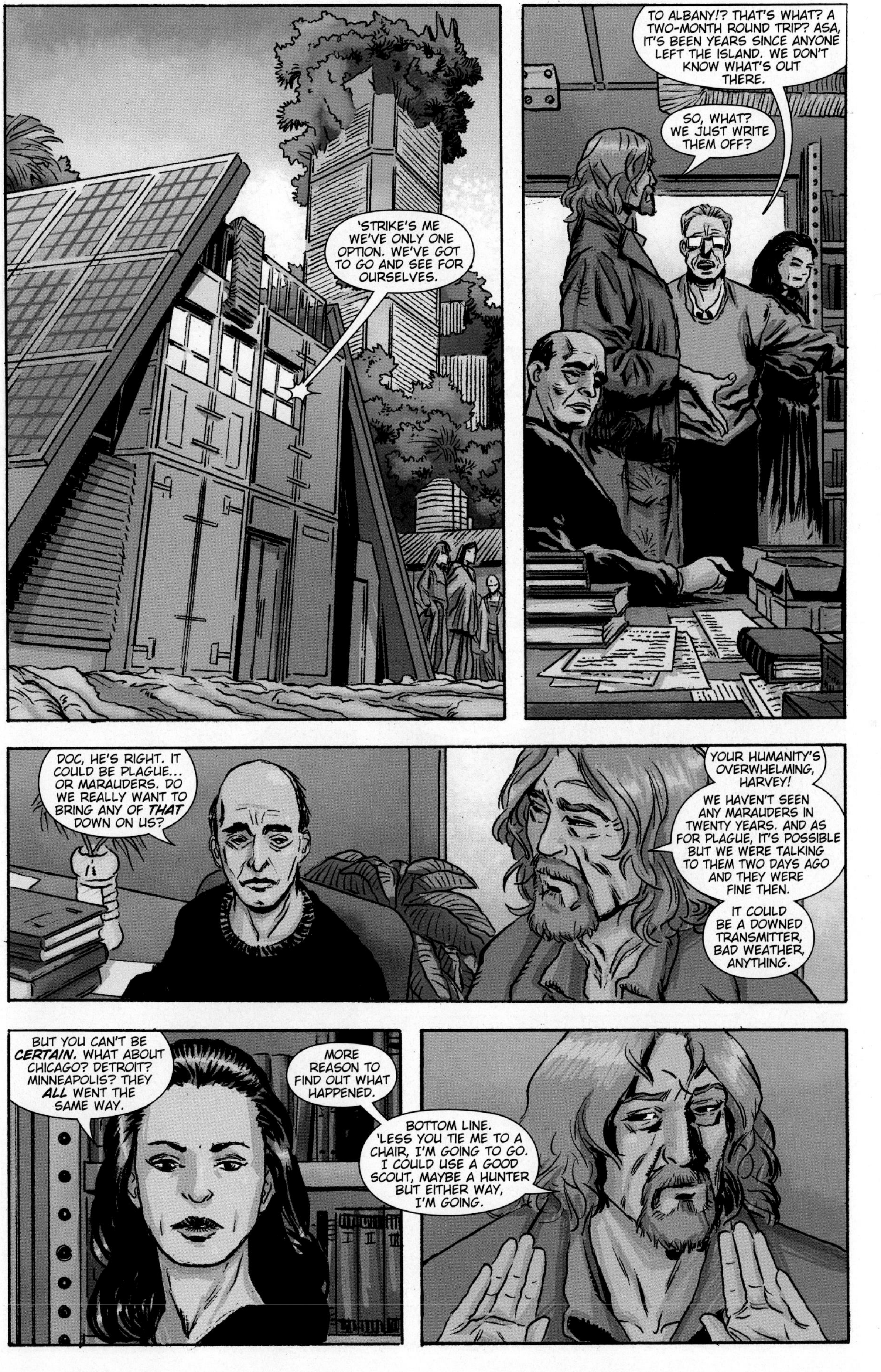
'STRIKE'S ME WE'VE ONLY ONE OPTION. WE'VE GOT TO GO AND SEE FOR OURSELVES.
TO ALBANY!? THAT'S WHAT? A TWO-MONTH ROUND TRIP? ASA, IT'S BEEN YEARS SINCE ANYONE LEFT THE ISLAND. WE DON'T KNOW WHAT'S OUT THERE.
SO, WHAT? WE JUST WRITE THEM OFF?
DOC, HE'S RIGHT. IT COULD BE PLAGUE... OR MARAUDERS. DO WE REALLY WANT TO BRING ANY OF THAT DOWN ON US?
YOUR HUMANITY'S OVERWHELMING, HARVEY!
WE HAVEN'T SEEN ANY MARAUDERS IN TWENTY YEARS. AND AS FOR PLAGUE, IT'S POSSIBLE BUT WE WERE TALKING TO THEM TWO DAYS AGO AND THEY WERE FINE THEN.
IT COULD BE A DOWNED TRANSMITTER, BAD WEATHER, ANYTHING.
BUT YOU CAN'T BE CERTAIN. WHAT ABOUT CHICAGO? DETROIT? MINNEAPOLIS? THEY ALL WENT THE SAME WAY.
MORE REASON TO FIND OUT WHAT HAPPENED.
BOTTOM LINE. 'LESS YOU TIE ME TO A CHAIR, I'M GOING TO GO. I COULD USE A GOOD SCOUT, MAYBE A HUNTER BUT EITHER WAY, I'M GOING.

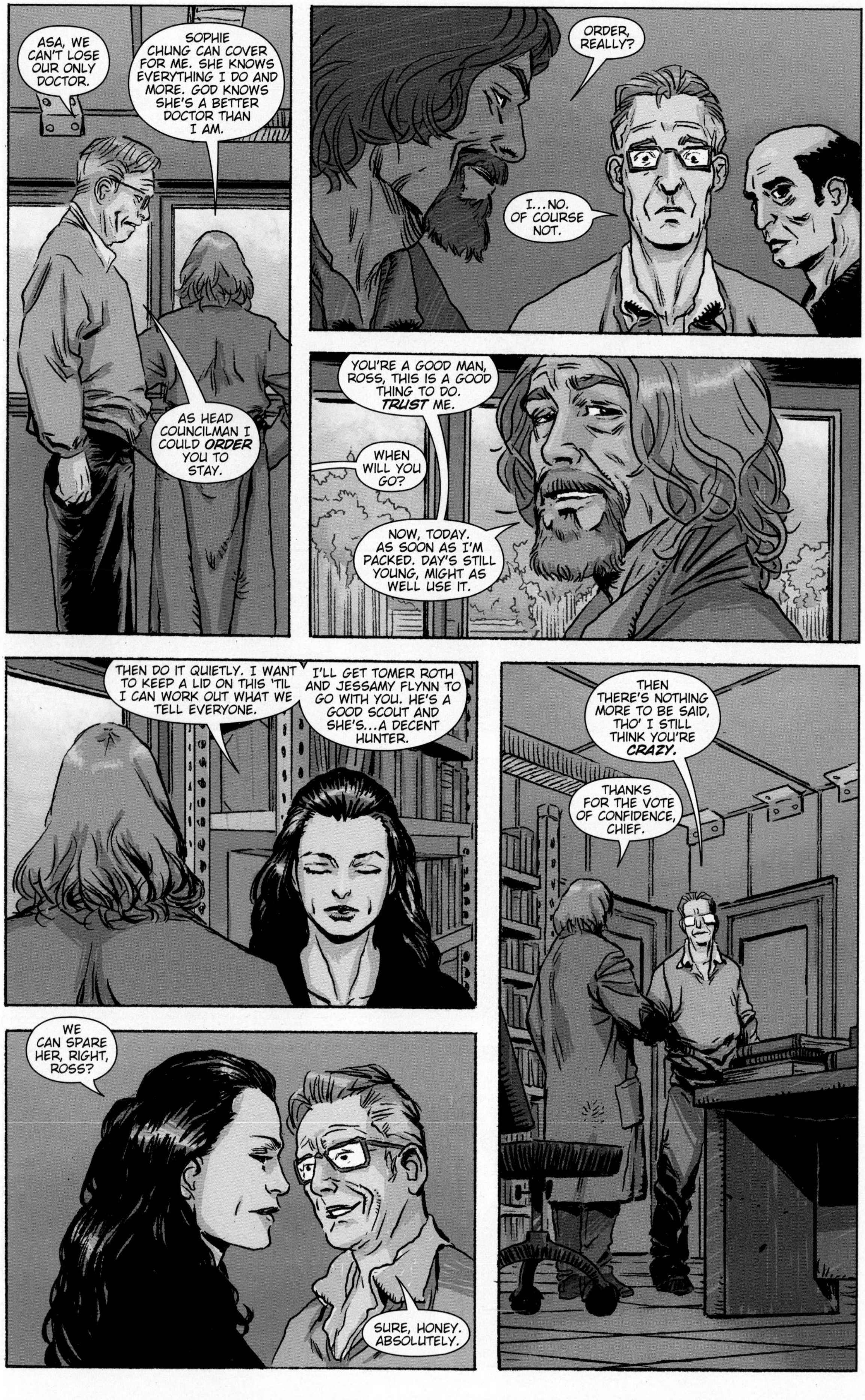
ASA, WE CAN'T LOSE OUR ONLY DOCTOR.
SOPHIE CHUNG CAN COVER FOR ME. SHE KNOWS EVERYTHING I DO AND MORE. GOD KNOWS SHE'S A BETTER DOCTOR THAN I AM.
AS HEAD COUNCILMAN I COULD ORDER YOU TO STAY.
ORDER, REALLY?
I...NO. OF COURSE NOT.
YOU'RE A GOOD MAN, ROSS, THIS IS A GOOD THING TO DO. TRUST ME.
WHEN WILL YOU GO?
NOW, TODAY. AS SOON AS I'M PACKED. DAY'S STILL YOUNG, MIGHT AS WELL USE IT.
THEN DO IT QUIETLY. I WANT TO KEEP A LID ON THIS 'TIL I CAN WORK OUT WHAT WE TELL EVERYONE.
I'LL GET TOMER ROTH AND JESSAMY FLYNN TO GO WITH YOU. HE'S A GOOD SCOUT AND SHE'S...A DECENT HUNTER.
WE CAN SPARE HER, RIGHT, ROSS?
SURE, HONEY. ABSOLUTELY.
THEN THERE'S NOTHING MORE TO BE SAID, THO' I STILL THINK YOU'RE CRAZY.
THANKS FOR THE VOTE OF CONFIDENCE, CHIEF.

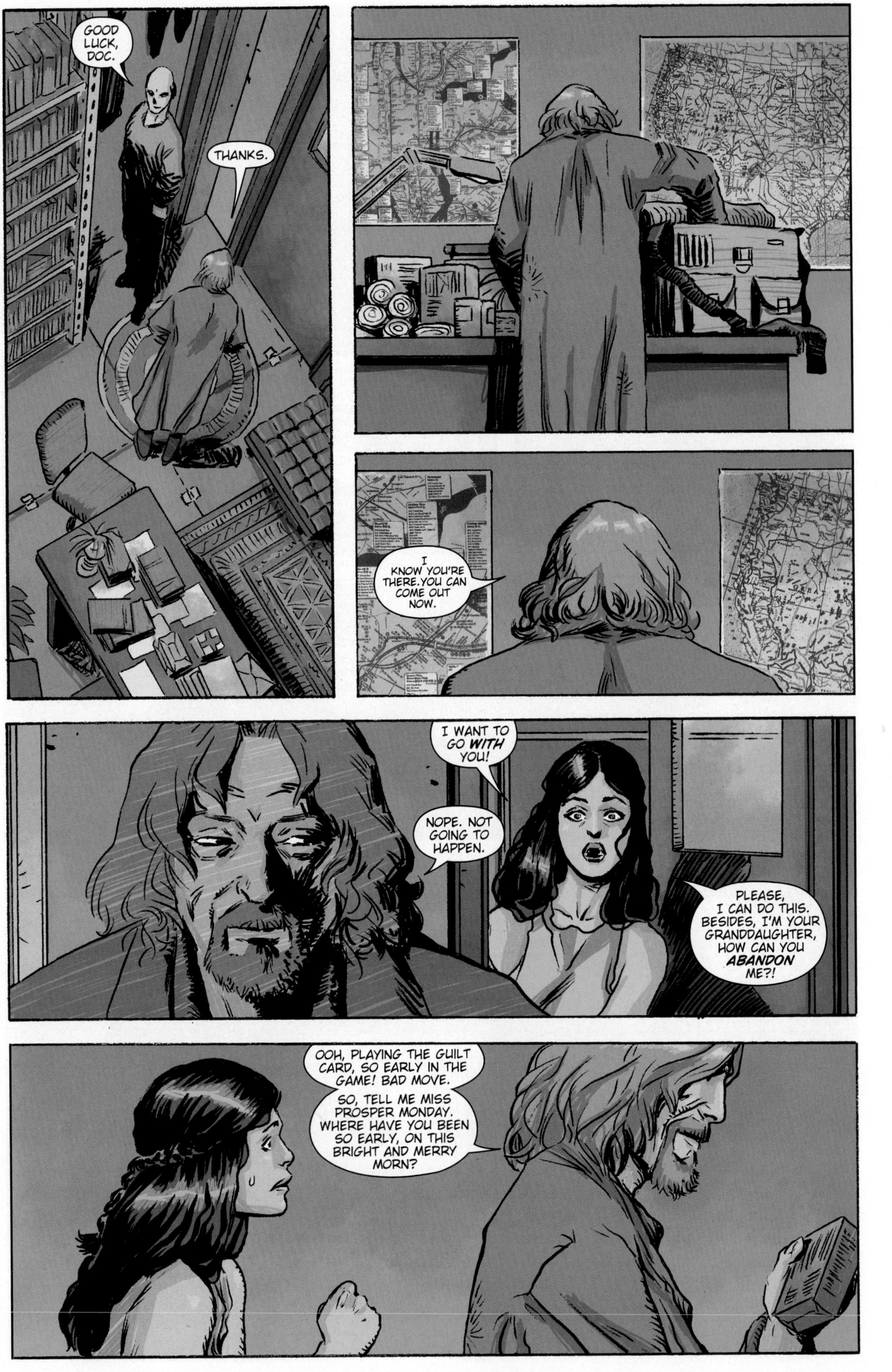
GOOD LUCK, DOC.
THANKS.
I KNOW YOU'RE THERE. YOU CAN COME OUT NOW.
I WANT TO GO WITH YOU!
NOPE. NOT GOING TO HAPPEN.
PLEASE, I CAN DO THIS. BESIDES, I'M YOUR GRANDDAUGHTER, HOW CAN YOU ABANDON ME?!
OOH, PLAYING THE GUILT CARD, SO EARLY IN THE GAME! BAD MOVE.
SO, TELL ME MISS PROSPER MONDAY. WHERE HAVE YOU BEEN SO EARLY, ON THIS BRIGHT AND MERRY MORN?

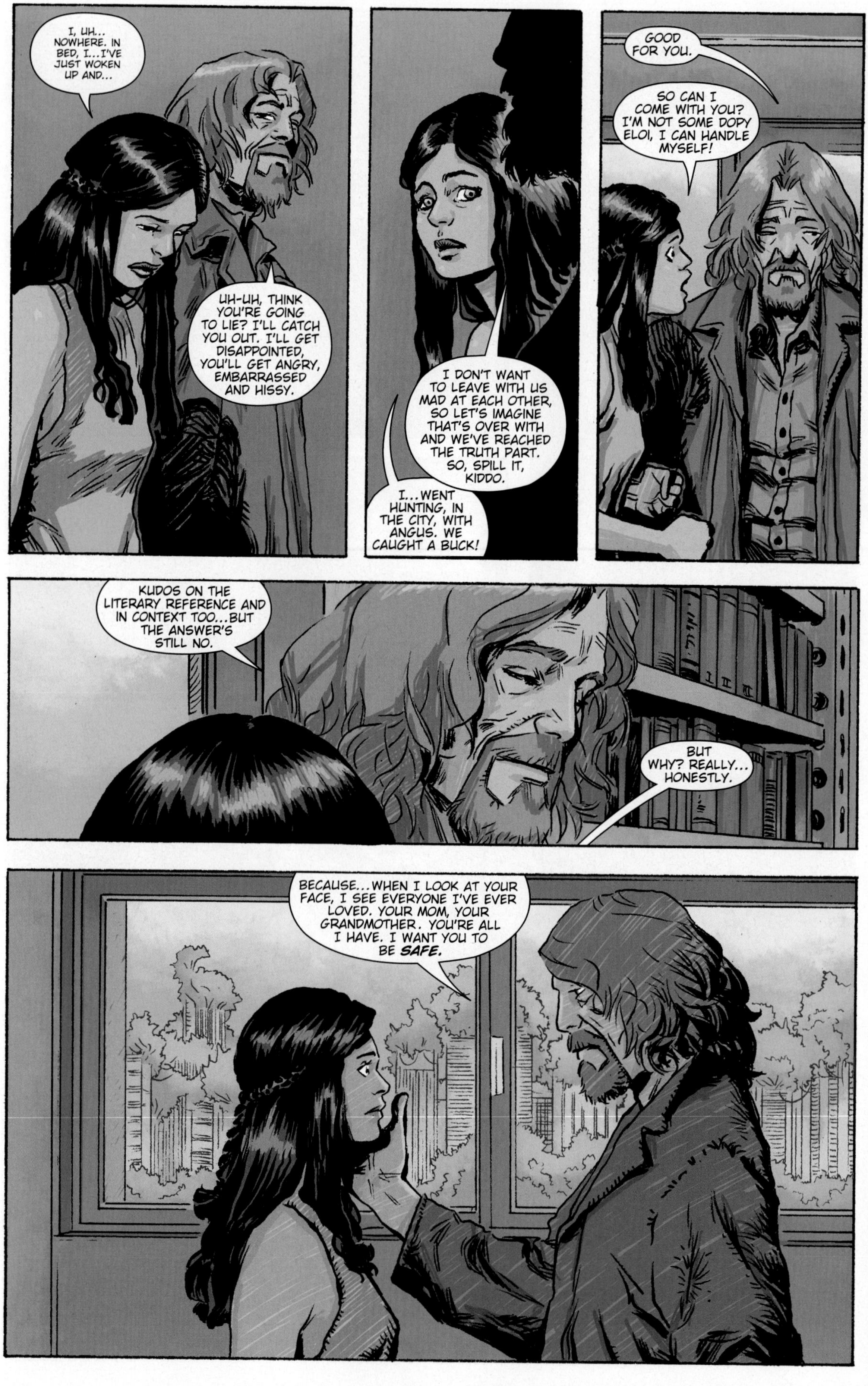

I, UH... NOWHERE. IN BED, I...I'VE JUST WOKEN UP AND...
UH-UH, THINK YOU'RE GOING TO LIE? I'LL CATCH YOU OUT. I'LL GET DISAPPOINTED, YOU'LL GET ANGRY, EMBARRASSED AND HISSY.
I DON'T WANT TO LEAVE WITH US MAD AT EACH OTHER, SO LET'S IMAGINE THAT'S OVER WITH AND WE'VE REACHED THE TRUTH PART. SO, SPILL IT, KIDDO.
I...WENT HUNTING, IN THE CITY, WITH ANGUS. WE CAUGHT A BUCK!
GOOD FOR YOU.
SO CAN I COME WITH YOU? I'M NOT SOME DOPY ELOI, I CAN HANDLE MYSELF!
KUDOS ON THE LITERARY REFERENCE AND IN CONTEXT TOO...BUT THE ANSWER'S STILL NO.
BUT WHY? REALLY... HONESTLY.
BECAUSE...WHEN I LOOK AT YOUR FACE, I SEE EVERYONE I'VE EVER LOVED. YOUR MOM, YOUR GRANDMOTHER. YOU'RE ALL I HAVE. I WANT YOU TO BE ***SAFE.***

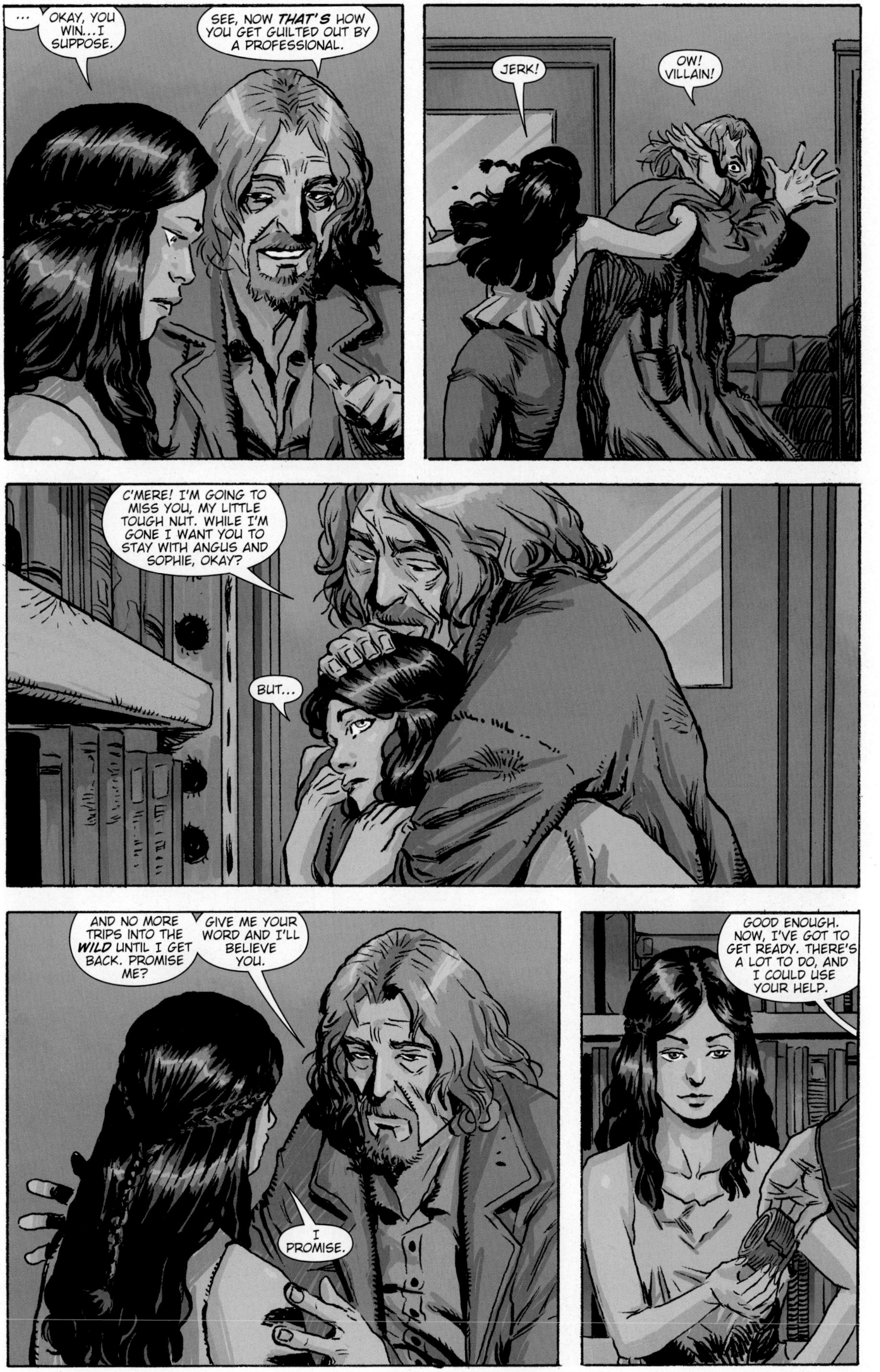
...
OKAY, YOU WIN...I SUPPOSE.
SEE, NOW ***THAT'S*** HOW YOU GET GUILTED OUT BY A PROFESSIONAL.
JERK!
OW! VILLAIN!
C'MERE! I'M GOING TO MISS YOU, MY LITTLE TOUGH NUT. WHILE I'M GONE I WANT YOU TO STAY WITH ANGUS AND SOPHIE, OKAY?
BUT...
AND NO MORE TRIPS INTO THE ***WILD*** UNTIL I GET BACK. PROMISE ME?
GIVE ME YOUR WORD AND I'LL BELIEVE YOU.
I PROMISE.
GOOD ENOUGH. NOW, I'VE GOT TO GET READY. THERE'S A LOT TO DO, AND I COULD USE YOUR HELP.

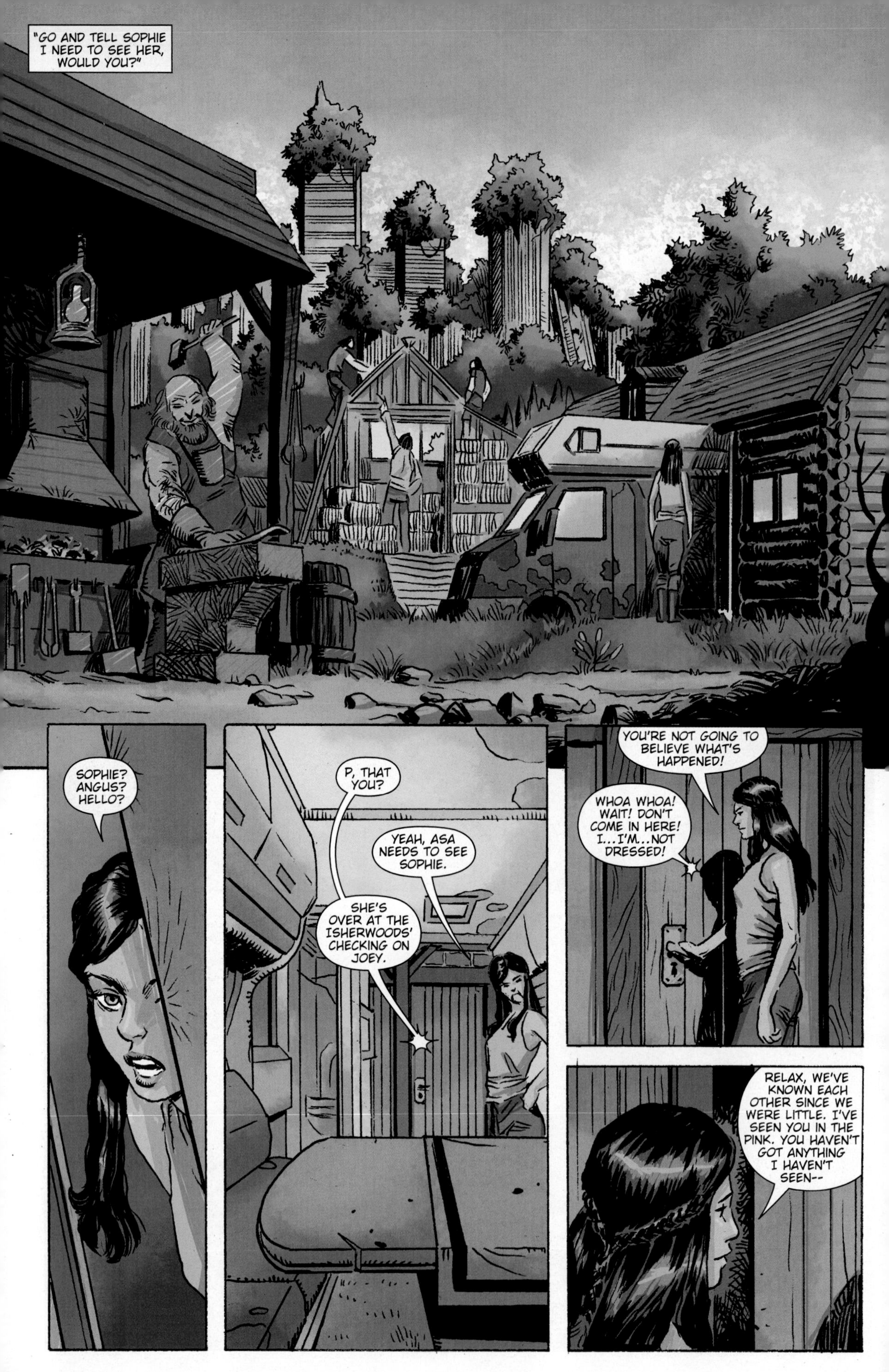
"GO AND TELL SOPHIE I NEED TO SEE HER, WOULD YOU?"
SOPHIE? ANGUS? HELLO?
P, THAT YOU?
YEAH, ASA NEEDS TO SEE SOPHIE.
SHE'S OVER AT THE ISHERWOODS' CHECKING ON JOEY.
YOU'RE NOT GOING TO BELIEVE WHAT'S HAPPENED!
WHOA WHOA! WAIT! DON'T COME IN HERE! I...I'M...NOT DRESSED!
RELAX, WE'VE KNOWN EACH OTHER SINCE WE WERE LITTLE. I'VE SEEN YOU IN THE PINK. YOU HAVEN'T GOT ANYTHING I HAVEN'T SEEN--

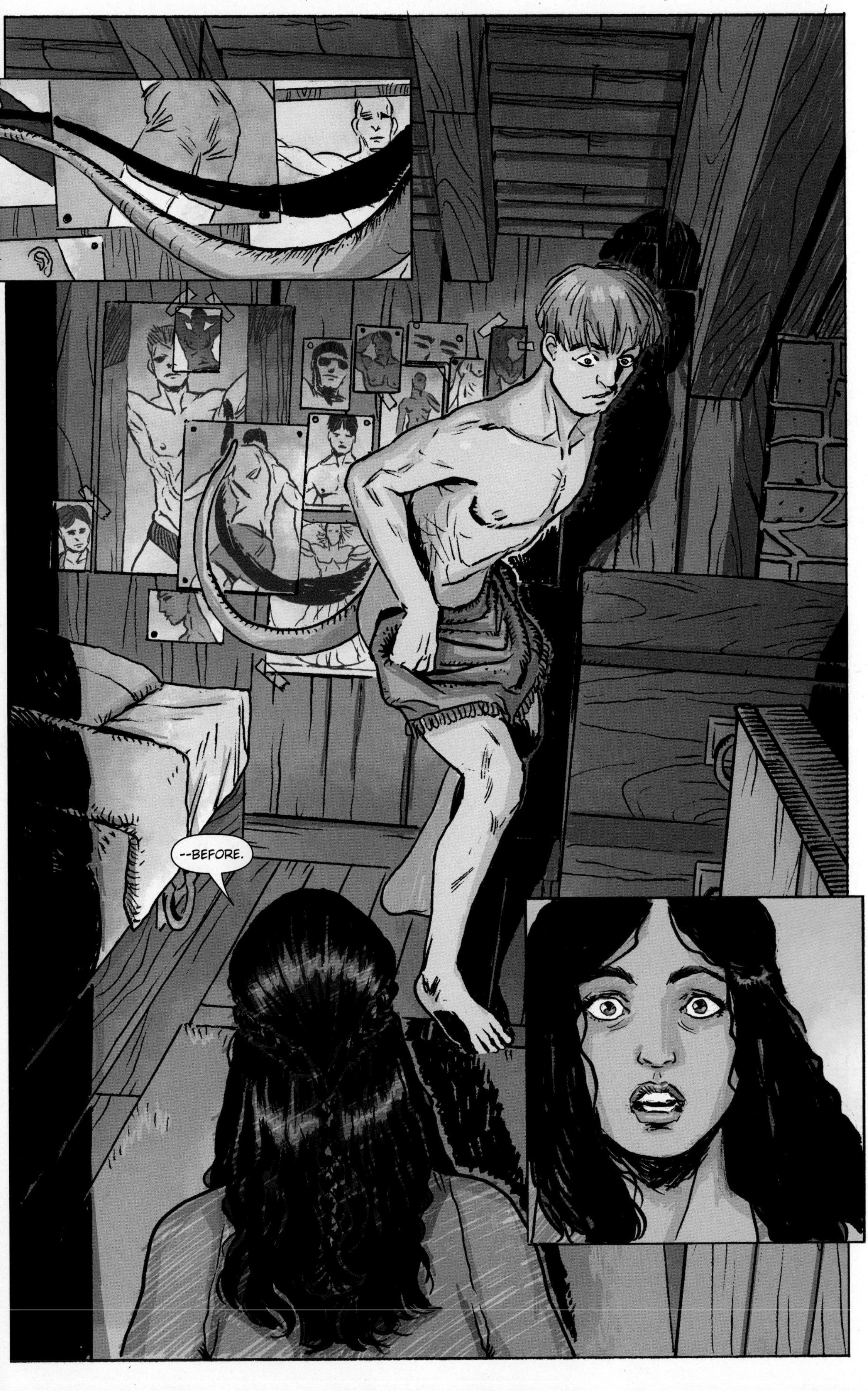
--BEFORE.

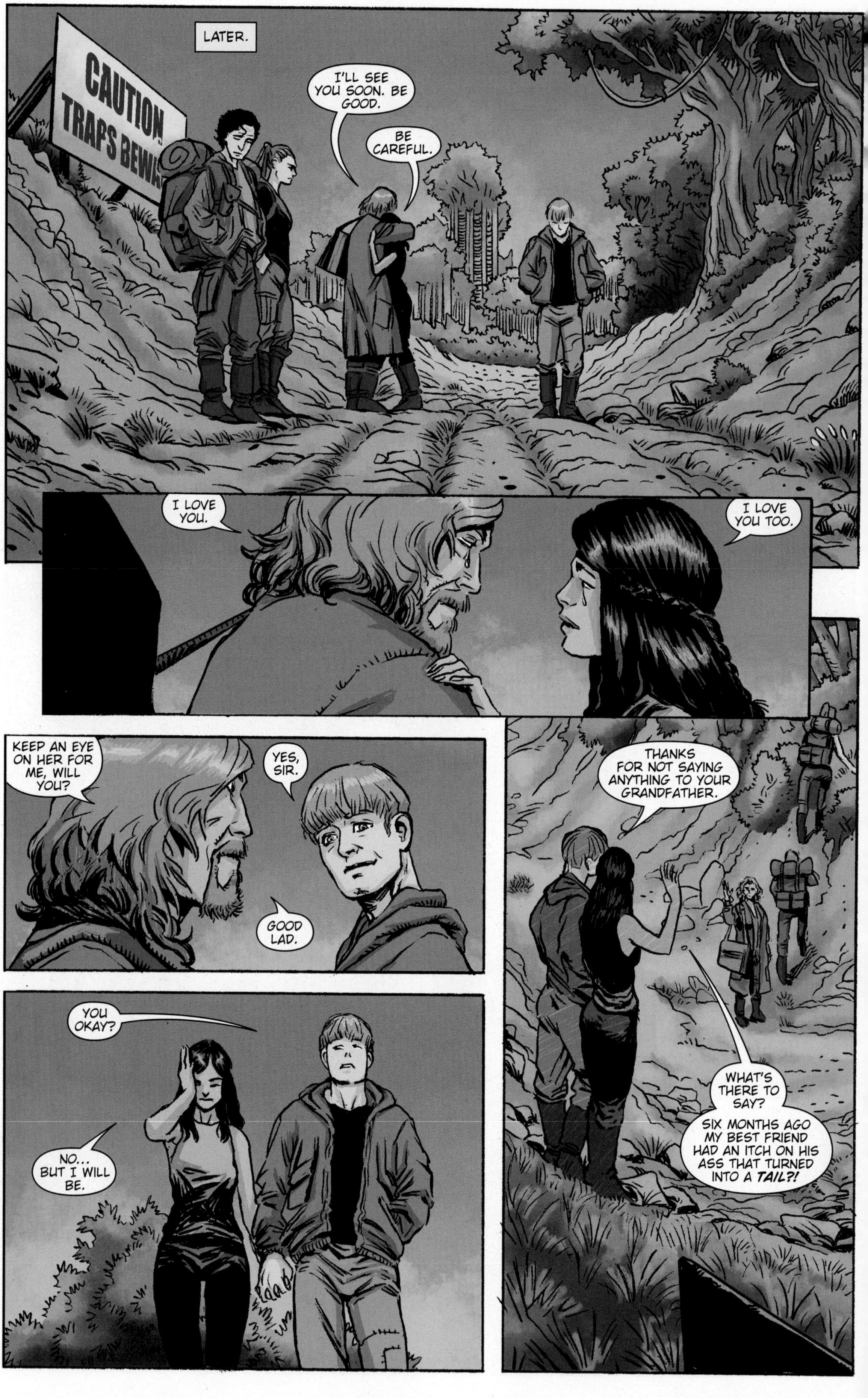
LATER.
CAUTION
TRAPS BEWA
I'LL SEE YOU SOON. BE GOOD.
BE CAREFUL.
I LOVE YOU.
I LOVE YOU TOO.
KEEP AN EYE ON HER FOR ME, WILL YOU?
YES, SIR.
GOOD LAD.
YOU OKAY?
NO... BUT I WILL BE.
THANKS FOR NOT SAYING ANYTHING TO YOUR GRANDFATHER.
WHAT'S THERE TO SAY?
SIX MONTHS AGO MY BEST FRIEND HAD AN ITCH ON HIS ASS THAT TURNED INTO A *TAIL?!*

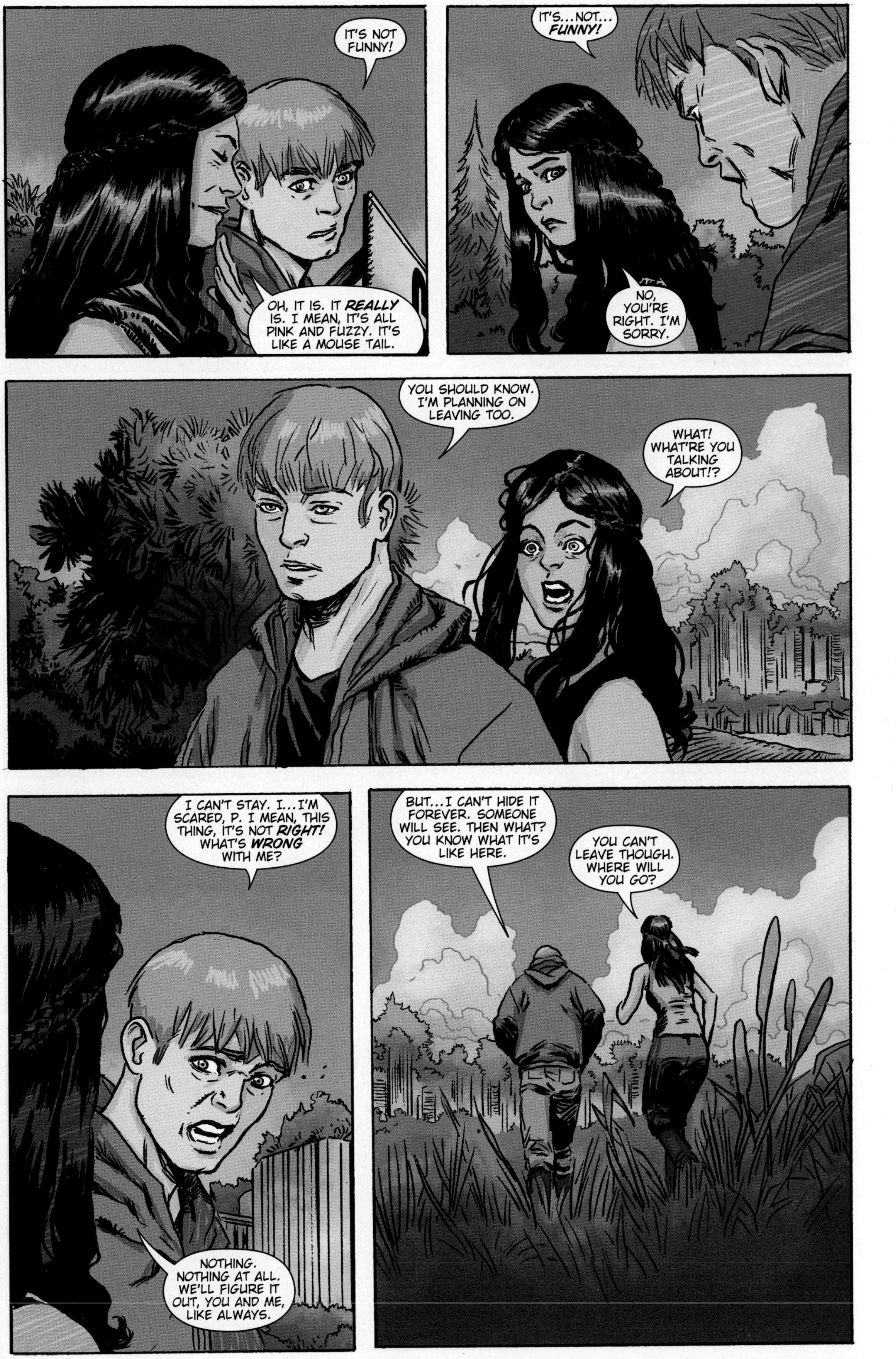
IT'S NOT FUNNY!
OH, IT IS. IT REALLY IS. I MEAN, IT'S ALL PINK AND FUZZY. IT'S LIKE A MOUSE TAIL.
IT'S...NOT... FUNNY!
NO, YOU'RE RIGHT. I'M SORRY.
YOU SHOULD KNOW. I'M PLANNING ON LEAVING TOO.
WHAT! WHAT'RE YOU TALKING ABOUT!?
I CAN'T STAY. I...I'M SCARED, P. I MEAN, THIS THING, IT'S NOT RIGHT! WHAT'S WRONG WITH ME?
NOTHING. NOTHING AT ALL. WE'LL FIGURE IT OUT, YOU AND ME, LIKE ALWAYS.
BUT...I CAN'T HIDE IT FOREVER. SOMEONE WILL SEE. THEN WHAT? YOU KNOW WHAT IT'S LIKE HERE.
YOU CAN'T LEAVE THOUGH. WHERE WILL YOU GO?

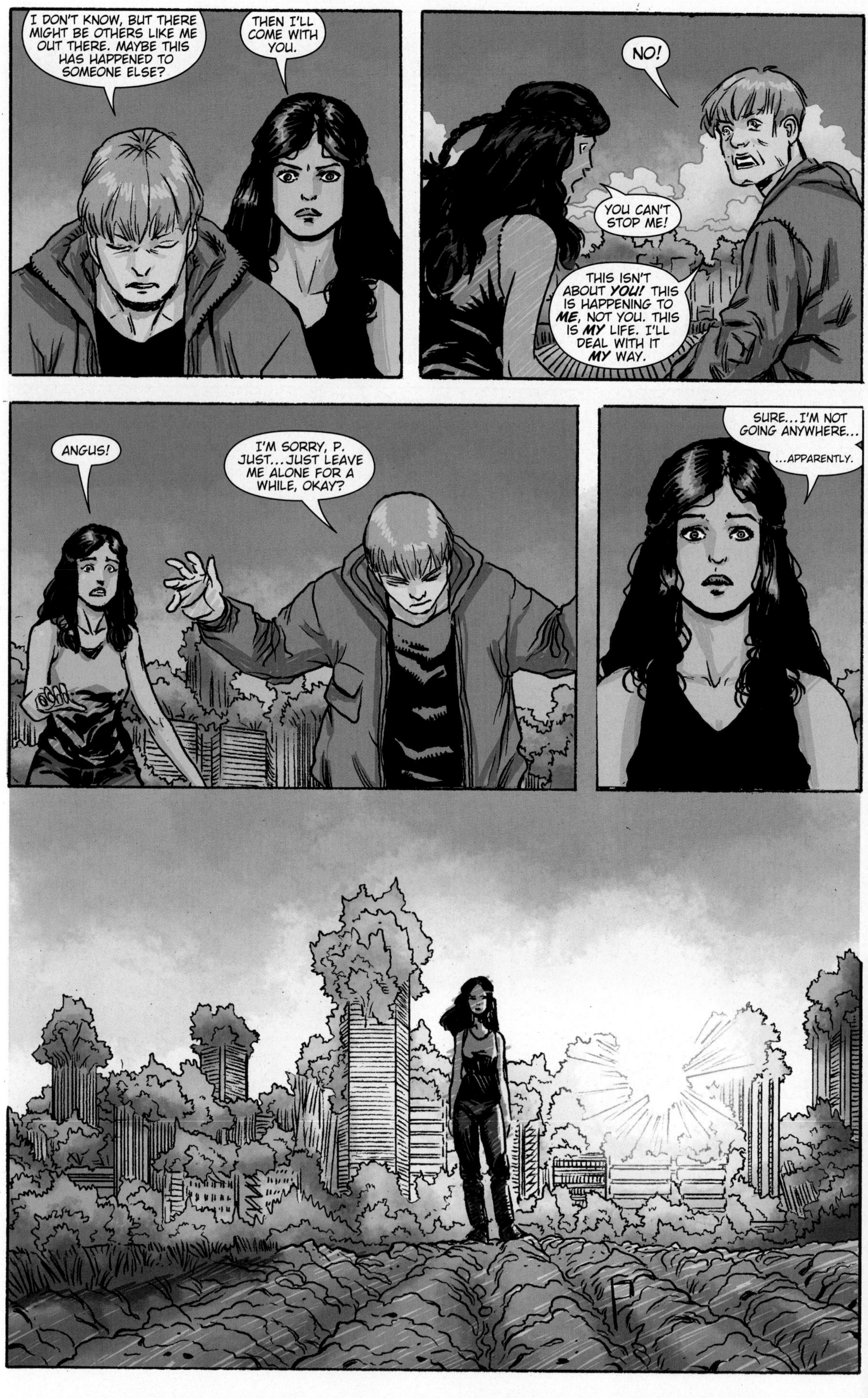
I DON'T KNOW, BUT THERE MIGHT BE OTHERS LIKE ME OUT THERE. MAYBE THIS HAS HAPPENED TO SOMEONE ELSE?
THEN I'LL COME WITH YOU.
NO!
YOU CAN'T STOP ME!
THIS ISN'T ABOUT *YOU!* THIS IS HAPPENING TO *ME*, NOT YOU. THIS IS *MY* LIFE. I'LL DEAL WITH IT *MY* WAY.
ANGUS!
I'M SORRY, P. JUST...JUST LEAVE ME ALONE FOR A WHILE, OKAY?
SURE...I'M NOT GOING ANYWHERE...
...APPARENTLY.

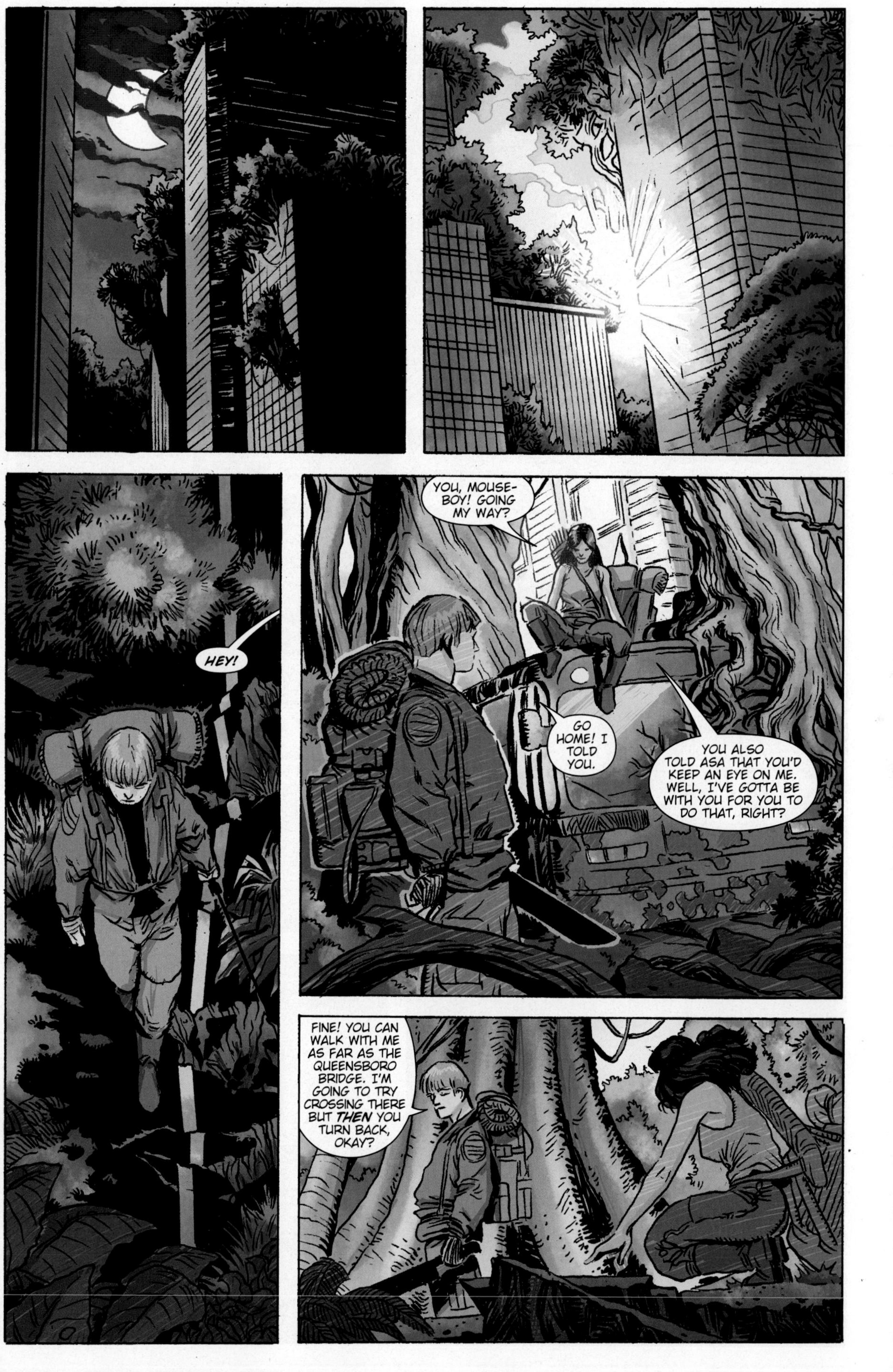
HEY!
YOU, MOUSE-BOY! GOING MY WAY?
GO HOME! I TOLD YOU.
YOU ALSO TOLD ASA THAT YOU'D KEEP AN EYE ON ME. WELL, I'VE GOTTA BE WITH YOU FOR YOU TO DO THAT, RIGHT?
FINE! YOU CAN WALK WITH ME AS FAR AS THE QUEENSBORO BRIDGE. I'M GOING TO TRY CROSSING THERE BUT *THEN* YOU TURN BACK, OKAY?

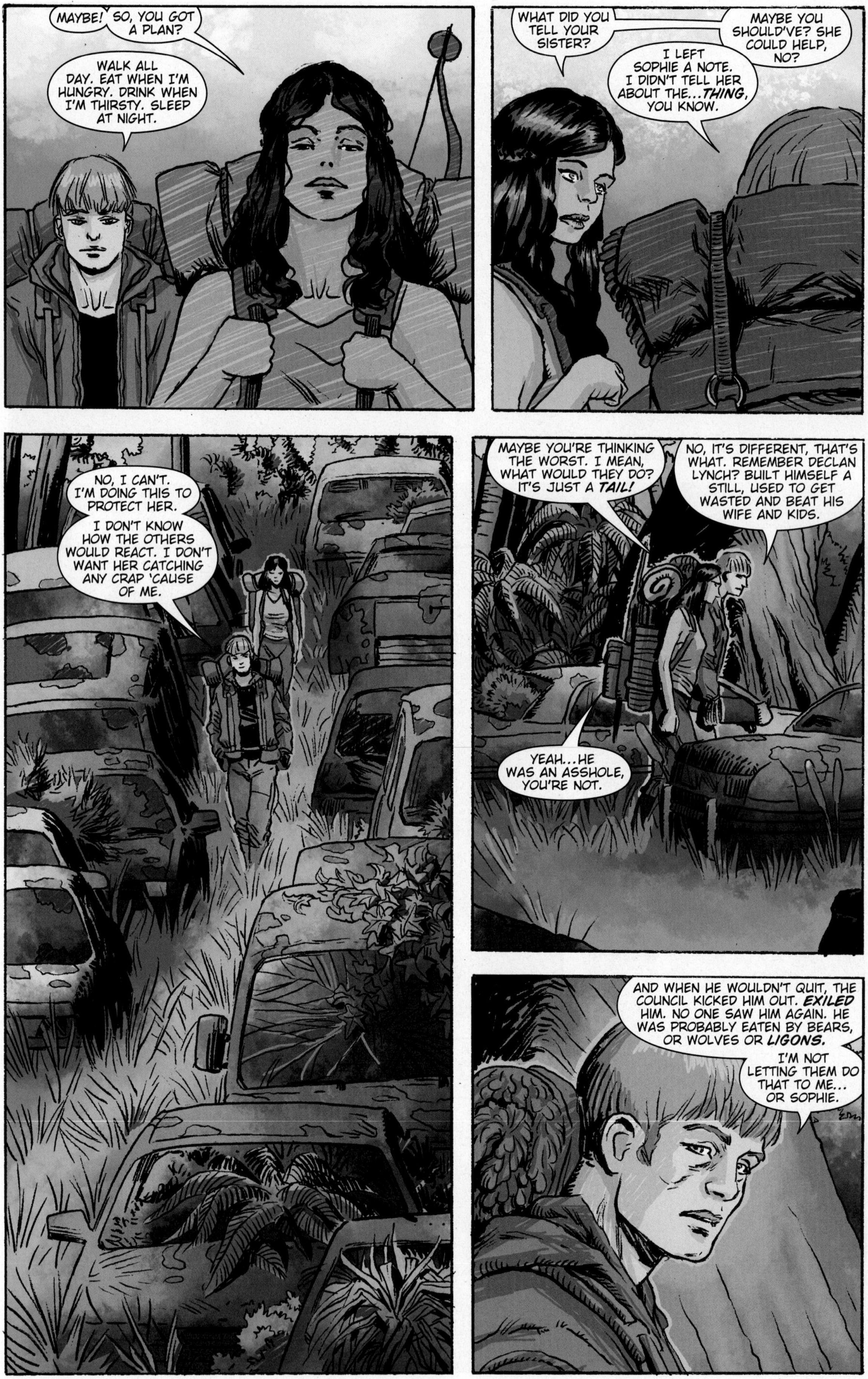
MAYBE!
SO, YOU GOT A PLAN?
WALK ALL DAY. EAT WHEN I'M HUNGRY. DRINK WHEN I'M THIRSTY. SLEEP AT NIGHT.
WHAT DID YOU TELL YOUR SISTER?
I LEFT SOPHIE A NOTE. I DIDN'T TELL HER ABOUT THE...THING, YOU KNOW.
MAYBE YOU SHOULD'VE? SHE COULD HELP, NO?
NO, I CAN'T. I'M DOING THIS TO PROTECT HER.
I DON'T KNOW HOW THE OTHERS WOULD REACT. I DON'T WANT HER CATCHING ANY CRAP 'CAUSE OF ME.
MAYBE YOU'RE THINKING THE WORST. I MEAN, WHAT WOULD THEY DO? IT'S JUST A TAIL!
NO, IT'S DIFFERENT, THAT'S WHAT. REMEMBER DECLAN LYNCH? BUILT HIMSELF A STILL, USED TO GET WASTED AND BEAT HIS WIFE AND KIDS.
YEAH...HE WAS AN ASSHOLE, YOU'RE NOT.
AND WHEN HE WOULDN'T QUIT, THE COUNCIL KICKED HIM OUT. EXILED HIM. NO ONE SAW HIM AGAIN. HE WAS PROBABLY EATEN BY BEARS, OR WOLVES OR LIGONS.
I'M NOT LETTING THEM DO THAT TO ME... OR SOPHIE.

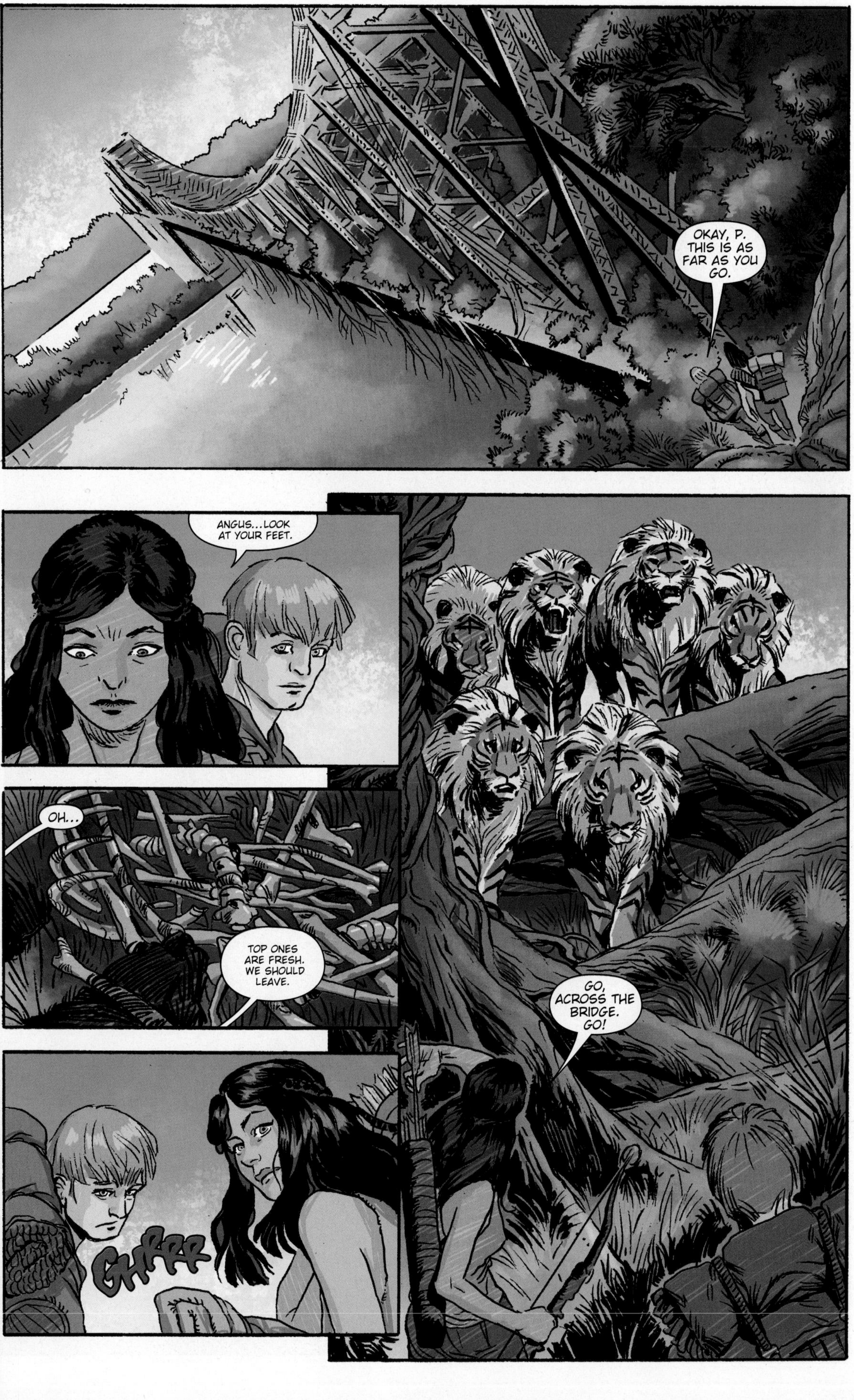
OKAY, P. THIS IS AS FAR AS YOU GO.
ANGUS...LOOK AT YOUR FEET.
OH...
TOP ONES ARE FRESH. WE SHOULD LEAVE.
GHRRR
GO, ACROSS THE BRIDGE. GO!

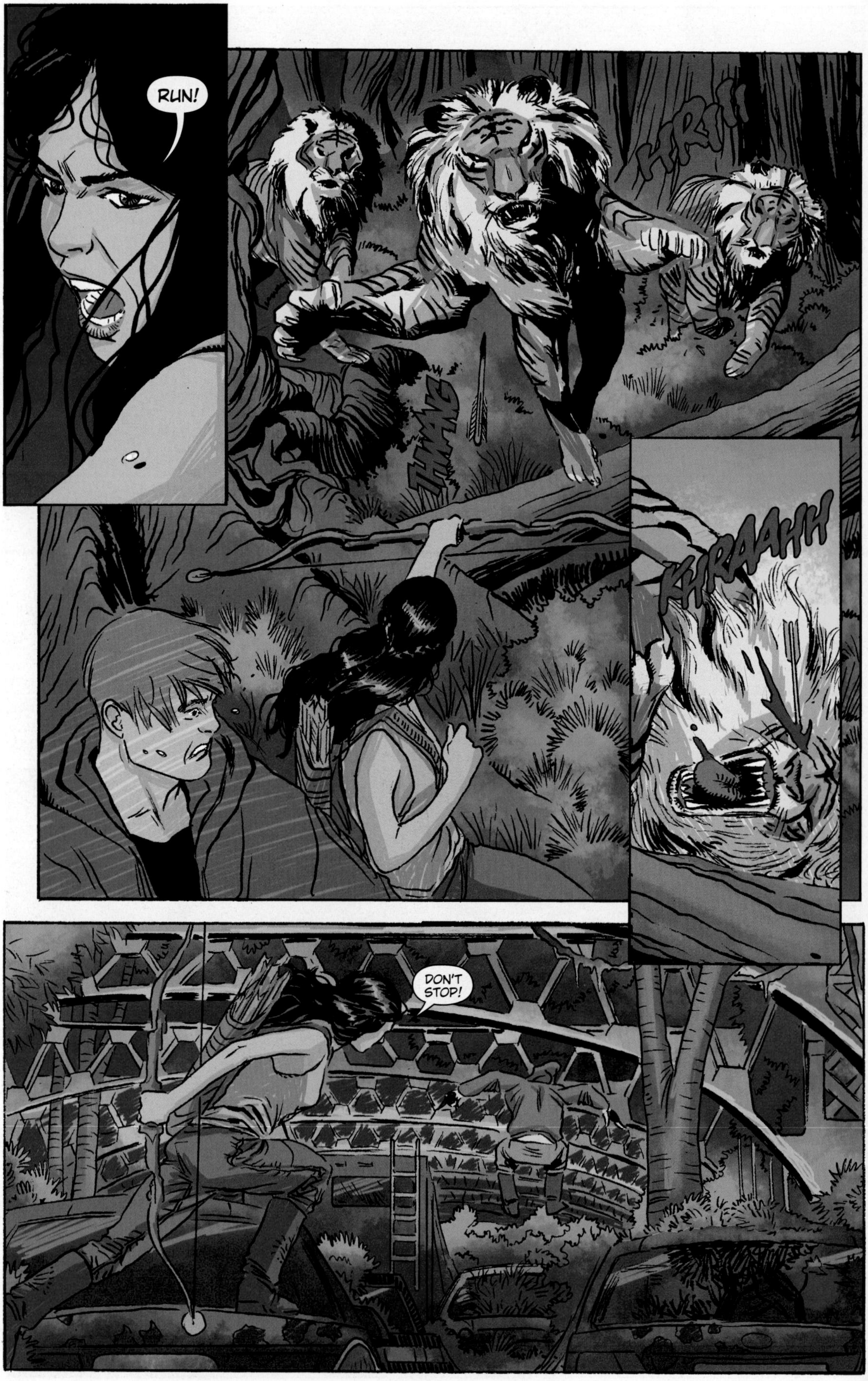
RUN!
HRRR
THWANG
KHRAAHH
DON'T STOP!

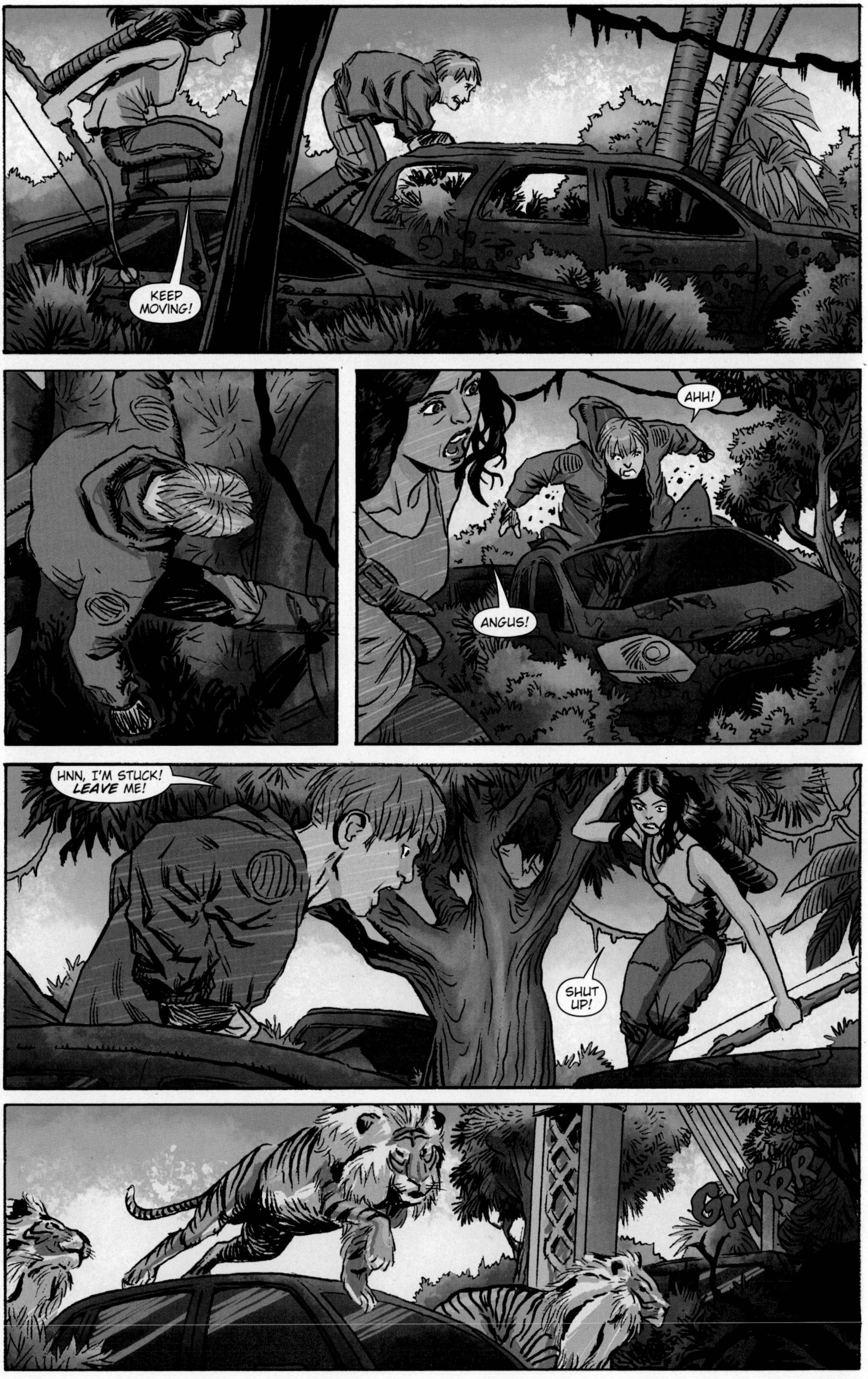
KEEP MOVING!
AHH!
ANGUS!
HNN, I'M STUCK! LEAVE ME!
SHUT UP!
GHRRR

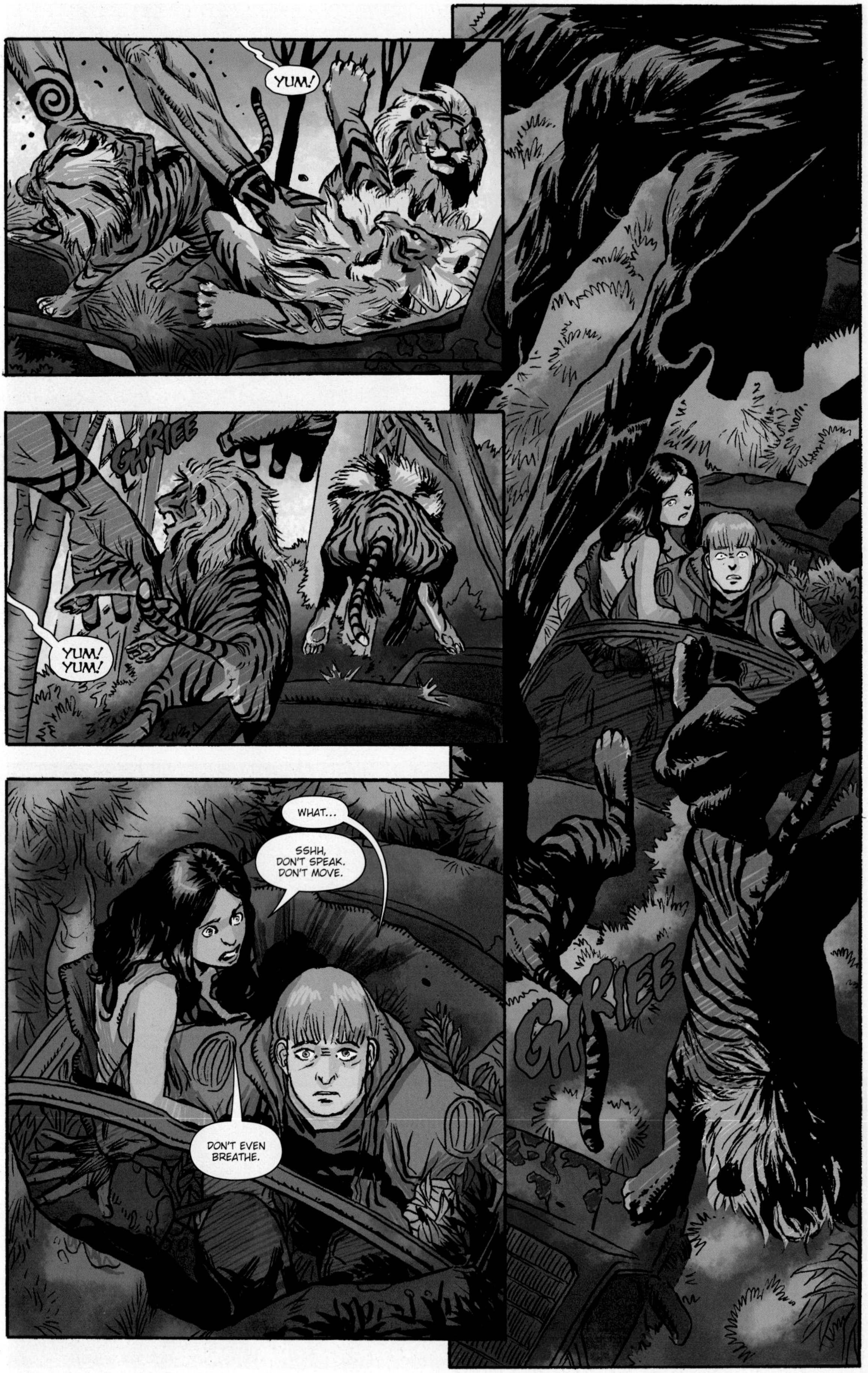

YUM!
GHRIEE
YUM! YUM!
WHAT...
SSHH, DON'T SPEAK. DON'T MOVE.
DON'T EVEN BREATHE.
GHRIEE

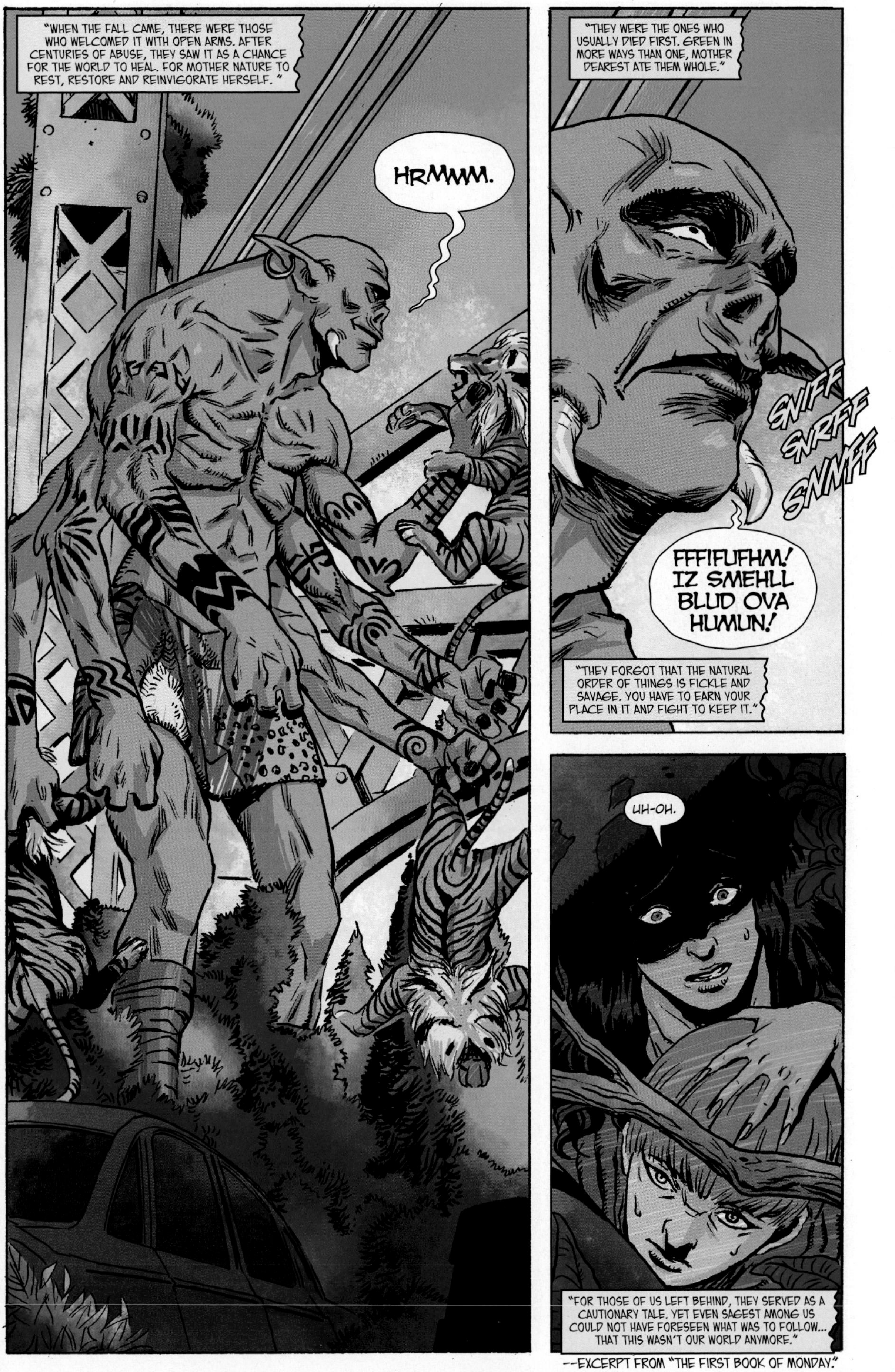
"WHEN THE FALL CAME, THERE WERE THOSE WHO WELCOMED IT WITH OPEN ARMS. AFTER CENTURIES OF ABUSE, THEY SAW IT AS A CHANCE FOR THE WORLD TO HEAL. FOR MOTHER NATURE TO REST, RESTORE AND REINVIGORATE HERSELF."
HRMMM.
"THEY WERE THE ONES WHO USUALLY DIED FIRST. GREEN IN MORE WAYS THAN ONE, MOTHER DEAREST ATE THEM WHOLE."
SNIFF
SNRFF
SNMFF
FFFIFUFHM! IZ SMEHLL BLUD OVA HUMUN!
"THEY FORGOT THAT THE NATURAL ORDER OF THINGS IS FICKLE AND SAVAGE. YOU HAVE TO EARN YOUR PLACE IN IT AND FIGHT TO KEEP IT."
UH-OH.
"FOR THOSE OF US LEFT BEHIND, THEY SERVED AS A CAUTIONARY TALE. YET EVEN SAGEST AMONG US COULD NOT HAVE FORESEEN WHAT WAS TO FOLLOW... THAT THIS WASN'T OUR WORLD ANYMORE."

--EXCERPT FROM "THE FIRST BOOK OF MONDAY."

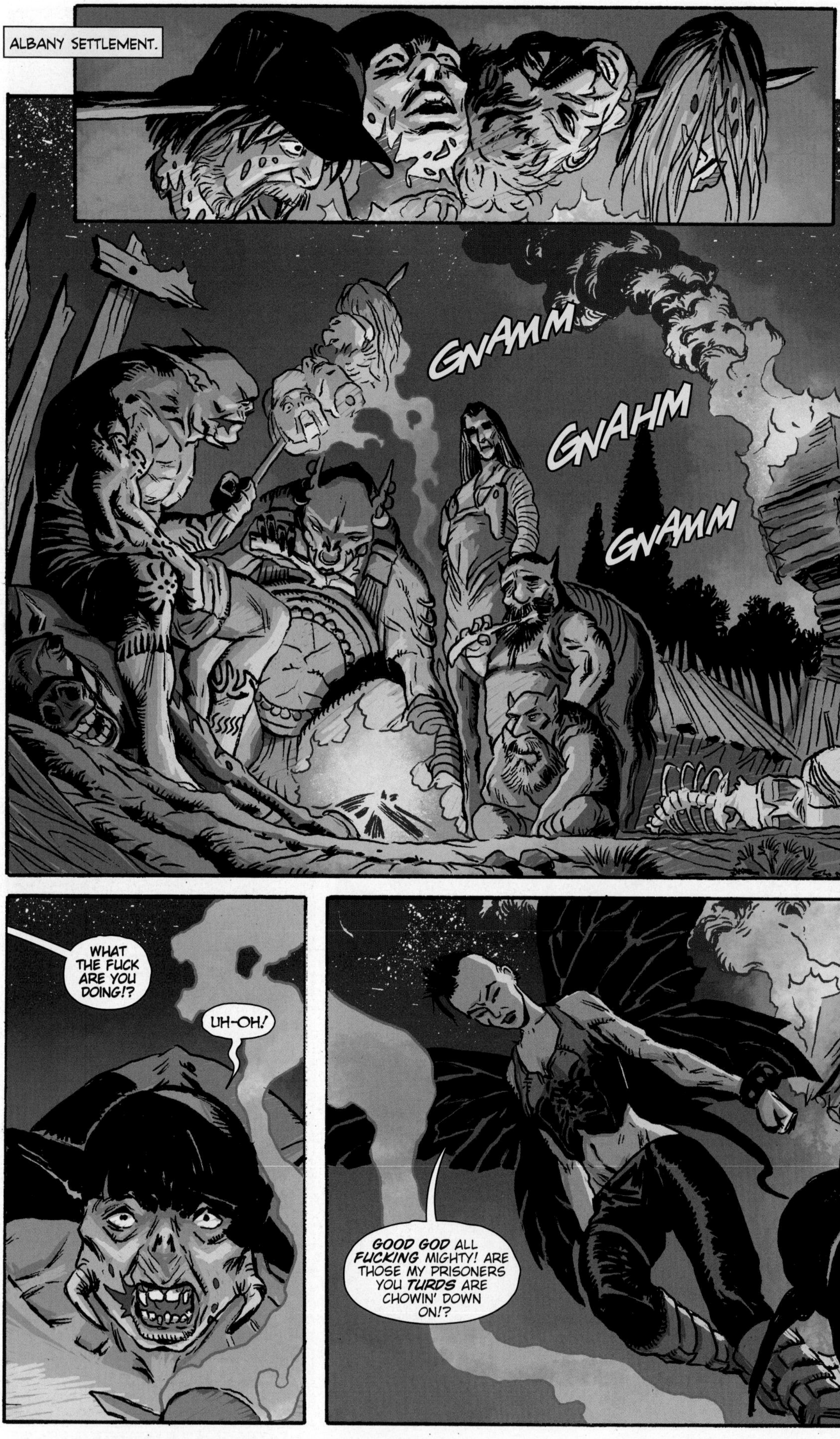
ALBANY SETTLEMENT.
GNAMM
GNAHM
GNAMM
WHAT THE FUCK ARE YOU DOING!?
UH-OH!
GOOD GOD ALL FUCKING MIGHTY! ARE THOSE MY PRISONERS YOU TURDS ARE CHOWIN' DOWN ON!?

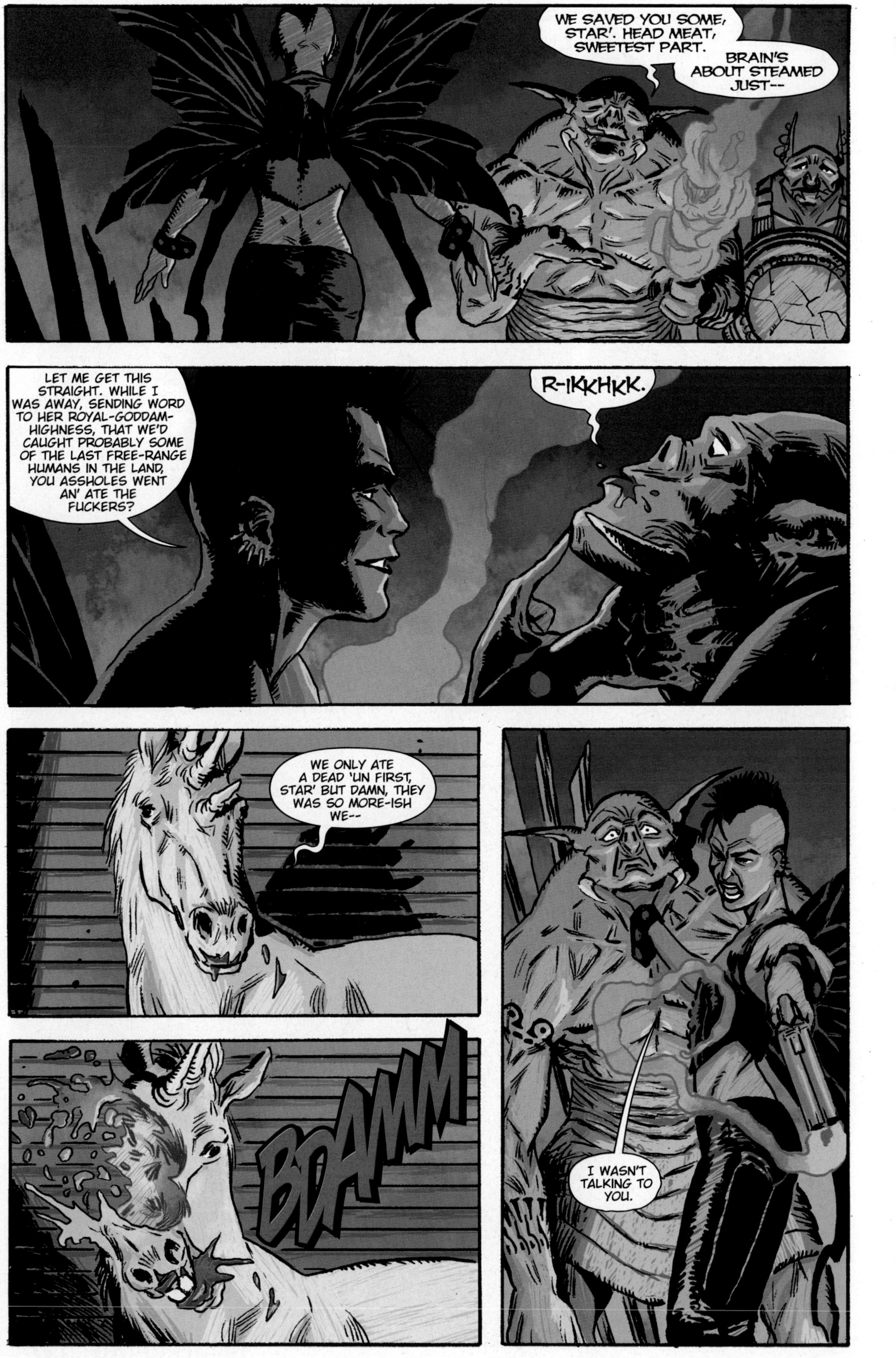
WE SAVED YOU SOME, STAR'. HEAD MEAT, SWEETEST PART.
BRAIN'S ABOUT STEAMED JUST--
LET ME GET THIS STRAIGHT. WHILE I WAS AWAY, SENDING WORD TO HER ROYAL-GODDAM-HIGHNESS, THAT WE'D CAUGHT PROBABLY SOME OF THE LAST FREE-RANGE HUMANS IN THE LAND, YOU ASSHOLES WENT AN' ATE THE FUCKERS?
R-IKKHKK.
WE ONLY ATE A DEAD 'UN FIRST, STAR' BUT DAMN, THEY WAS SO MORE-ISH WE--
BOAMM
I WASN'T TALKING TO YOU.

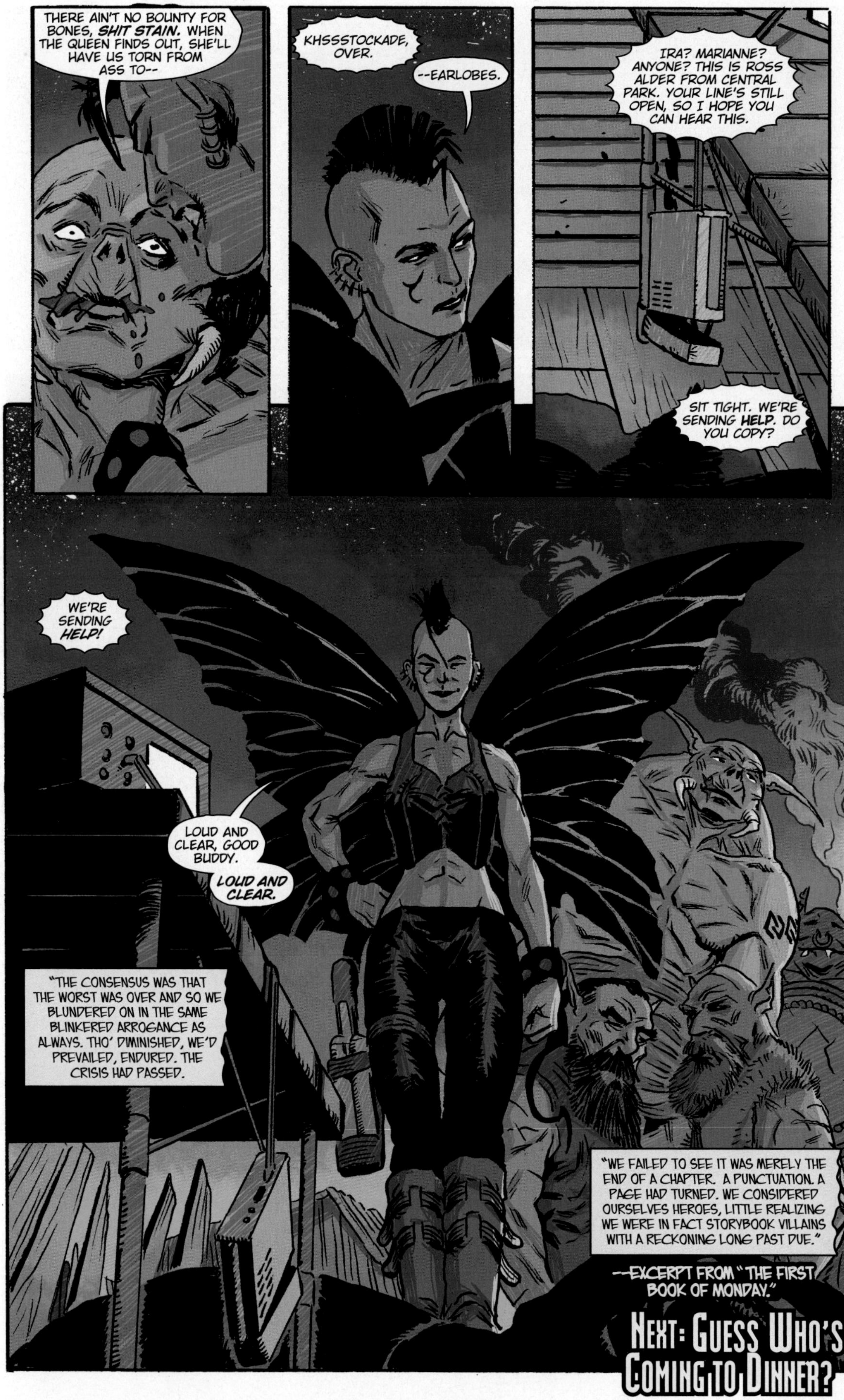
THERE AIN'T NO BOUNTY FOR BONES, SHIT STAIN. WHEN THE QUEEN FINDS OUT, SHE'LL HAVE US TORN FROM ASS TO--
KHSSSTOCKADE, OVER.
--EARLOBES.
IRA? MARIANNE? ANYONE? THIS IS ROSS ALDER FROM CENTRAL PARK. YOUR LINE'S STILL OPEN, SO I HOPE YOU CAN HEAR THIS.
SIT TIGHT. WE'RE SENDING HELP. DO YOU COPY?
WE'RE SENDING HELP!
LOUD AND CLEAR, GOOD BUDDY.
LOUD AND CLEAR.
"THE CONSENSUS WAS THAT THE WORST WAS OVER AND SO WE BLUNDERED ON IN THE SAME BLINKERED ARROGANCE AS ALWAYS. THO' DIMINISHED, WE'D PREVAILED, ENDURED. THE CRISIS HAD PASSED.
"WE FAILED TO SEE IT WAS MERELY THE END OF A CHAPTER. A PUNCTUATION. A PAGE HAD TURNED. WE CONSIDERED OURSELVES HEROES, LITTLE REALIZING WE WERE IN FACT STORYBOOK VILLAINS WITH A RECKONING LONG PAST DUE."
—EXCERPT FROM "THE FIRST BOOK OF MONDAY."
NEXT: GUESS WHO'S COMING TO DINNER?

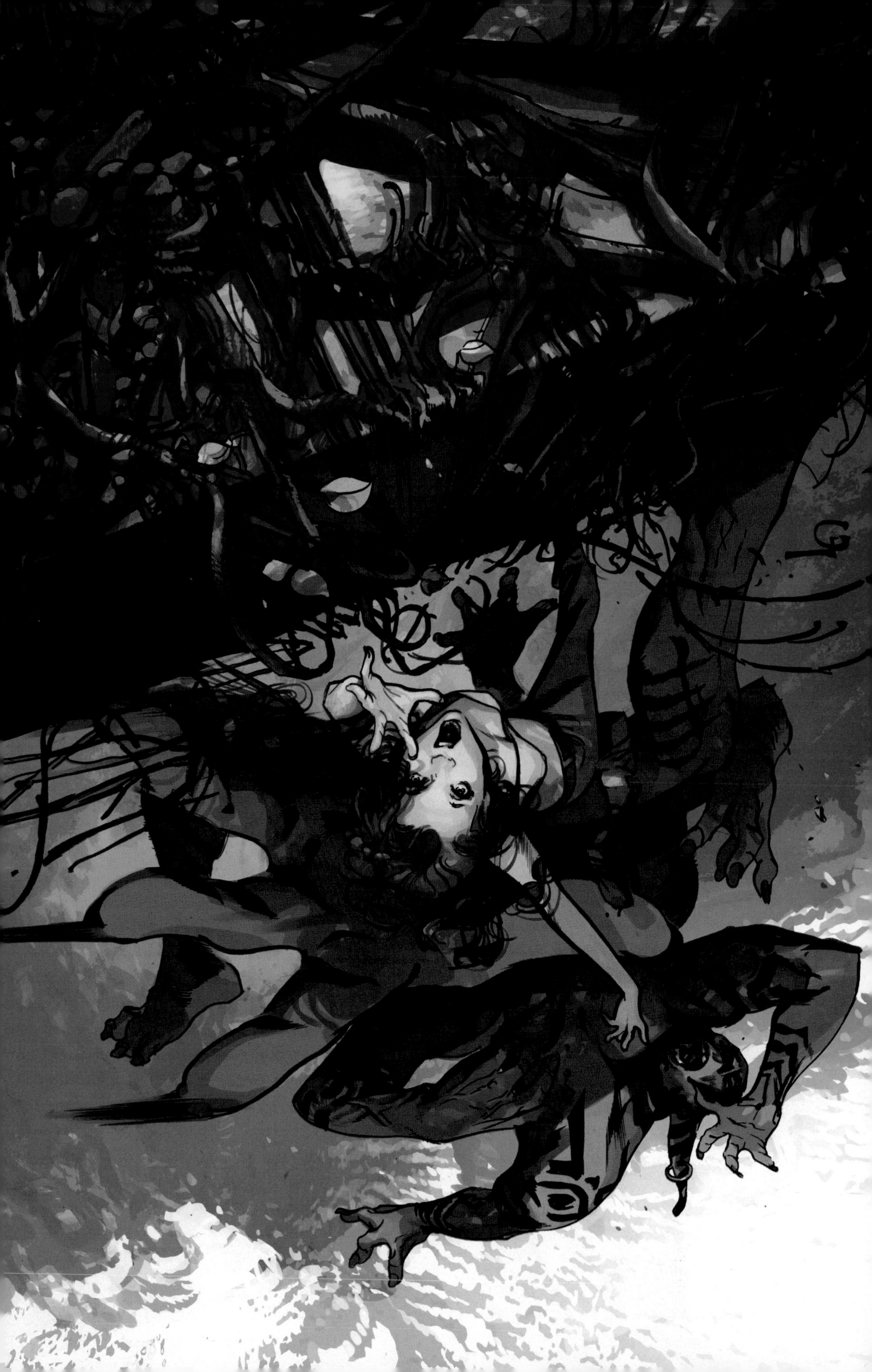

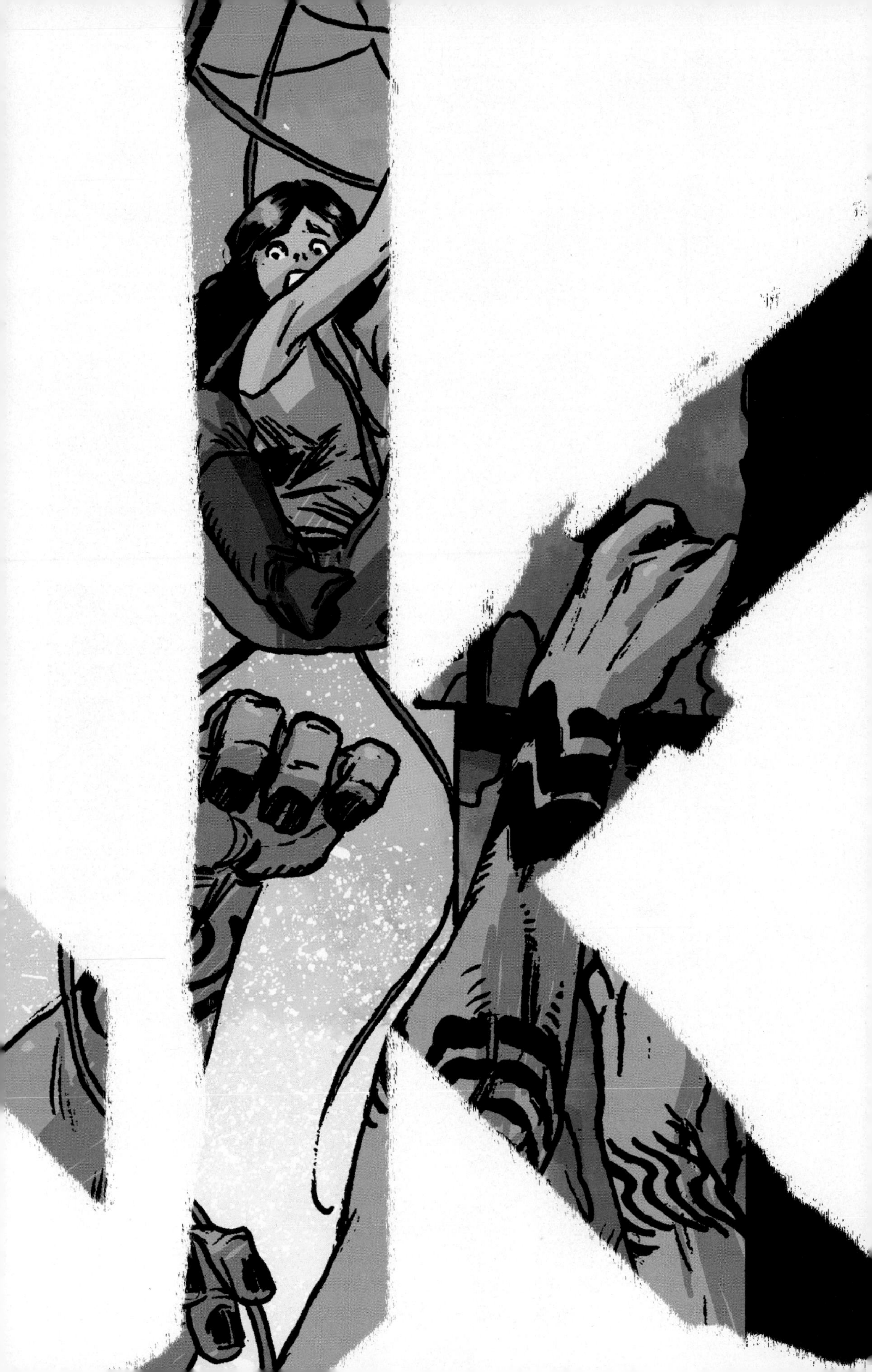

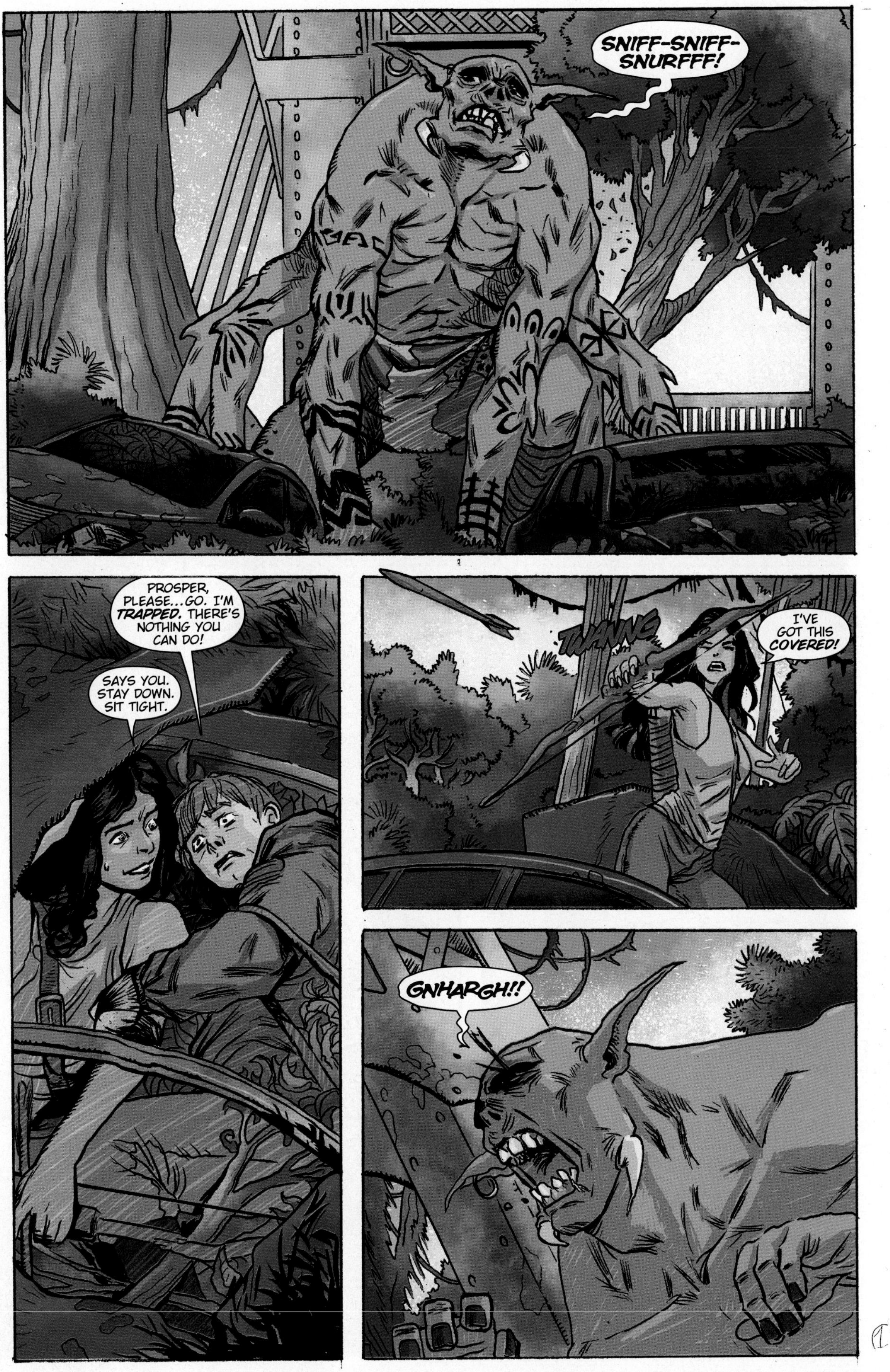
SNIFF-SNIFF-SNURFFF!
PROSPER, PLEASE...GO. I'M TRAPPED. THERE'S NOTHING YOU CAN DO!
SAYS YOU. STAY DOWN. SIT TIGHT.
TWANG
I'VE GOT THIS COVERED!
GNHARGH!!

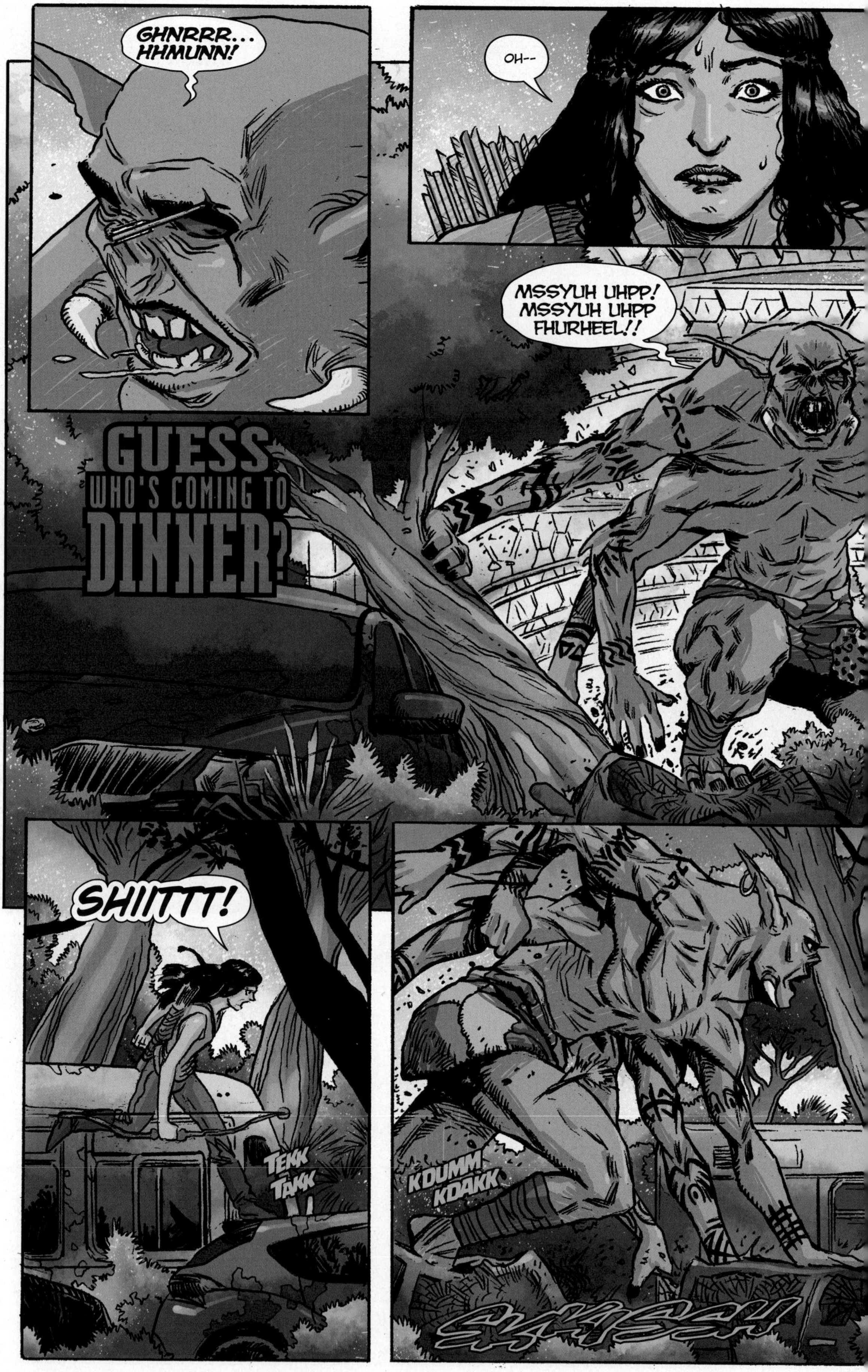
GHNRRR... HHMUNN!
OH--
MSSYUH UHPP! MSSYUH UHPP FHURHEEL!!
GUESS WHO'S COMING TO DINNER?
SHIITTT!
TEKK TAKK
KDUMM KDAKK
SKRASCH

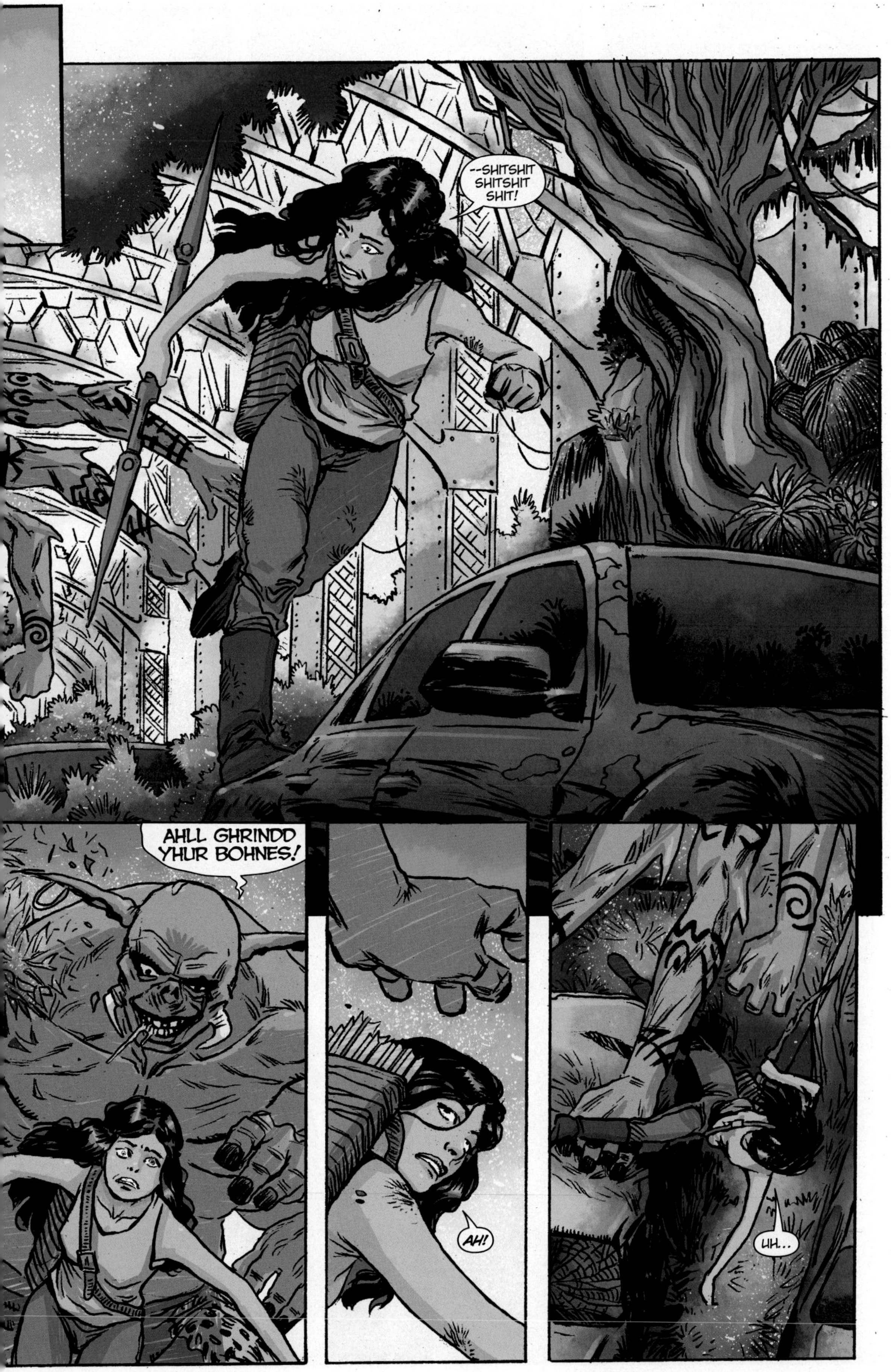
--SHITSHIT SHITSHIT SHIT!
AHLL GHRINDD YHUR BOHNES!
AH!
UH...

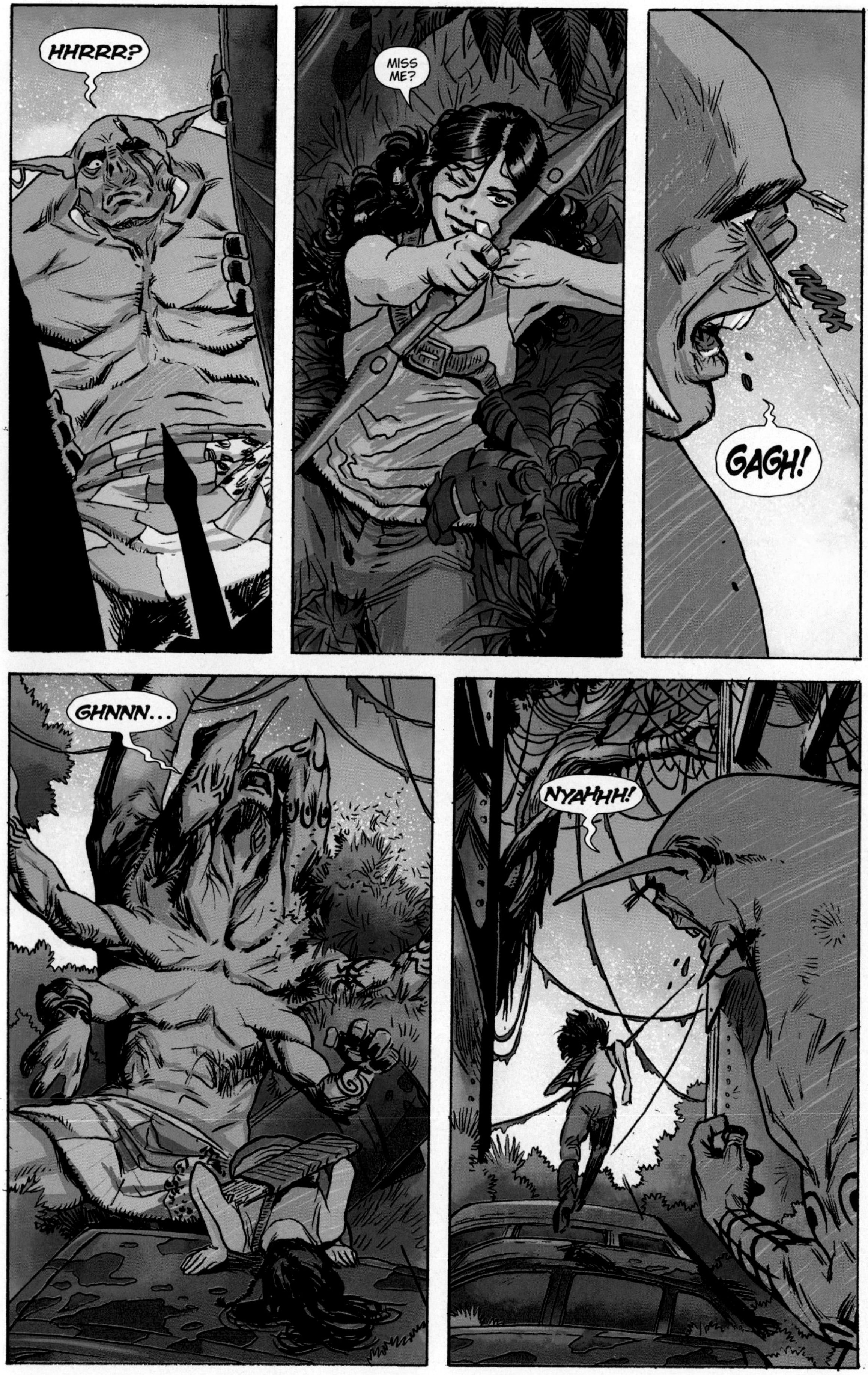
HHRRR?
MISS ME?
THOK
GAGH!
GHNNN...
NYAHHH!

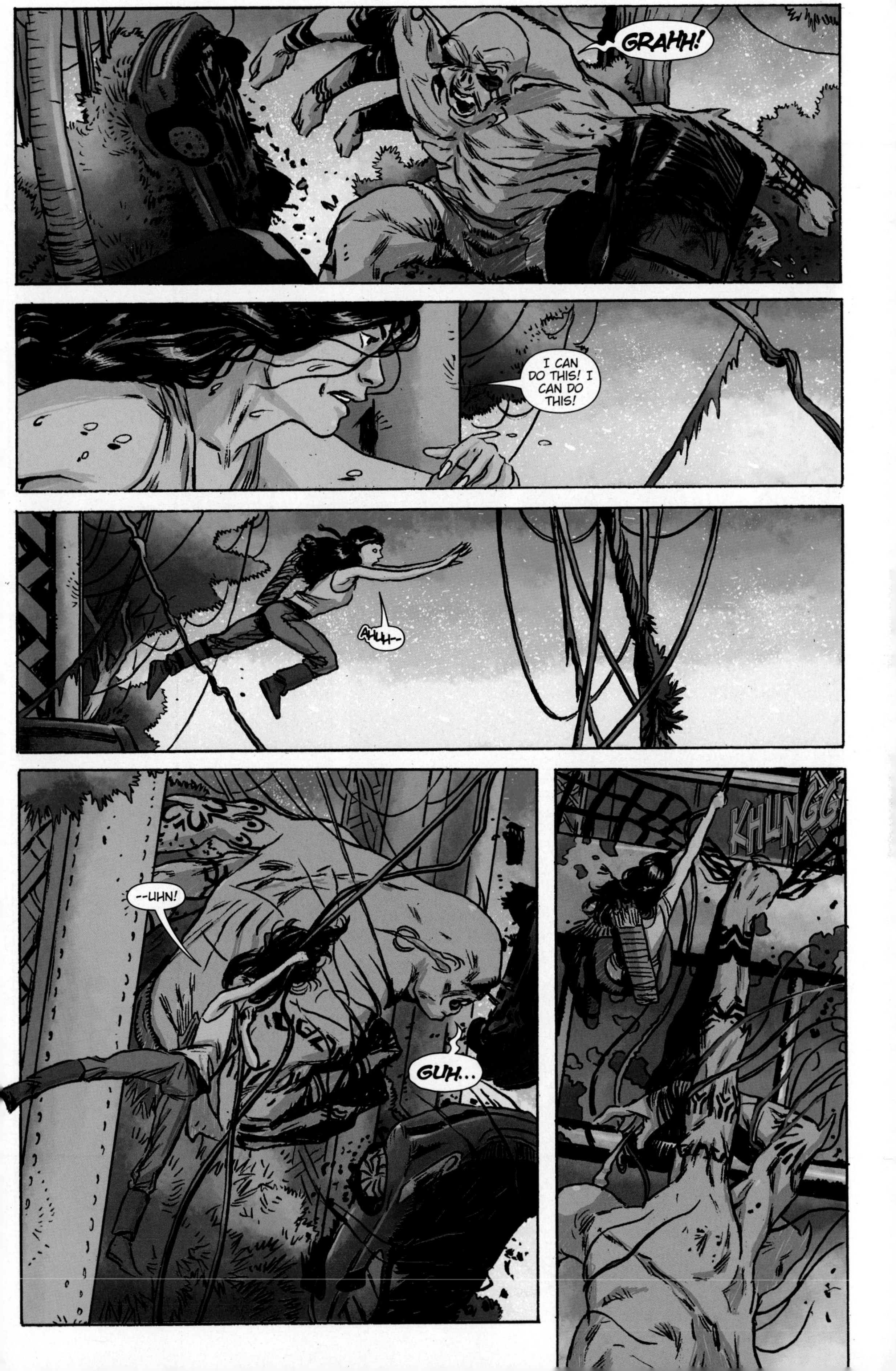
GRAHH!
I CAN DO THIS! I CAN DO THIS!
AHHH--
--UHN!
GUH...
KHUNGG

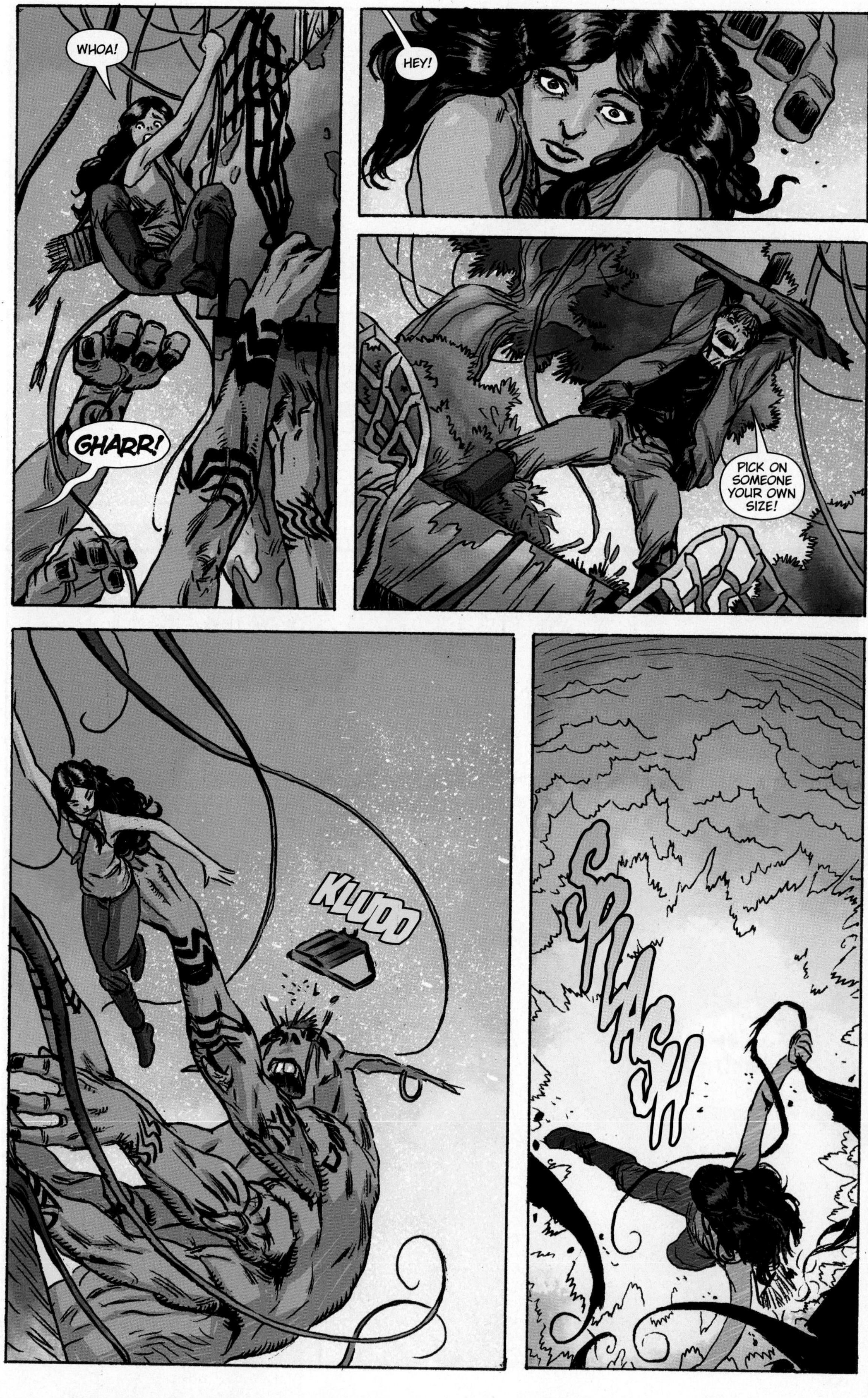
WHOA!
GHARR!
HEY!
PICK ON SOMEONE YOUR OWN SIZE!
KLUDD
SPLASH

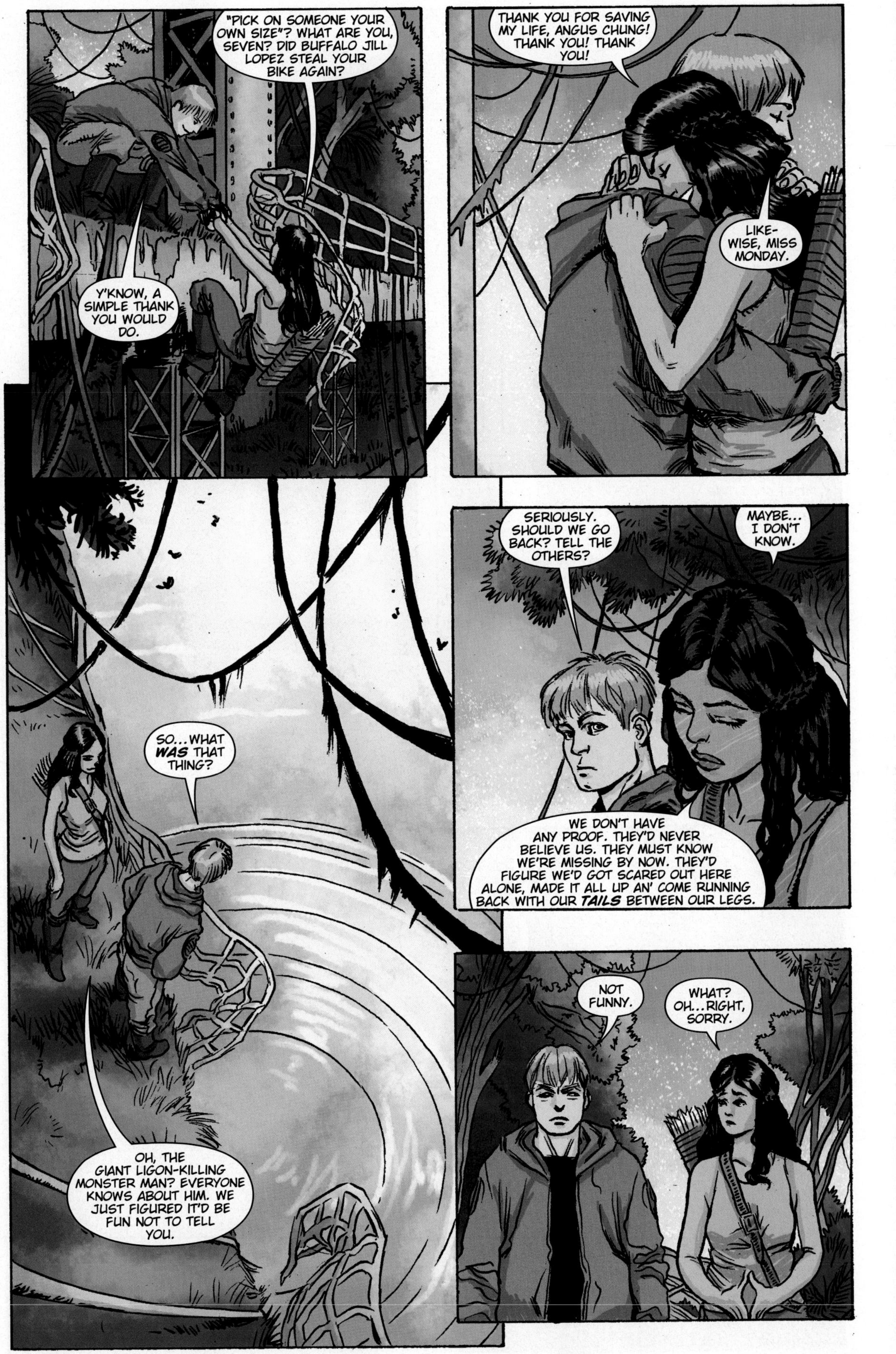
"PICK ON SOMEONE YOUR OWN SIZE"? WHAT ARE YOU, SEVEN? DID BUFFALO JILL LOPEZ STEAL YOUR BIKE AGAIN?
Y'KNOW, A SIMPLE THANK YOU WOULD DO.
THANK YOU FOR SAVING MY LIFE, ANGUS CHUNG! THANK YOU! THANK YOU!
LIKE-WISE, MISS MONDAY.
SO...WHAT ***WAS*** THAT THING?
OH, THE GIANT LIGON-KILLING MONSTER MAN? EVERYONE KNOWS ABOUT HIM. WE JUST FIGURED IT'D BE FUN NOT TO TELL YOU.
SERIOUSLY. SHOULD WE GO BACK? TELL THE OTHERS?
MAYBE... I DON'T KNOW.
WE DON'T HAVE ANY PROOF. THEY'D NEVER BELIEVE US. THEY MUST KNOW WE'RE MISSING BY NOW. THEY'D FIGURE WE'D GOT SCARED OUT HERE ALONE, MADE IT ALL UP AN' COME RUNNING BACK WITH OUR ***TAILS*** BETWEEN OUR LEGS.
NOT FUNNY.
WHAT? OH...RIGHT, SORRY.

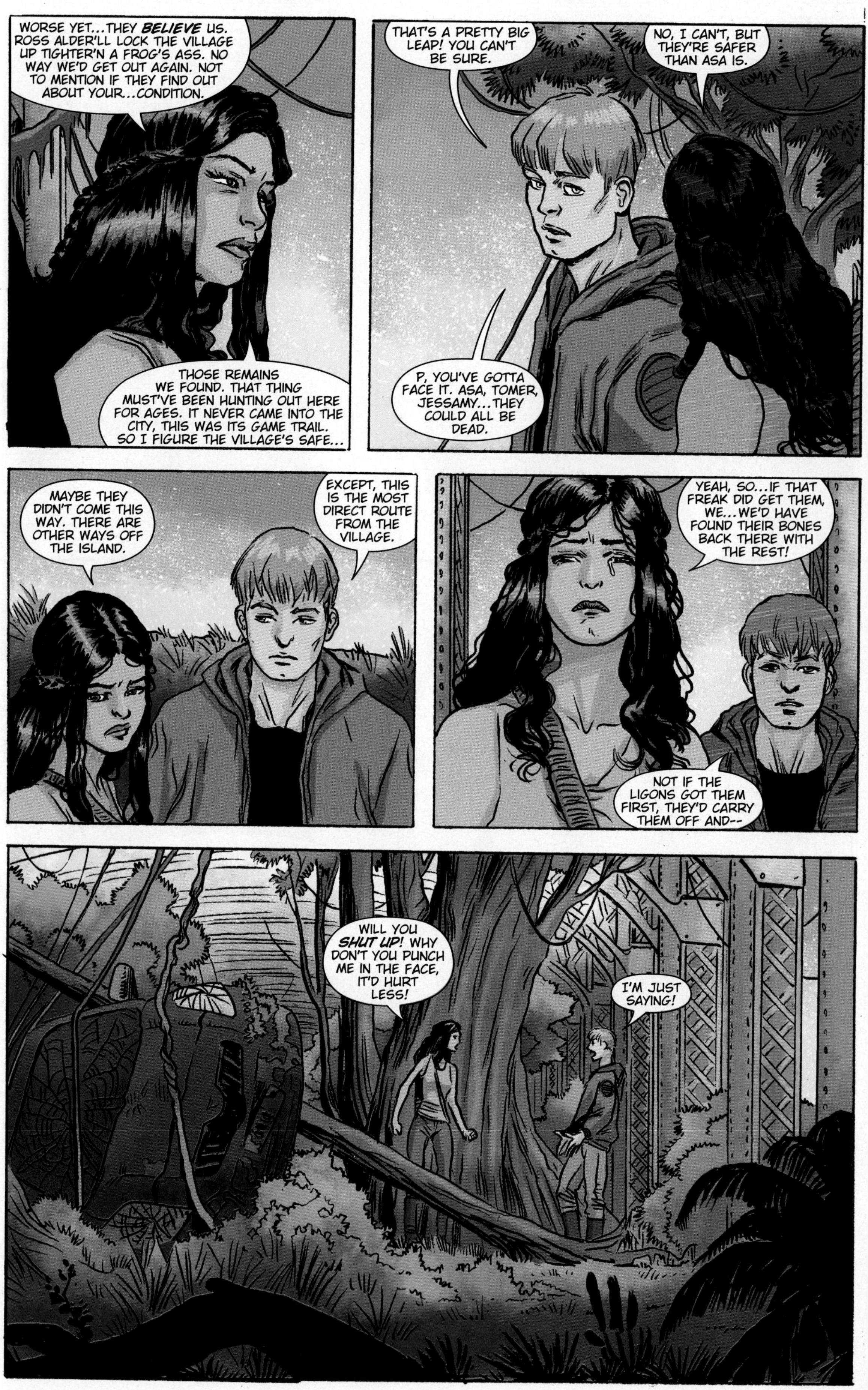
WORSE YET...THEY **BELIEVE** US. ROSS ALDER'LL LOCK THE VILLAGE UP TIGHTER'N A FROG'S ASS. NO WAY WE'D GET OUT AGAIN. NOT TO MENTION IF THEY FIND OUT ABOUT YOUR...CONDITION.
THOSE REMAINS WE FOUND. THAT THING MUST'VE BEEN HUNTING OUT HERE FOR AGES. IT NEVER CAME INTO THE CITY, THIS WAS ITS GAME TRAIL. SO I FIGURE THE VILLAGE'S SAFE...
THAT'S A PRETTY BIG LEAP! YOU CAN'T BE SURE.
NO, I CAN'T, BUT THEY'RE SAFER THAN ASA IS.
P, YOU'VE GOTTA FACE IT. ASA, TOMER, JESSAMY...THEY COULD ALL BE DEAD.
MAYBE THEY DIDN'T COME THIS WAY. THERE ARE OTHER WAYS OFF THE ISLAND.
EXCEPT, THIS IS THE MOST DIRECT ROUTE FROM THE VILLAGE.
YEAH, SO...IF THAT FREAK DID GET THEM, WE...WE'D HAVE FOUND THEIR BONES BACK THERE WITH THE REST!
NOT IF THE LIGONS GOT THEM FIRST, THEY'D CARRY THEM OFF AND--
WILL YOU **SHUT UP**! WHY DON'T YOU PUNCH ME IN THE FACE, IT'D HURT LESS!
I'M JUST SAYING!

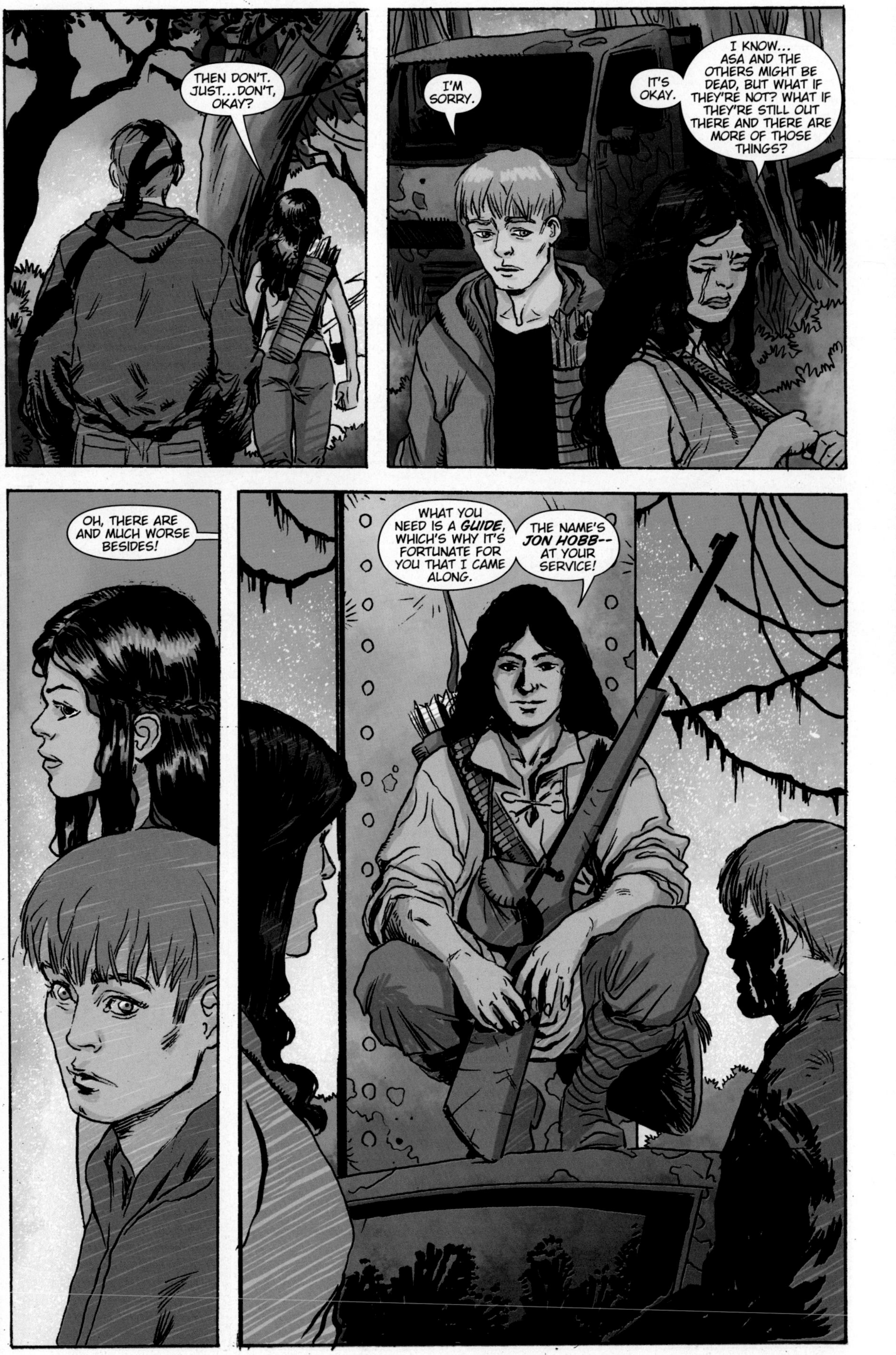
THEN DON'T. JUST...DON'T, OKAY?
I'M SORRY.
IT'S OKAY.
I KNOW... ASA AND THE OTHERS MIGHT BE DEAD, BUT WHAT IF THEY'RE NOT? WHAT IF THEY'RE STILL OUT THERE AND THERE ARE MORE OF THOSE THINGS?
OH, THERE ARE AND MUCH WORSE BESIDES!
WHAT YOU NEED IS A GUIDE, WHICH'S WHY IT'S FORTUNATE FOR YOU THAT I CAME ALONG.
THE NAME'S JON HOBB-- AT YOUR SERVICE!

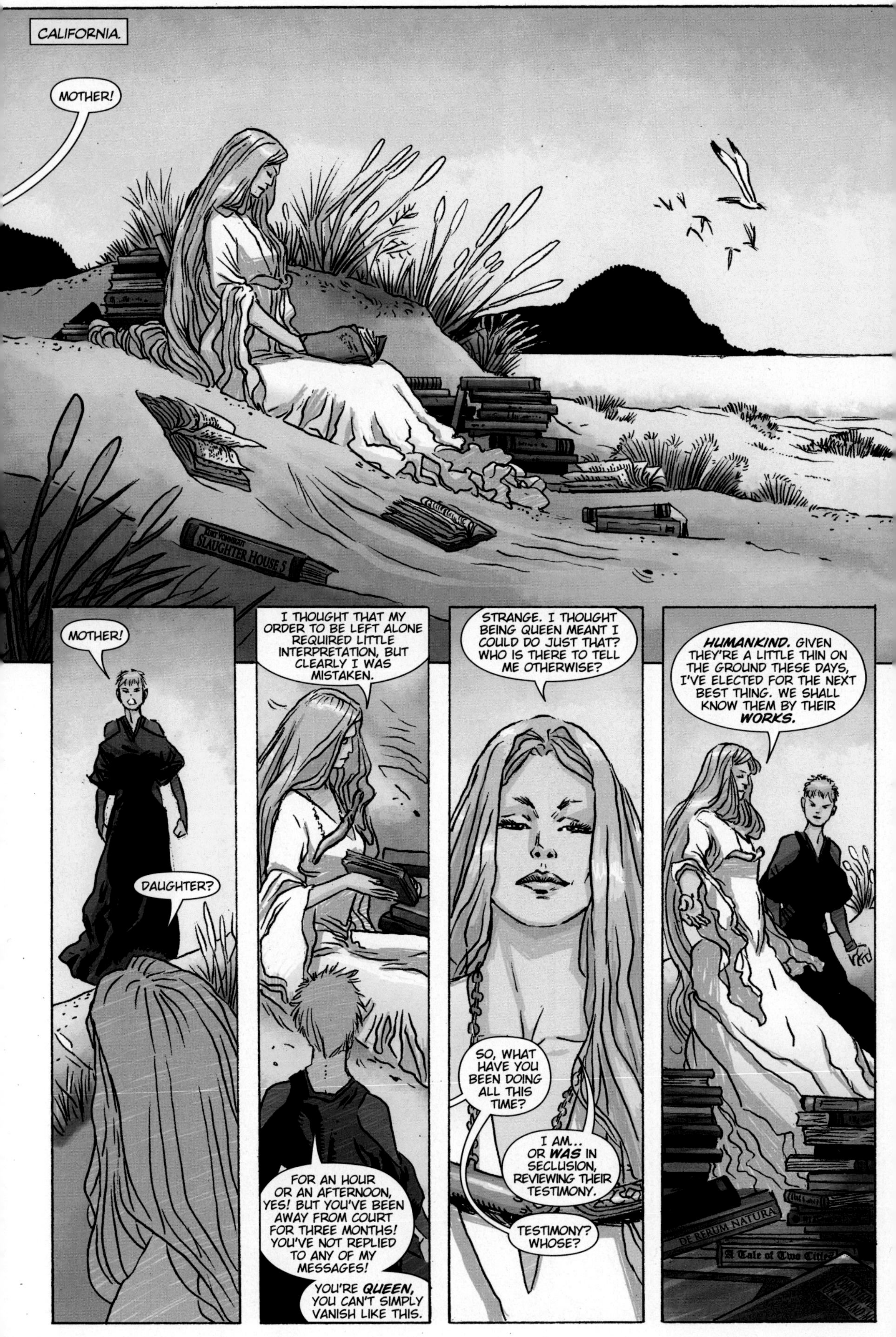
CALIFORNIA.
MOTHER!
KURT VONNEGUT SLAUGHTER HOUSE 5
MOTHER!
DAUGHTER?
I THOUGHT THAT MY ORDER TO BE LEFT ALONE REQUIRED LITTLE INTERPRETATION, BUT CLEARLY I WAS MISTAKEN.
FOR AN HOUR OR AN AFTERNOON, YES! BUT YOU'VE BEEN AWAY FROM COURT FOR THREE MONTHS! YOU'VE NOT REPLIED TO ANY OF MY MESSAGES!
YOU'RE QUEEN, YOU CAN'T SIMPLY VANISH LIKE THIS.
STRANGE. I THOUGHT BEING QUEEN MEANT I COULD DO JUST THAT? WHO IS THERE TO TELL ME OTHERWISE?
SO, WHAT HAVE YOU BEEN DOING ALL THIS TIME?
I AM... OR WAS IN SECLUSION, REVIEWING THEIR TESTIMONY.
TESTIMONY? WHOSE?
HUMANKIND. GIVEN THEY'RE A LITTLE THIN ON THE GROUND THESE DAYS, I'VE ELECTED FOR THE NEXT BEST THING. WE SHALL KNOW THEM BY THEIR WORKS.
DE RERUM NATURA
A Tale of Two Cities

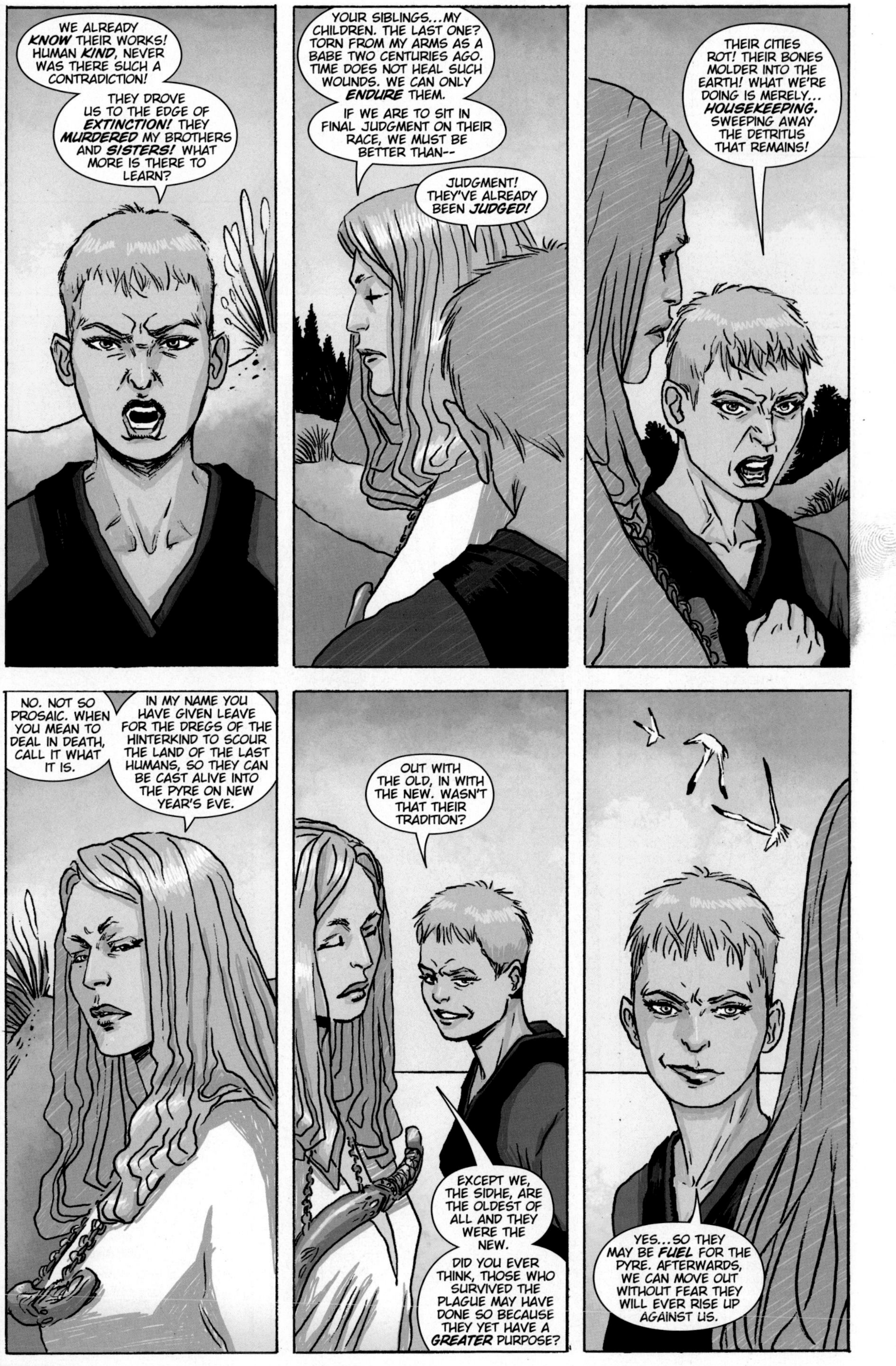
WE ALREADY KNOW THEIR WORKS! HUMAN KIND, NEVER WAS THERE SUCH A CONTRADICTION!
THEY DROVE US TO THE EDGE OF EXTINCTION! THEY MURDERED MY BROTHERS AND SISTERS! WHAT MORE IS THERE TO LEARN?
YOUR SIBLINGS... MY CHILDREN. THE LAST ONE? TORN FROM MY ARMS AS A BABE TWO CENTURIES AGO. TIME DOES NOT HEAL SUCH WOUNDS. WE CAN ONLY ENDURE THEM.
IF WE ARE TO SIT IN FINAL JUDGMENT ON THEIR RACE, WE MUST BE BETTER THAN--
JUDGMENT! THEY'VE ALREADY BEEN JUDGED!
THEIR CITIES ROT! THEIR BONES MOLDER INTO THE EARTH! WHAT WE'RE DOING IS MERELY... HOUSEKEEPING. SWEEPING AWAY THE DETRITUS THAT REMAINS!
NO. NOT SO PROSAIC. WHEN YOU MEAN TO DEAL IN DEATH, CALL IT WHAT IT IS.
IN MY NAME YOU HAVE GIVEN LEAVE FOR THE DREGS OF THE HINTERKIND TO SCOUR THE LAND OF THE LAST HUMANS, SO THEY CAN BE CAST ALIVE INTO THE PYRE ON NEW YEAR'S EVE.
OUT WITH THE OLD, IN WITH THE NEW. WASN'T THAT THEIR TRADITION?
EXCEPT WE, THE SIDHE, ARE THE OLDEST OF ALL AND THEY WERE THE NEW.
DID YOU EVER THINK, THOSE WHO SURVIVED THE PLAGUE MAY HAVE DONE SO BECAUSE THEY YET HAVE A GREATER PURPOSE?
YES... SO THEY MAY BE FUEL FOR THE PYRE. AFTERWARDS, WE CAN MOVE OUT WITHOUT FEAR THEY WILL EVER RISE UP AGAINST US.

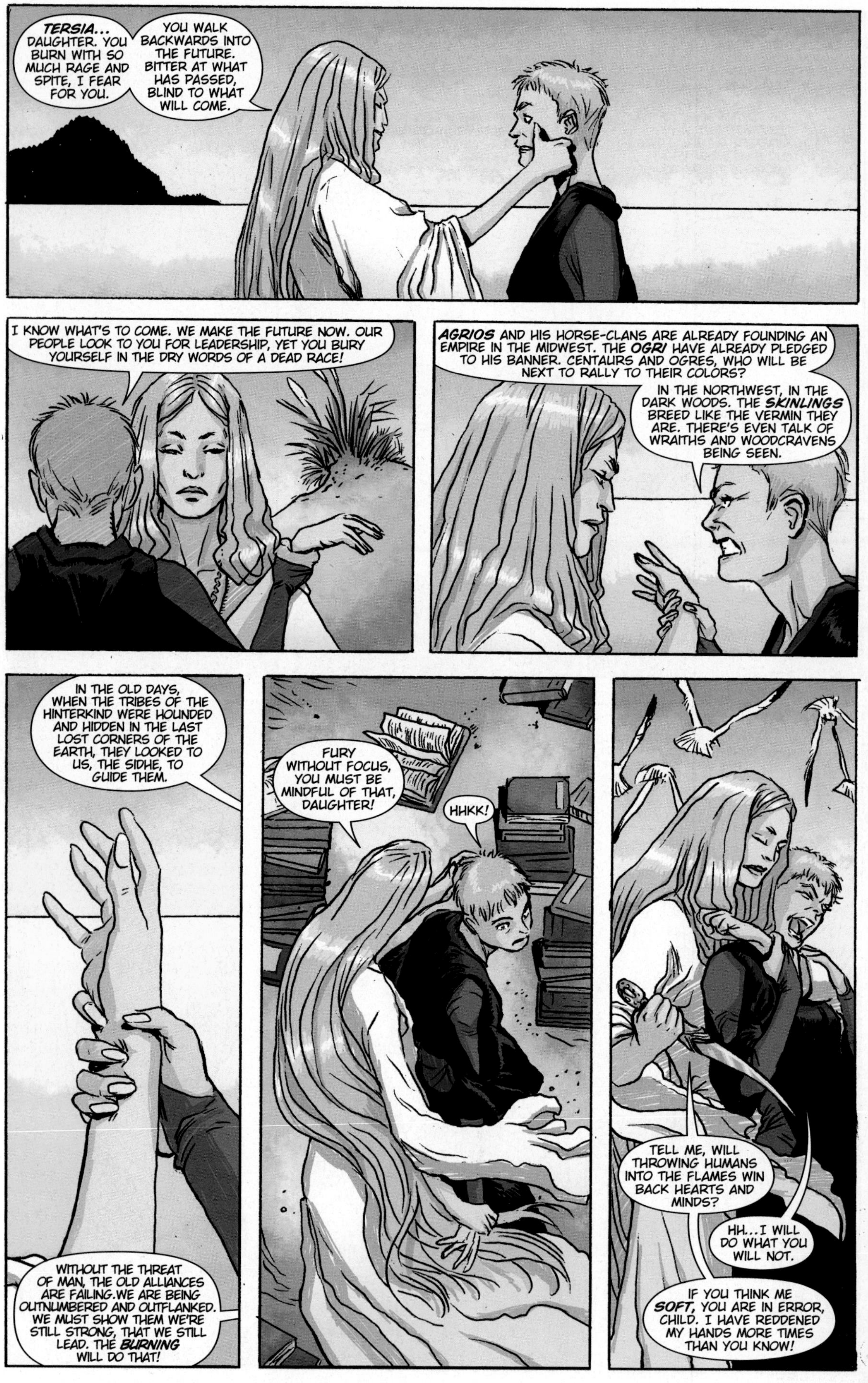
TERSIA... DAUGHTER. YOU BURN WITH SO MUCH RAGE AND SPITE, I FEAR FOR YOU.
YOU WALK BACKWARDS INTO THE FUTURE. BITTER AT WHAT HAS PASSED, BLIND TO WHAT WILL COME.
I KNOW WHAT'S TO COME. WE MAKE THE FUTURE NOW. OUR PEOPLE LOOK TO YOU FOR LEADERSHIP, YET YOU BURY YOURSELF IN THE DRY WORDS OF A DEAD RACE!
AGRIOS AND HIS HORSE-CLANS ARE ALREADY FOUNDING AN EMPIRE IN THE MIDWEST. THE OGRI HAVE ALREADY PLEDGED TO HIS BANNER. CENTAURS AND OGRES, WHO WILL BE NEXT TO RALLY TO THEIR COLORS?
IN THE NORTHWEST, IN THE DARK WOODS. THE SKINLINGS BREED LIKE THE VERMIN THEY ARE. THERE'S EVEN TALK OF WRAITHS AND WOODCRAVENS BEING SEEN.
IN THE OLD DAYS, WHEN THE TRIBES OF THE HINTERKIND WERE HOUNDED AND HIDDEN IN THE LAST LOST CORNERS OF THE EARTH, THEY LOOKED TO US, THE SIDHE, TO GUIDE THEM.
WITHOUT THE THREAT OF MAN, THE OLD ALLIANCES ARE FAILING. WE ARE BEING OUTNUMBERED AND OUTFLANKED. WE MUST SHOW THEM WE'RE STILL STRONG, THAT WE STILL LEAD. THE BURNING WILL DO THAT!
FURY WITHOUT FOCUS, YOU MUST BE MINDFUL OF THAT, DAUGHTER!
HHKK!
TELL ME, WILL THROWING HUMANS INTO THE FLAMES WIN BACK HEARTS AND MINDS?
HH...I WILL DO WHAT YOU WILL NOT.
IF YOU THINK ME SOFT, YOU ARE IN ERROR, CHILD. I HAVE REDDENED MY HANDS MORE TIMES THAN YOU KNOW!

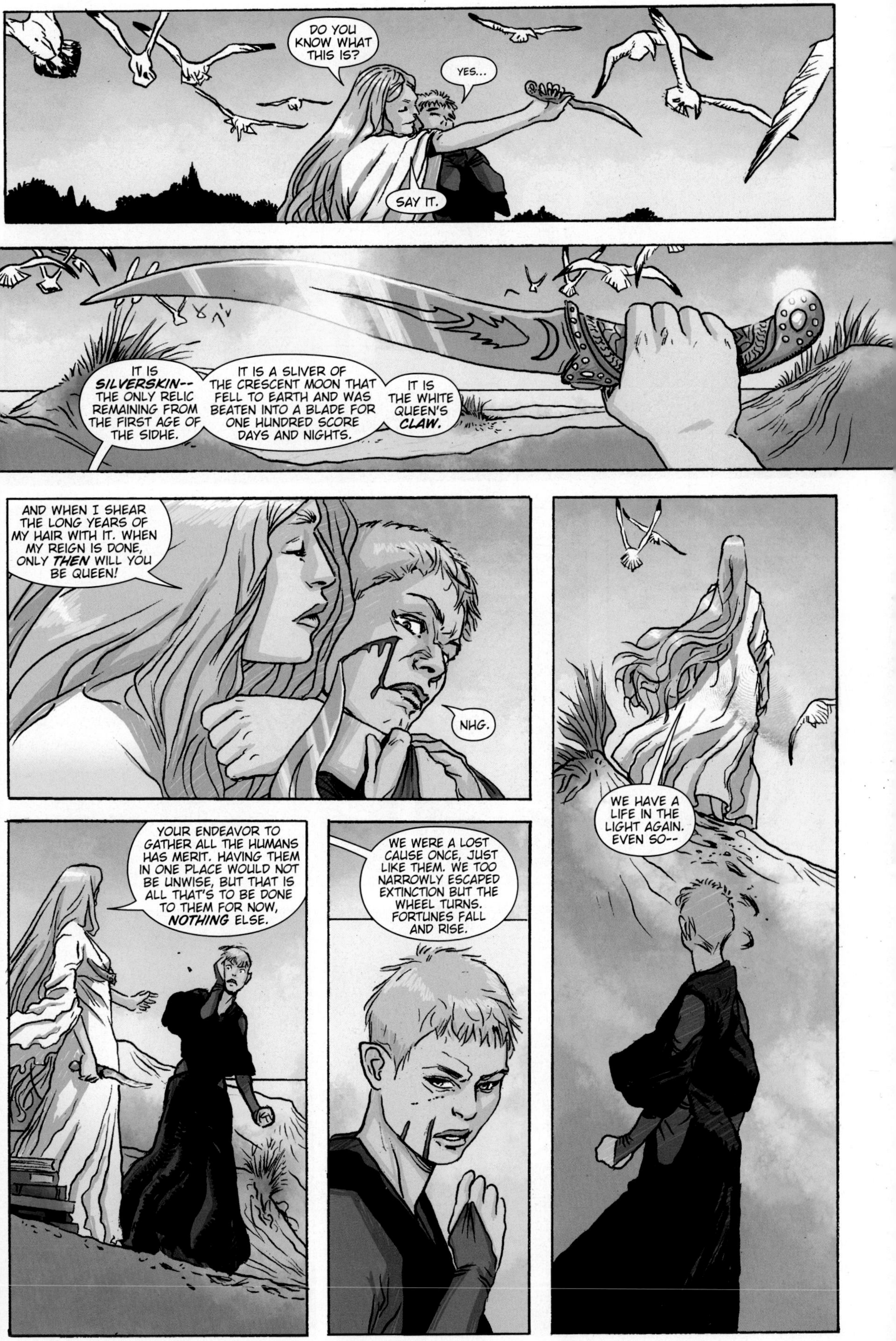
DO YOU KNOW WHAT THIS IS?
YES...
SAY IT.
IT IS SILVERSKIN-- THE ONLY RELIC REMAINING FROM THE FIRST AGE OF THE SIDHE.
IT IS A SLIVER OF THE CRESCENT MOON THAT FELL TO EARTH AND WAS BEATEN INTO A BLADE FOR ONE HUNDRED SCORE DAYS AND NIGHTS.
IT IS THE WHITE QUEEN'S CLAW.
AND WHEN I SHEAR THE LONG YEARS OF MY HAIR WITH IT. WHEN MY REIGN IS DONE, ONLY THEN WILL YOU BE QUEEN!
NHG.
WE HAVE A LIFE IN THE LIGHT AGAIN. EVEN SO--
YOUR ENDEAVOR TO GATHER ALL THE HUMANS HAS MERIT. HAVING THEM IN ONE PLACE WOULD NOT BE UNWISE, BUT THAT IS ALL THAT'S TO BE DONE TO THEM FOR NOW, NOTHING ELSE.
WE WERE A LOST CAUSE ONCE, JUST LIKE THEM. WE TOO NARROWLY ESCAPED EXTINCTION BUT THE WHEEL TURNS. FORTUNES FALL AND RISE.

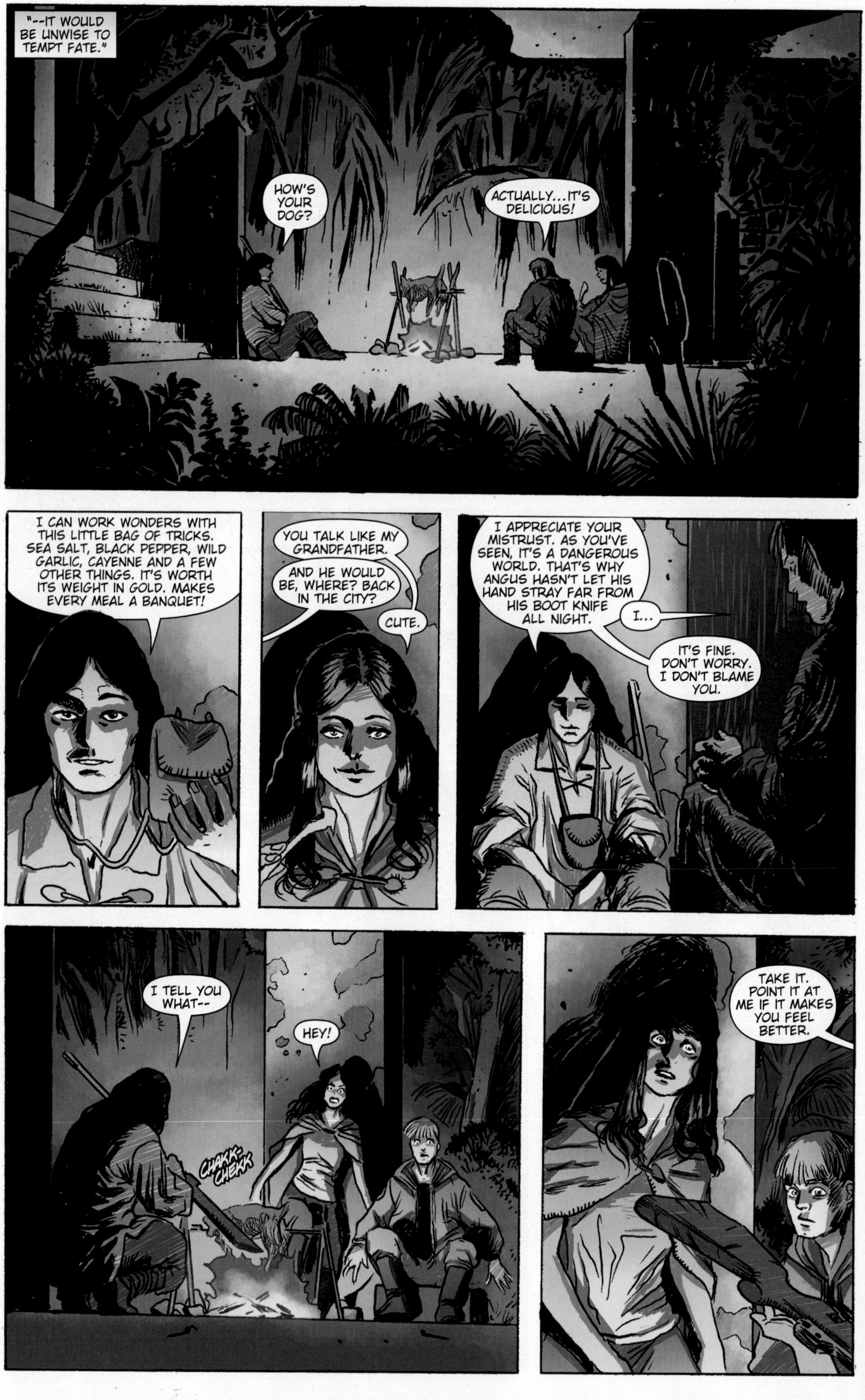
"--IT WOULD BE UNWISE TO TEMPT FATE."
HOW'S YOUR DOG?
ACTUALLY... IT'S DELICIOUS!
I CAN WORK WONDERS WITH THIS LITTLE BAG OF TRICKS. SEA SALT, BLACK PEPPER, WILD GARLIC, CAYENNE AND A FEW OTHER THINGS. IT'S WORTH ITS WEIGHT IN GOLD. MAKES EVERY MEAL A BANQUET!
YOU TALK LIKE MY GRANDFATHER.
AND HE WOULD BE, WHERE? BACK IN THE CITY?
CUTE.
I APPRECIATE YOUR MISTRUST. AS YOU'VE SEEN, IT'S A DANGEROUS WORLD. THAT'S WHY ANGUS HASN'T LET HIS HAND STRAY FAR FROM HIS BOOT KNIFE ALL NIGHT.
I...
IT'S FINE. DON'T WORRY. I DON'T BLAME YOU.
I TELL YOU WHAT--
HEY!
CHAKK-CHEKK
TAKE IT. POINT IT AT ME IF IT MAKES YOU FEEL BETTER.

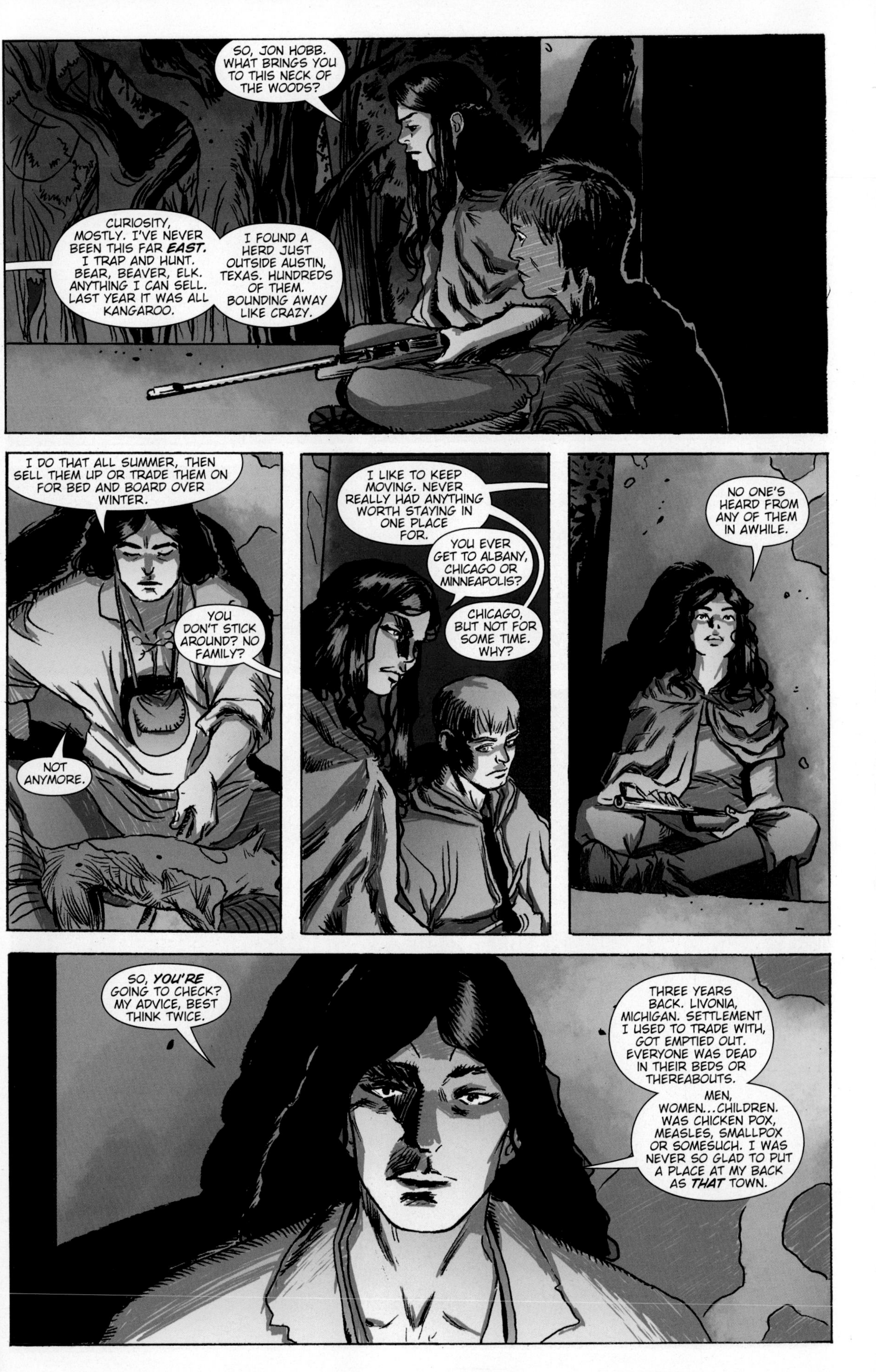
SO, JON HOBB. WHAT BRINGS YOU TO THIS NECK OF THE WOODS?
CURIOSITY, MOSTLY. I'VE NEVER BEEN THIS FAR **EAST.** I TRAP AND HUNT. BEAR, BEAVER, ELK. ANYTHING I CAN SELL. LAST YEAR IT WAS ALL KANGAROO.
I FOUND A HERD JUST OUTSIDE AUSTIN, TEXAS. HUNDREDS OF THEM. BOUNDING AWAY LIKE CRAZY.
I DO THAT ALL SUMMER, THEN SELL THEM UP OR TRADE THEM ON FOR BED AND BOARD OVER WINTER.
YOU DON'T STICK AROUND? NO FAMILY?
NOT ANYMORE.
I LIKE TO KEEP MOVING. NEVER REALLY HAD ANYTHING WORTH STAYING IN ONE PLACE FOR.
YOU EVER GET TO ALBANY, CHICAGO OR MINNEAPOLIS?
CHICAGO, BUT NOT FOR SOME TIME. WHY?
NO ONE'S HEARD FROM ANY OF THEM IN AWHILE.
SO, **YOU'RE** GOING TO CHECK? MY ADVICE, BEST THINK TWICE.
THREE YEARS BACK. LIVONIA, MICHIGAN. SETTLEMENT I USED TO TRADE WITH, GOT EMPTIED OUT. EVERYONE WAS DEAD IN THEIR BEDS OR THEREABOUTS.
MEN, WOMEN...CHILDREN. WAS CHICKEN POX, MEASLES, SMALLPOX OR SOMESUCH. I WAS NEVER SO GLAD TO PUT A PLACE AT MY BACK AS ***THAT*** TOWN.

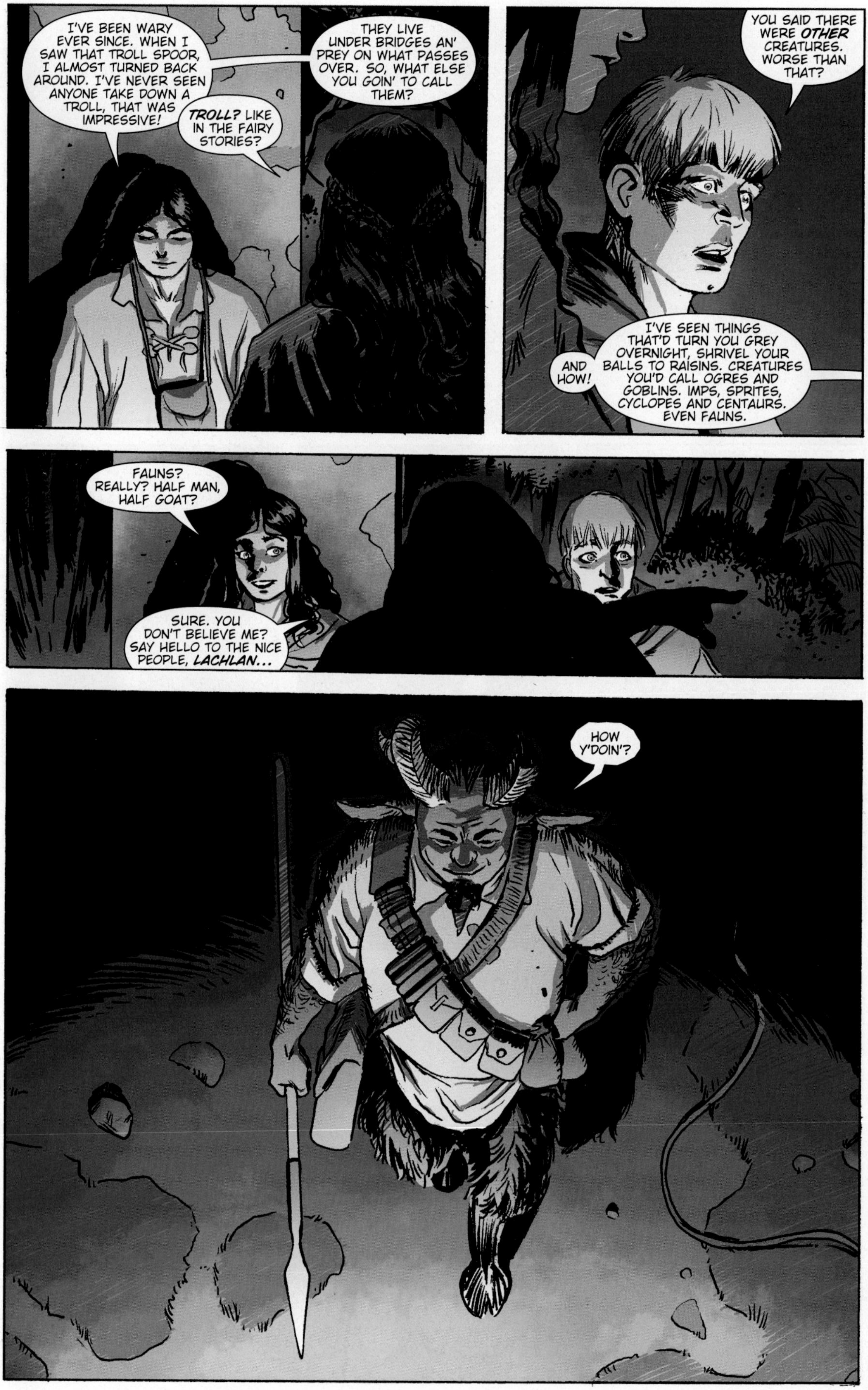
I'VE BEEN WARY EVER SINCE. WHEN I SAW THAT TROLL SPOOR, I ALMOST TURNED BACK AROUND. I'VE NEVER SEEN ANYONE TAKE DOWN A TROLL, THAT WAS IMPRESSIVE!
TROLL? LIKE IN THE FAIRY STORIES?
THEY LIVE UNDER BRIDGES AN' PREY ON WHAT PASSES OVER. SO, WHAT ELSE YOU GOIN' TO CALL THEM?
YOU SAID THERE WERE OTHER CREATURES. WORSE THAN THAT?
AND HOW!
I'VE SEEN THINGS THAT'D TURN YOU GREY OVERNIGHT, SHRIVEL YOUR BALLS TO RAISINS. CREATURES YOU'D CALL OGRES AND GOBLINS. IMPS, SPRITES, CYCLOPES AND CENTAURS. EVEN FAUNS.
FAUNS? REALLY? HALF MAN, HALF GOAT?
SURE. YOU DON'T BELIEVE ME? SAY HELLO TO THE NICE PEOPLE, LACHLAN...
HOW Y'DOIN'?

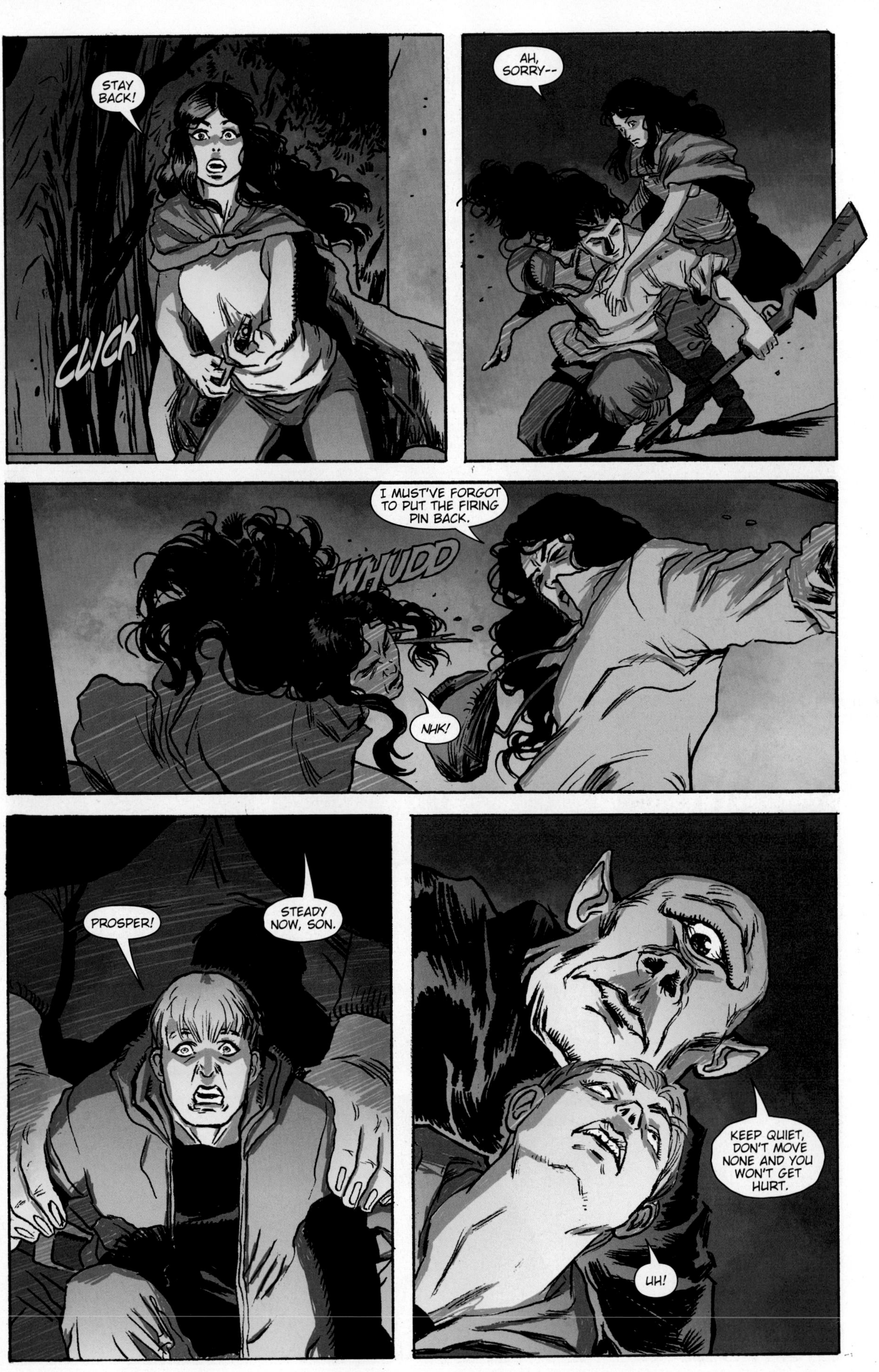
STAY BACK!
CLICK
AH, SORRY--
I MUST'VE FORGOT TO PUT THE FIRING PIN BACK.
WHUDD
NHK!
PROSPER!
STEADY NOW, SON.
KEEP QUIET, DON'T MOVE NONE AND YOU WON'T GET HURT.
UH!

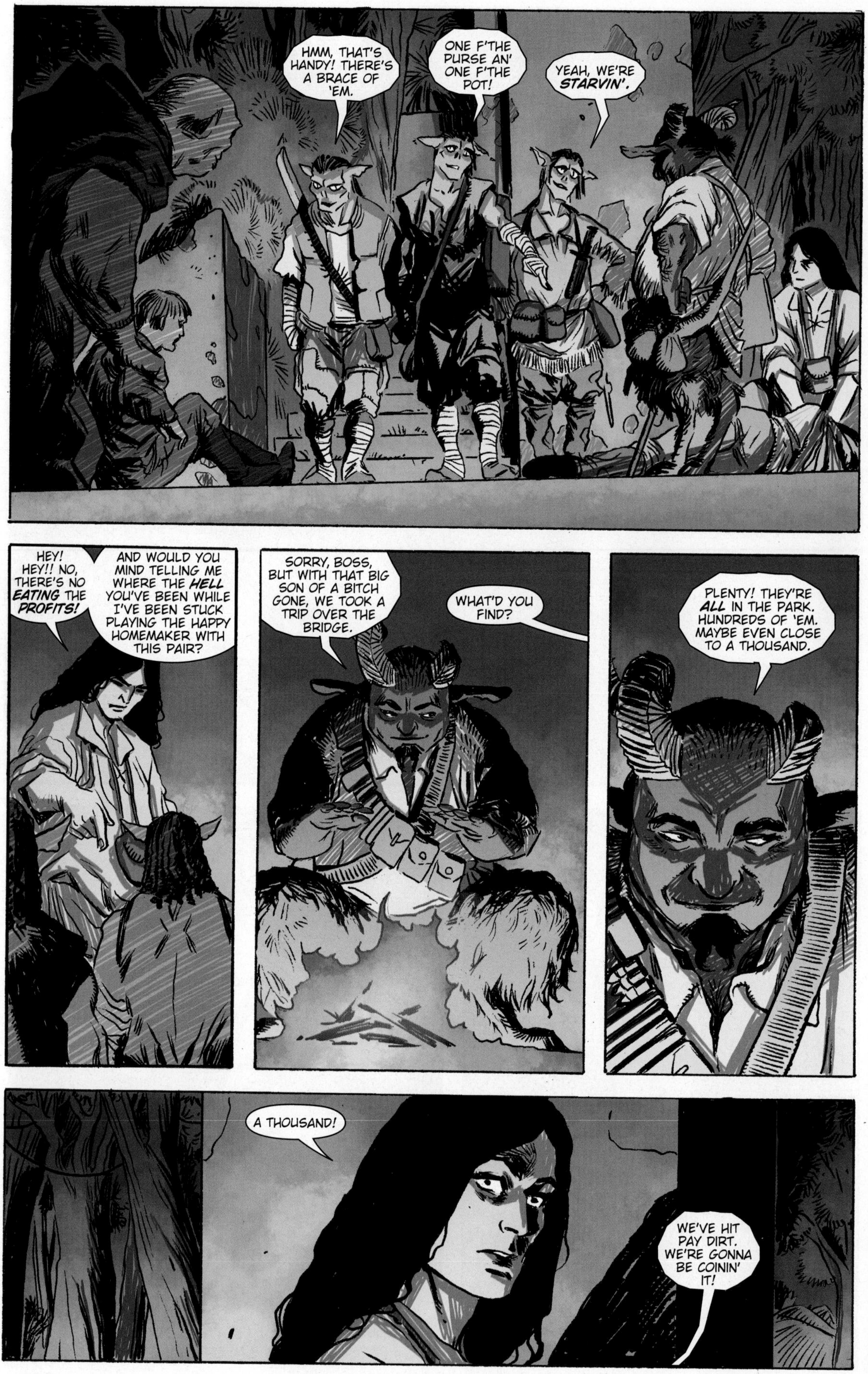
HMM, THAT'S HANDY! THERE'S A BRACE OF 'EM.
ONE F'THE PURSE AN' ONE F'THE POT!
YEAH, WE'RE STARVIN'.
HEY! HEY!! NO, THERE'S NO EATING THE PROFITS!
AND WOULD YOU MIND TELLING ME WHERE THE HELL YOU'VE BEEN WHILE I'VE BEEN STUCK PLAYING THE HAPPY HOMEMAKER WITH THIS PAIR?
SORRY, BOSS, BUT WITH THAT BIG SON OF A BITCH GONE, WE TOOK A TRIP OVER THE BRIDGE.
WHAT'D YOU FIND?
PLENTY! THEY'RE ALL IN THE PARK. HUNDREDS OF 'EM. MAYBE EVEN CLOSE TO A THOUSAND.
A THOUSAND!
WE'VE HIT PAY DIRT. WE'RE GONNA BE COININ' IT!

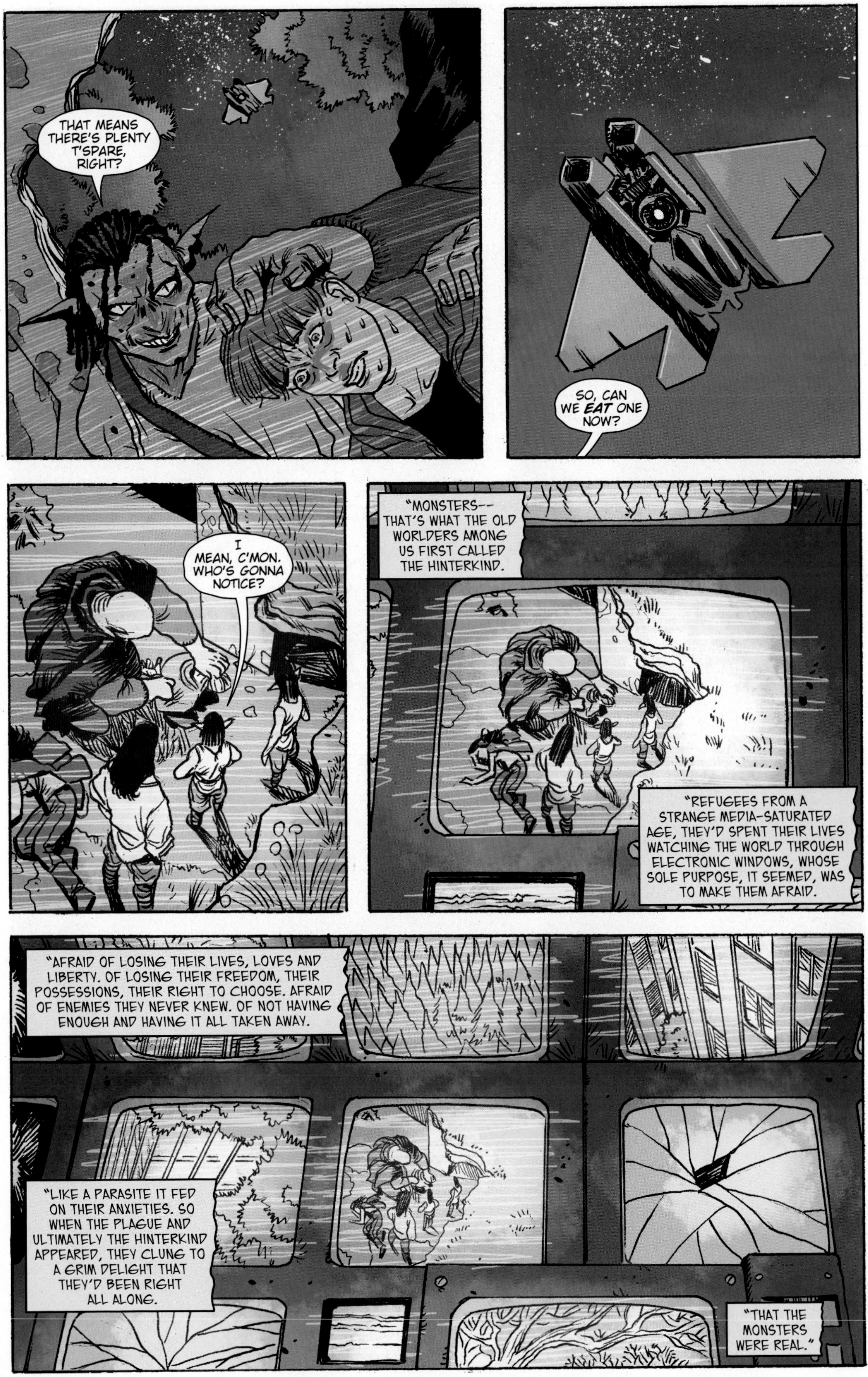
THAT MEANS THERE'S PLENTY T'SPARE, RIGHT?
SO, CAN WE EAT ONE NOW?
I MEAN, C'MON. WHO'S GONNA NOTICE?
"MONSTERS-- THAT'S WHAT THE OLD WORLDERS AMONG US FIRST CALLED THE HINTERKIND.
"REFUGEES FROM A STRANGE MEDIA-SATURATED AGE, THEY'D SPENT THEIR LIVES WATCHING THE WORLD THROUGH ELECTRONIC WINDOWS, WHOSE SOLE PURPOSE, IT SEEMED, WAS TO MAKE THEM AFRAID.
"AFRAID OF LOSING THEIR LIVES, LOVES AND LIBERTY. OF LOSING THEIR FREEDOM, THEIR POSSESSIONS, THEIR RIGHT TO CHOOSE. AFRAID OF ENEMIES THEY NEVER KNEW. OF NOT HAVING ENOUGH AND HAVING IT ALL TAKEN AWAY.
"LIKE A PARASITE IT FED ON THEIR ANXIETIES. SO WHEN THE PLAGUE AND ULTIMATELY THE HINTERKIND APPEARED, THEY CLUNG TO A GRIM DELIGHT THAT THEY'D BEEN RIGHT ALL ALONG.
"THAT THE MONSTERS WERE REAL."

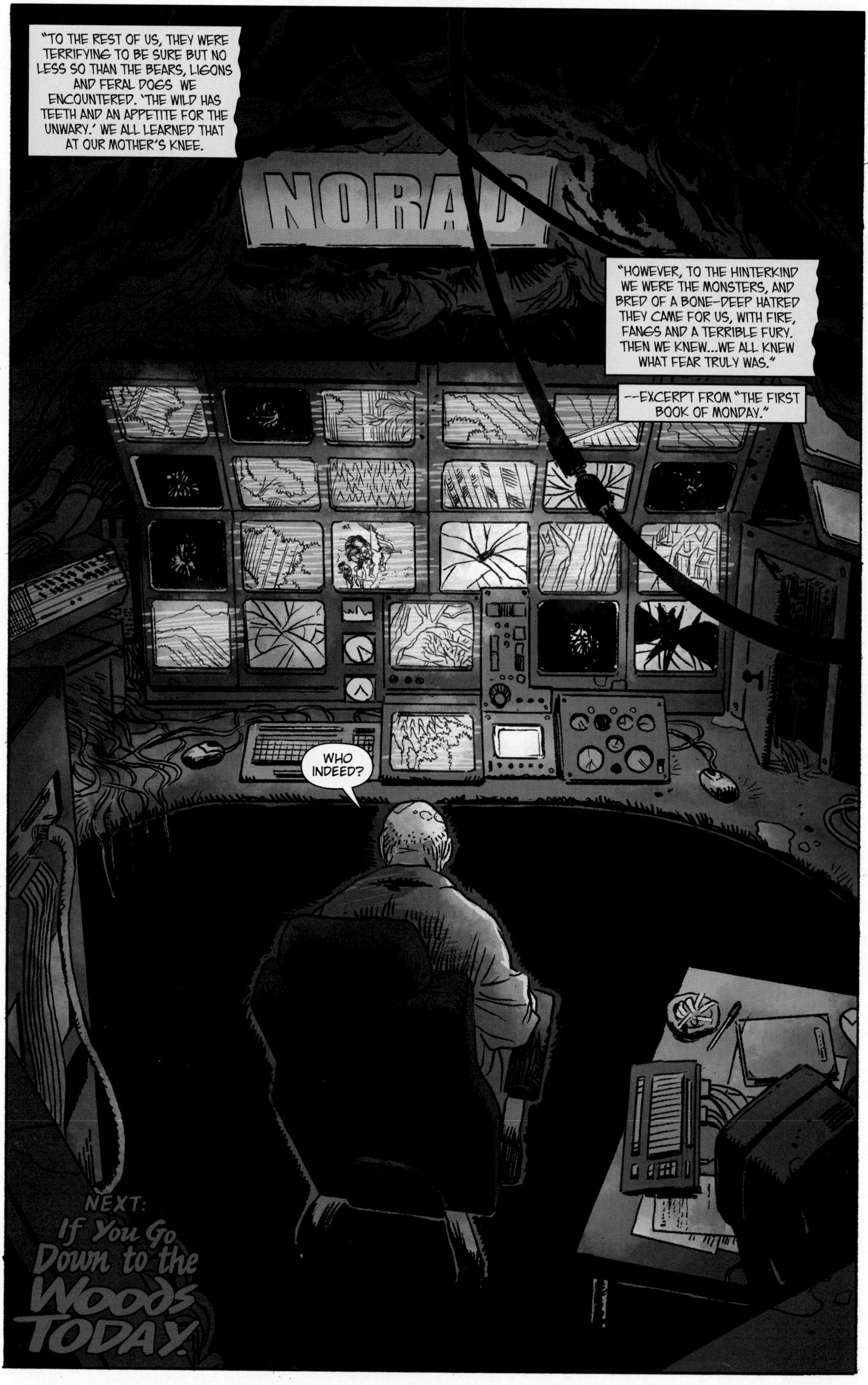
"TO THE REST OF US, THEY WERE TERRIFYING TO BE SURE BUT NO LESS SO THAN THE BEARS, LIGONS AND FERAL DOGS WE ENCOUNTERED. 'THE WILD HAS TEETH AND AN APPETITE FOR THE UNWARY.' WE ALL LEARNED THAT AT OUR MOTHER'S KNEE.
NORAD
"HOWEVER, TO THE HINTERKIND WE WERE THE MONSTERS, AND BRED OF A BONE-DEEP HATRED THEY CAME FOR US, WITH FIRE, FANGS AND A TERRIBLE FURY. THEN WE KNEW...WE ALL KNEW WHAT FEAR TRULY WAS."
--EXCERPT FROM "THE FIRST BOOK OF MONDAY."
WHO INDEED?
NEXT: If You Go Down to the Woods TODAY.

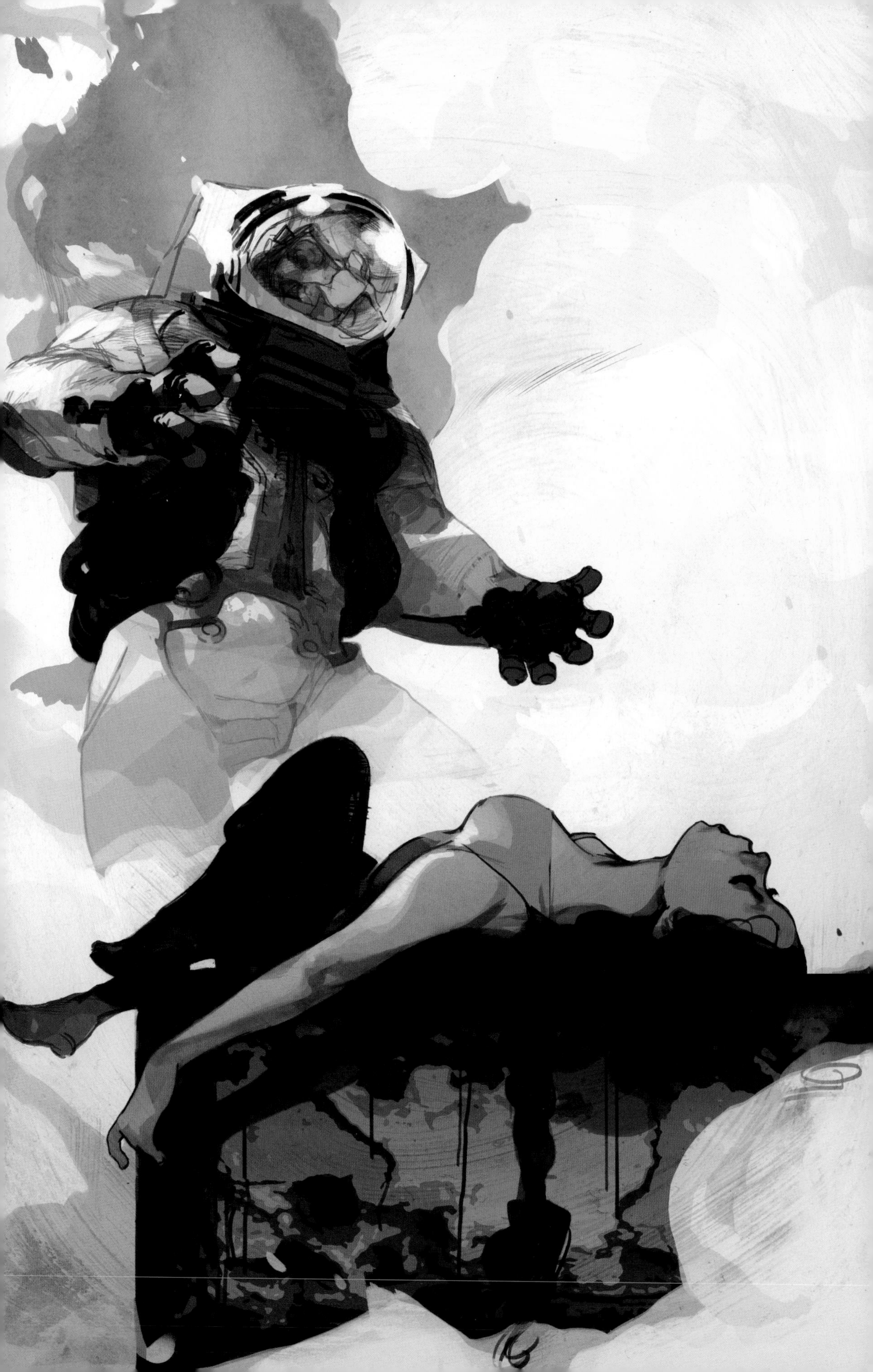

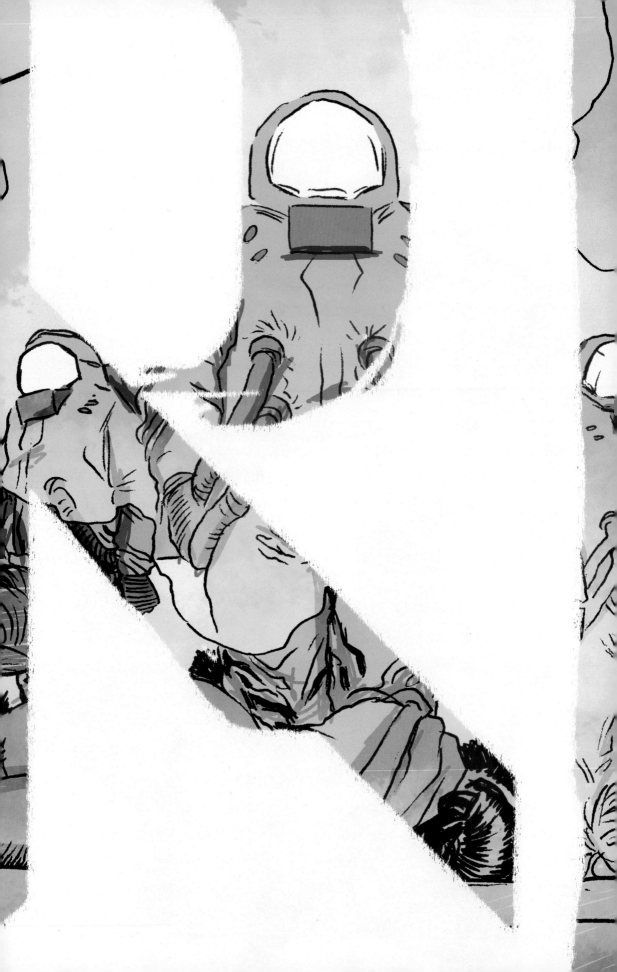

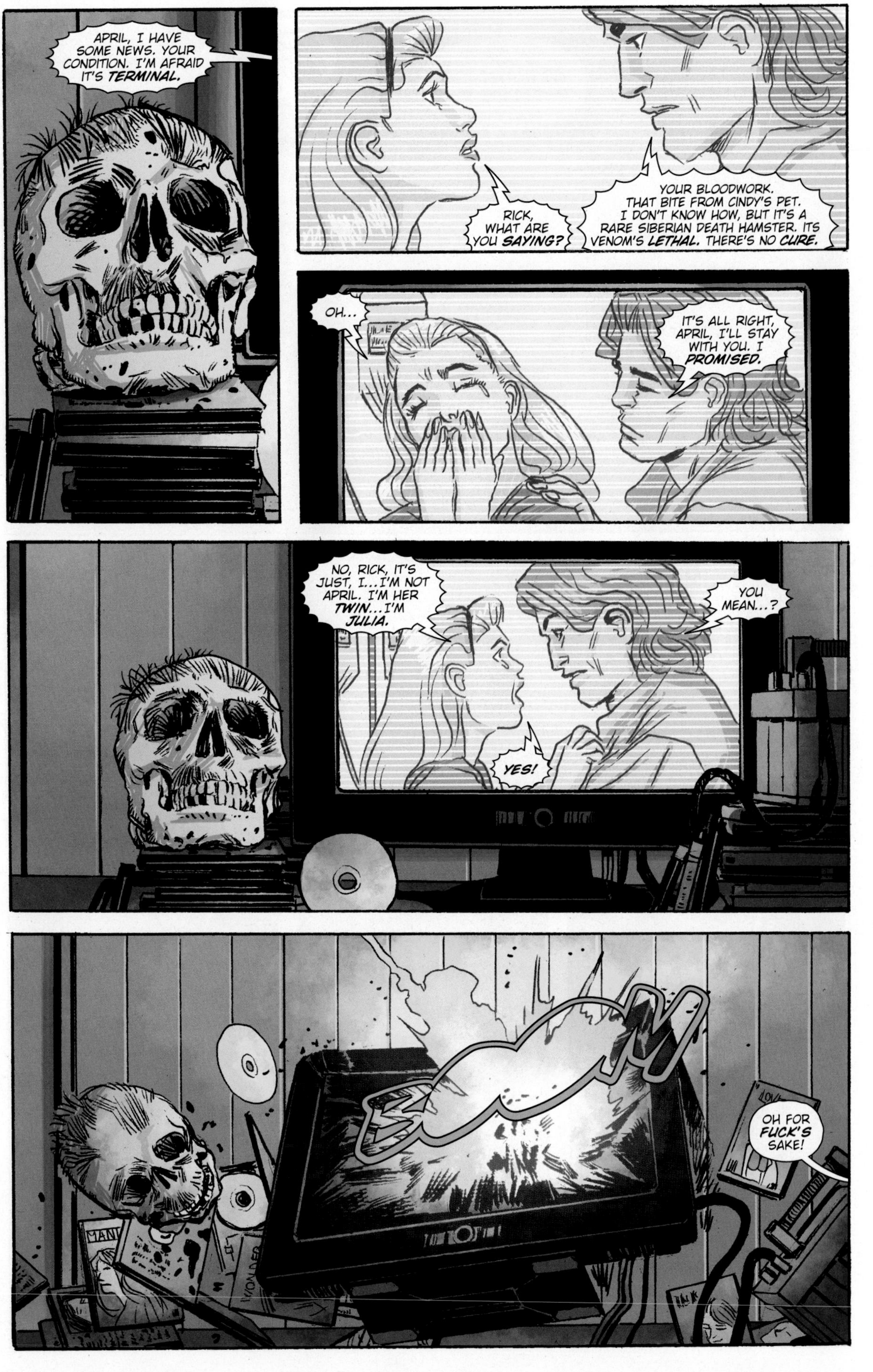
APRIL, I HAVE SOME NEWS. YOUR CONDITION. I'M AFRAID IT'S TERMINAL.
RICK, WHAT ARE YOU SAYING?
YOUR BLOODWORK. THAT BITE FROM CINDY'S PET. I DON'T KNOW HOW, BUT IT'S A RARE SIBERIAN DEATH HAMSTER. ITS VENOM'S LETHAL. THERE'S NO CURE.
OH...
IT'S ALL RIGHT, APRIL, I'LL STAY WITH YOU. I PROMISED.
NO, RICK, IT'S JUST, I...I'M NOT APRIL. I'M HER TWIN...I'M JULIA.
YOU MEAN...?
YES!
OH FOR FUCK'S SAKE!

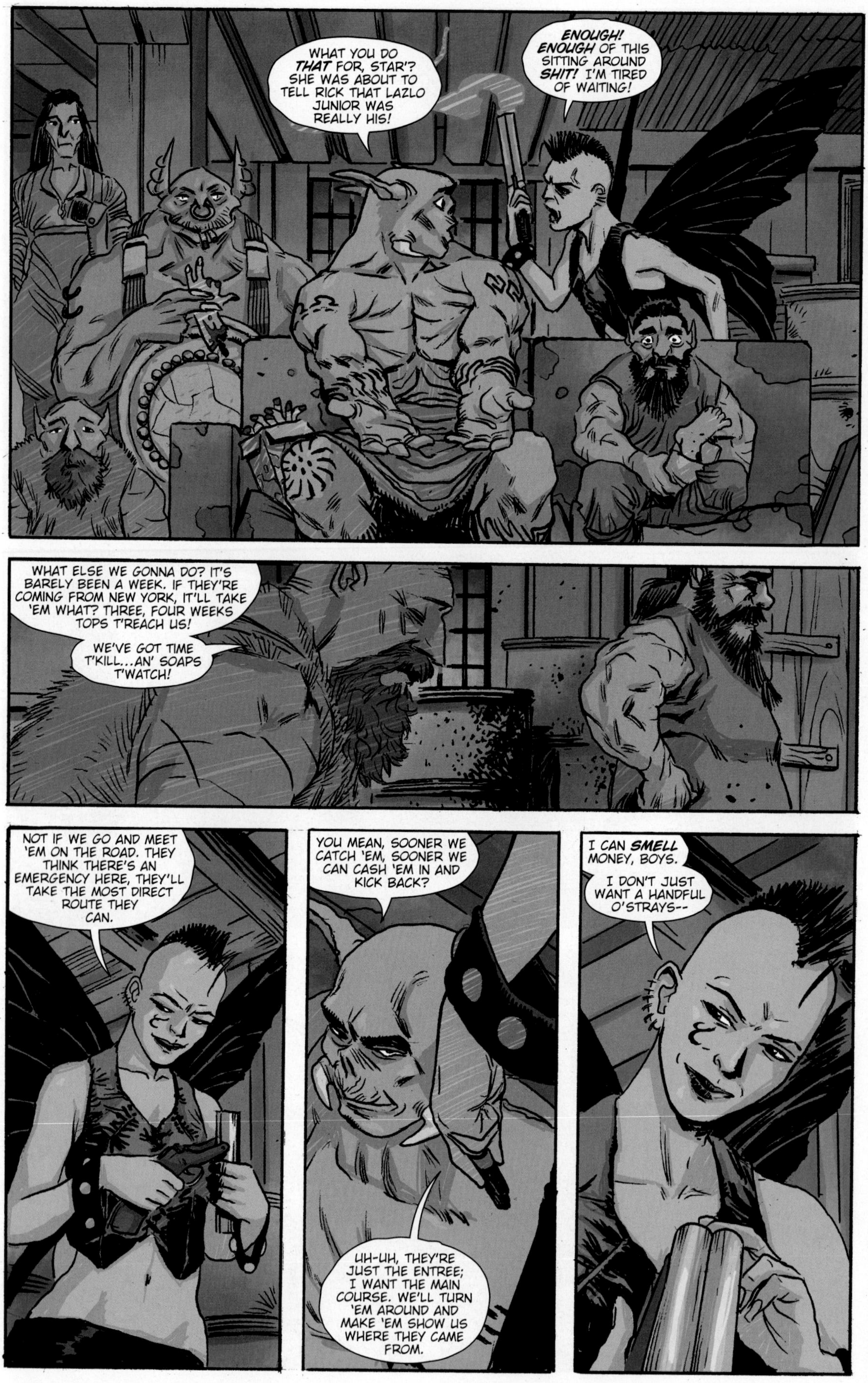
WHAT YOU DO THAT FOR, STAR'? SHE WAS ABOUT TO TELL RICK THAT LAZLO JUNIOR WAS REALLY HIS!
ENOUGH! ENOUGH OF THIS SITTING AROUND SHIT! I'M TIRED OF WAITING!
WHAT ELSE WE GONNA DO? IT'S BARELY BEEN A WEEK. IF THEY'RE COMING FROM NEW YORK, IT'LL TAKE 'EM WHAT? THREE, FOUR WEEKS TOPS T'REACH US!
WE'VE GOT TIME T'KILL...AN' SOAPS T'WATCH!
NOT IF WE GO AND MEET 'EM ON THE ROAD. THEY THINK THERE'S AN EMERGENCY HERE, THEY'LL TAKE THE MOST DIRECT ROUTE THEY CAN.
YOU MEAN, SOONER WE CATCH 'EM, SOONER WE CAN CASH 'EM IN AND KICK BACK?
UH-UH, THEY'RE JUST THE ENTREE; I WANT THE MAIN COURSE. WE'LL TURN 'EM AROUND AND MAKE 'EM SHOW US WHERE THEY CAME FROM.
I CAN SMELL MONEY, BOYS.
I DON'T JUST WANT A HANDFUL O'STRAYS--

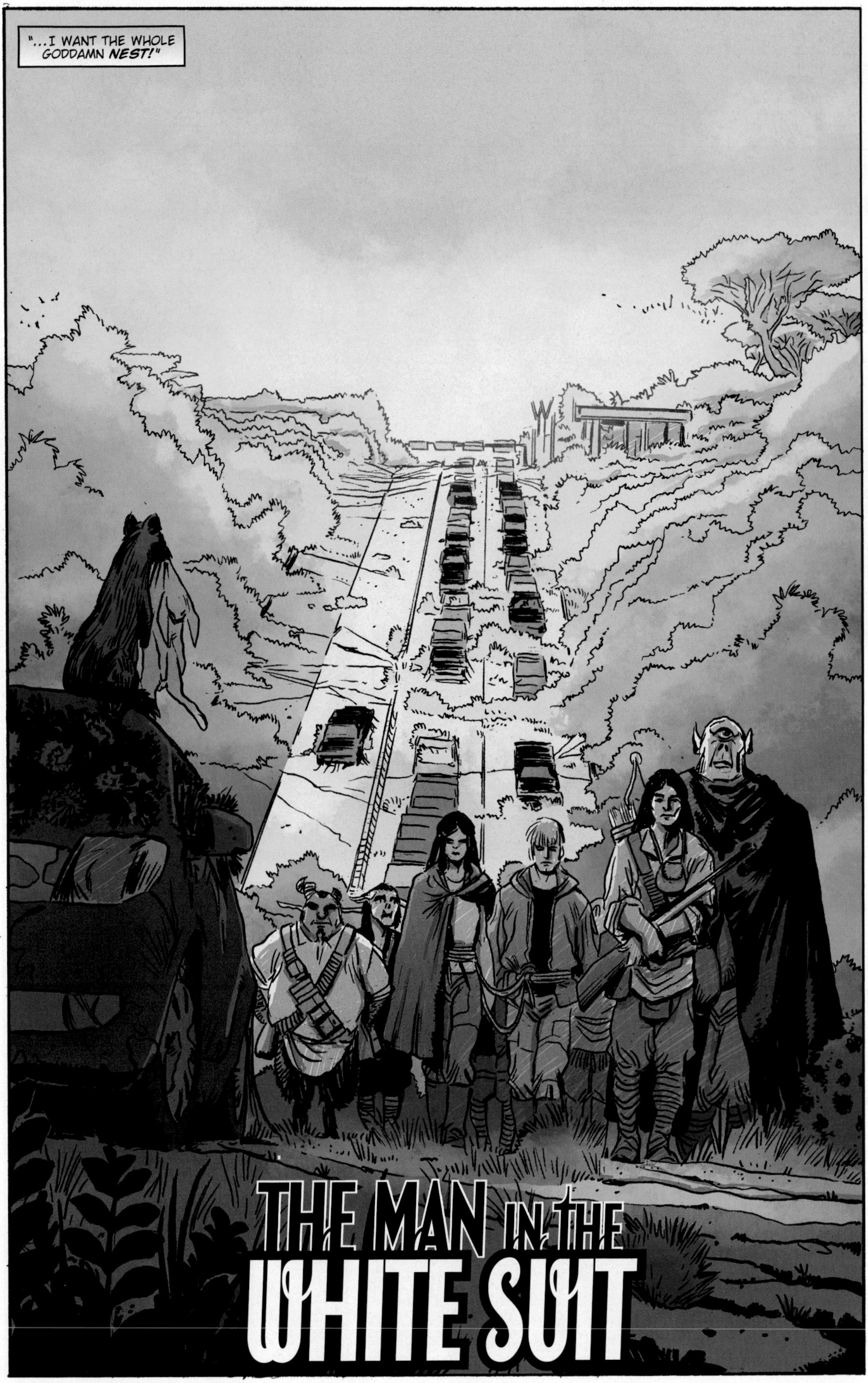
"...I WANT THE WHOLE GODDAMN NEST!"
THE MAN IN THE WHITE SUIT

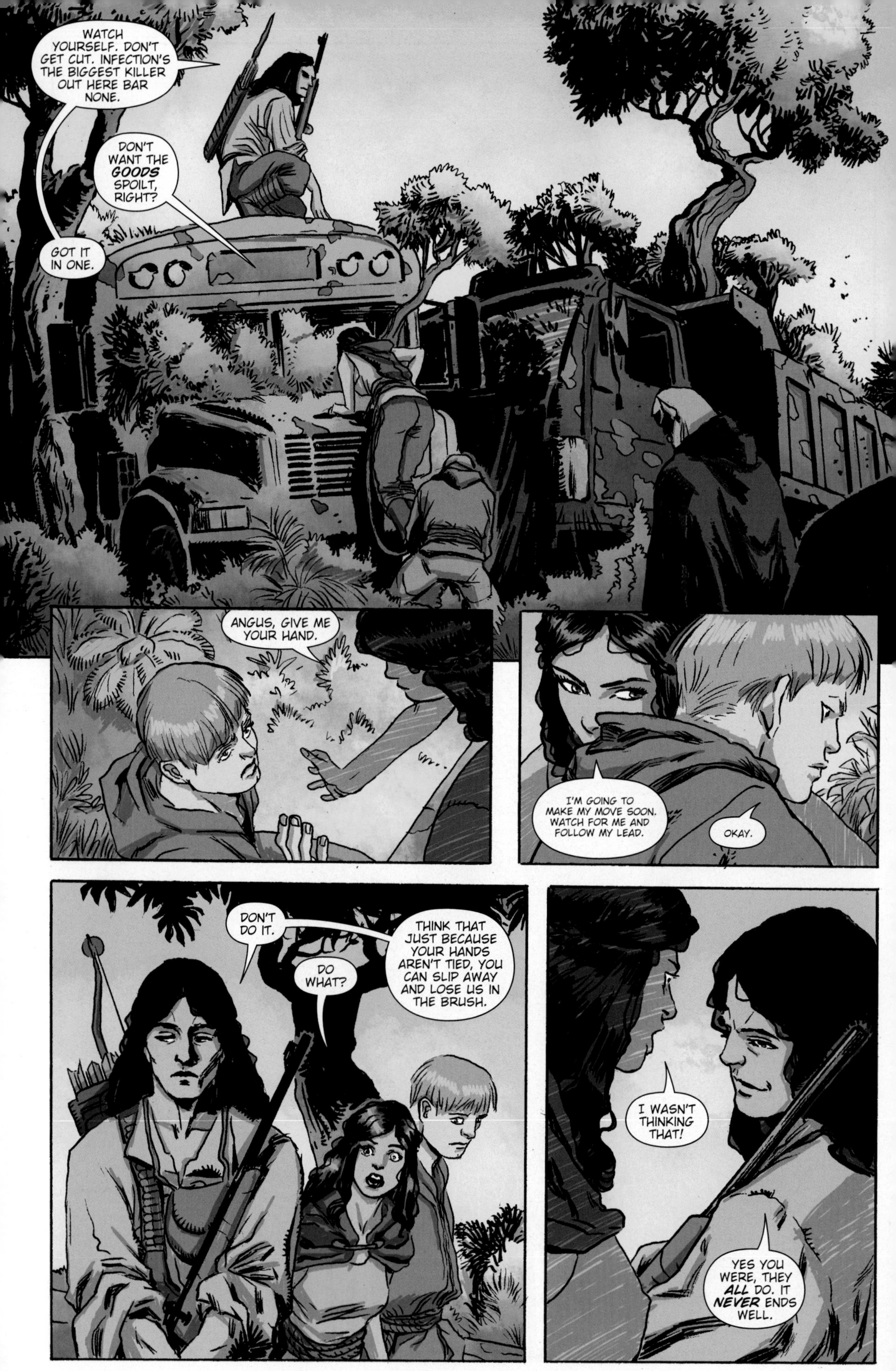
WATCH YOURSELF. DON'T GET CUT. INFECTION'S THE BIGGEST KILLER OUT HERE BAR NONE.
DON'T WANT THE GOODS SPOILT, RIGHT?
GOT IT IN ONE.
ANGUS, GIVE ME YOUR HAND.
I'M GOING TO MAKE MY MOVE SOON. WATCH FOR ME AND FOLLOW MY LEAD.
OKAY.
DON'T DO IT.
DO WHAT?
THINK THAT JUST BECAUSE YOUR HANDS AREN'T TIED, YOU CAN SLIP AWAY AND LOSE US IN THE BRUSH.
I WASN'T THINKING THAT!
YES YOU WERE, THEY ALL DO. IT NEVER ENDS WELL.

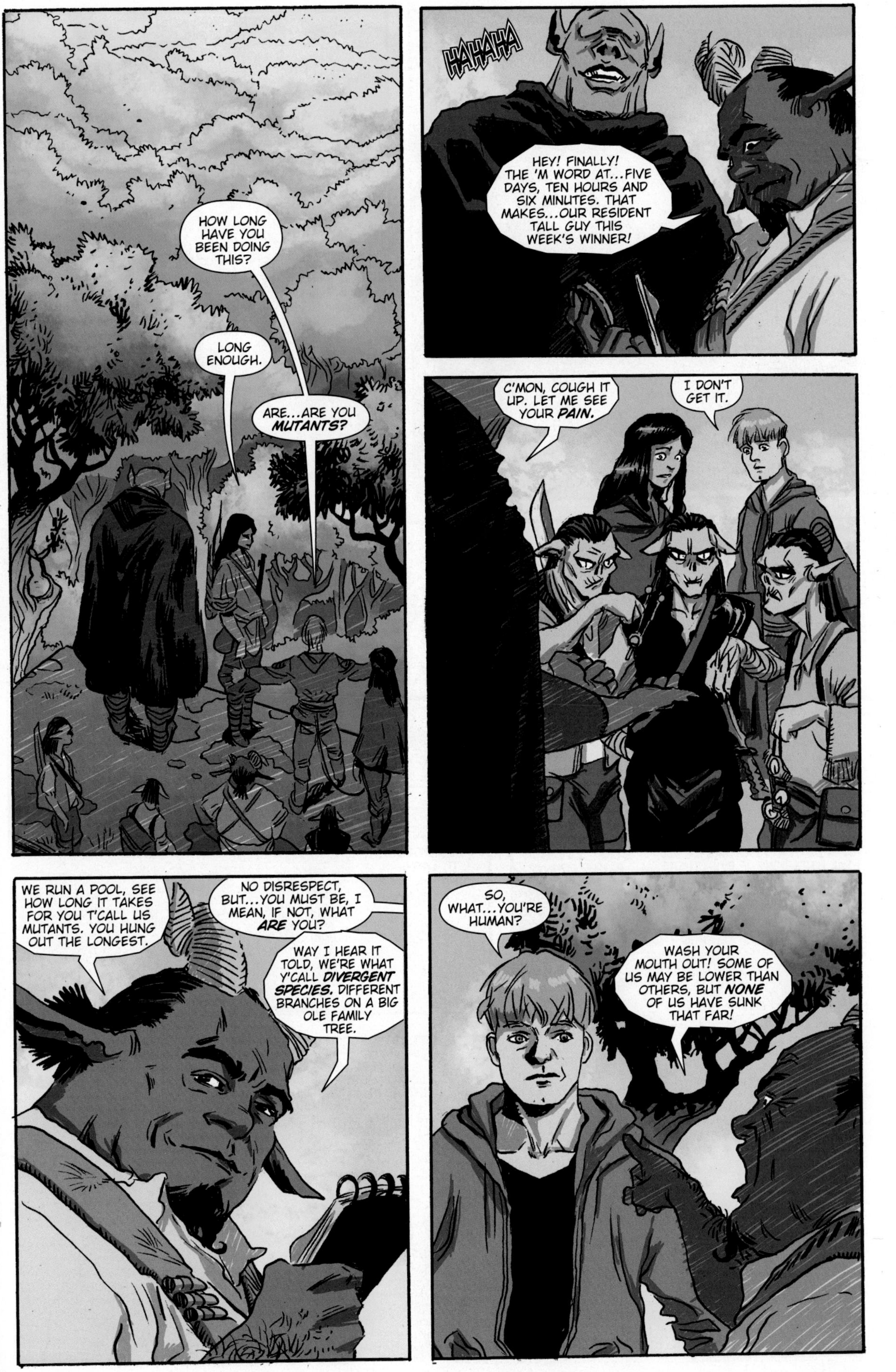

HOW LONG HAVE YOU BEEN DOING THIS?
LONG ENOUGH.
ARE...ARE YOU MUTANTS?
HAHAHA
HEY! FINALLY! THE 'M WORD AT...FIVE DAYS, TEN HOURS AND SIX MINUTES. THAT MAKES...OUR RESIDENT TALL GUY THIS WEEK'S WINNER!
C'MON, COUGH IT UP. LET ME SEE YOUR PAIN.
I DON'T GET IT.
WE RUN A POOL, SEE HOW LONG IT TAKES FOR YOU T'CALL US MUTANTS. YOU HUNG OUT THE LONGEST.
NO DISRESPECT, BUT...YOU MUST BE, I MEAN, IF NOT, WHAT ARE YOU?
WAY I HEAR IT TOLD, WE'RE WHAT Y'CALL DIVERGENT SPECIES. DIFFERENT BRANCHES ON A BIG OLE FAMILY TREE.
SO, WHAT...YOU'RE HUMAN?
WASH YOUR MOUTH OUT! SOME OF US MAY BE LOWER THAN OTHERS, BUT NONE OF US HAVE SUNK THAT FAR!

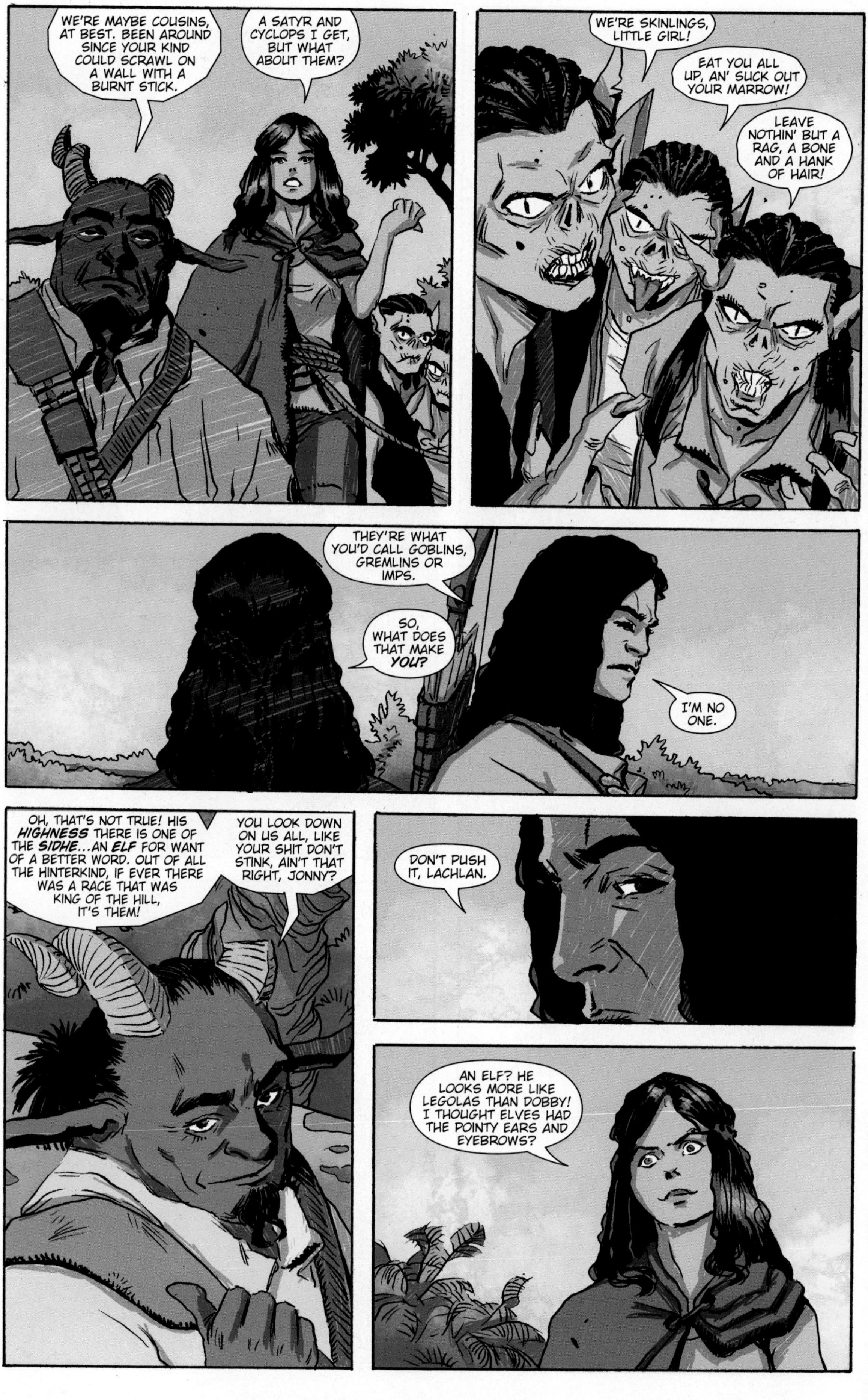
WE'RE MAYBE COUSINS, AT BEST. BEEN AROUND SINCE YOUR KIND COULD SCRAWL ON A WALL WITH A BURNT STICK.
A SATYR AND CYCLOPS I GET, BUT WHAT ABOUT THEM?
WE'RE SKINLINGS, LITTLE GIRL!
EAT YOU ALL UP, AN' SUCK OUT YOUR MARROW!
LEAVE NOTHIN' BUT A RAG, A BONE AND A HANK OF HAIR!
THEY'RE WHAT YOU'D CALL GOBLINS, GREMLINS OR IMPS.
SO, WHAT DOES THAT MAKE YOU?
I'M NO ONE.
OH, THAT'S NOT TRUE! HIS HIGHNESS THERE IS ONE OF THE SIDHE...AN ELF FOR WANT OF A BETTER WORD. OUT OF ALL THE HINTERKIND, IF EVER THERE WAS A RACE THAT WAS KING OF THE HILL, IT'S THEM!
YOU LOOK DOWN ON US ALL, LIKE YOUR SHIT DON'T STINK, AIN'T THAT RIGHT, JONNY?
DON'T PUSH IT, LACHLAN.
AN ELF? HE LOOKS MORE LIKE LEGOLAS THAN DOBBY! I THOUGHT ELVES HAD THE POINTY EARS AND EYEBROWS?

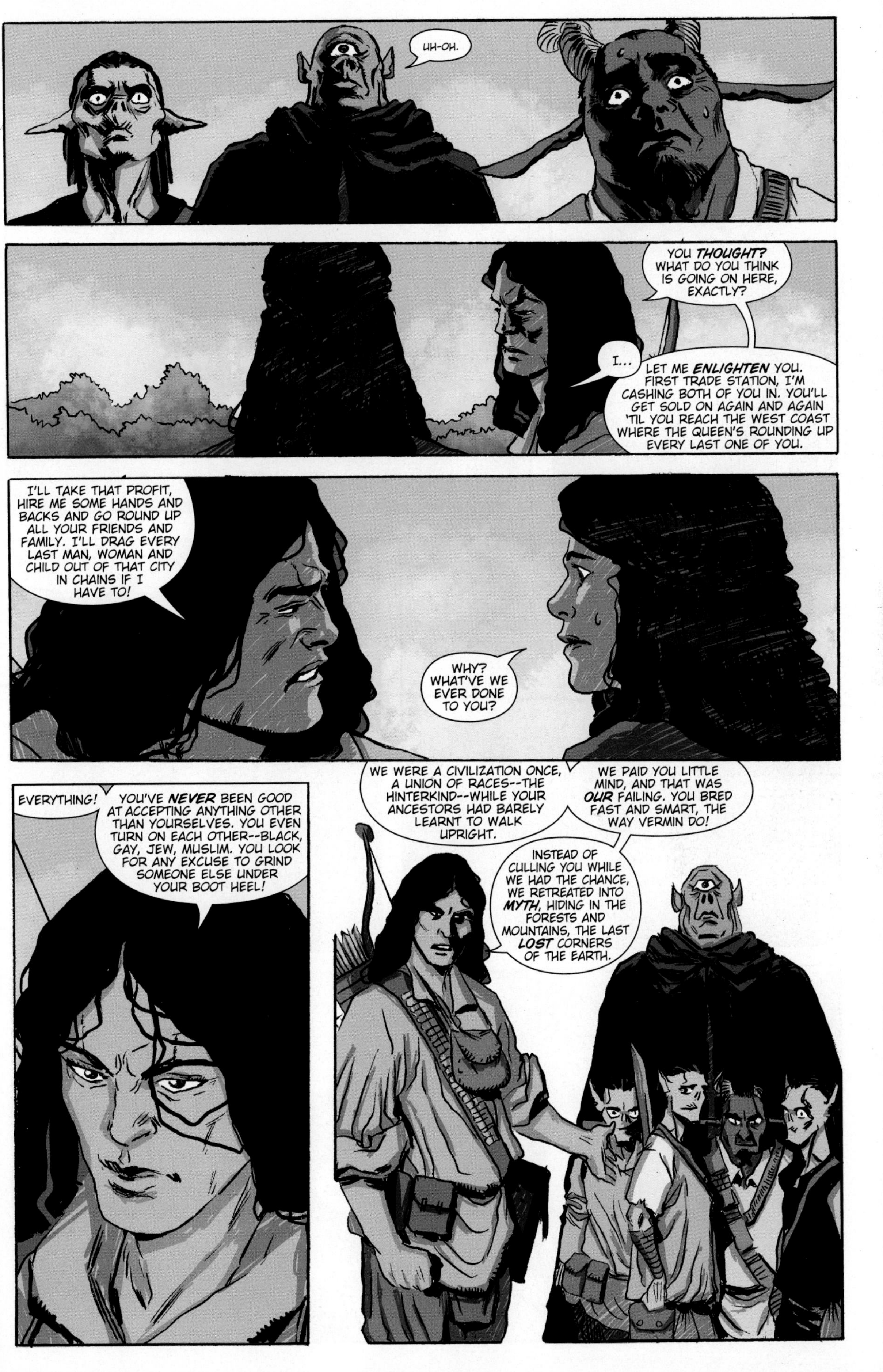
UH-OH.
YOU *THOUGHT?* WHAT DO YOU THINK IS GOING ON HERE, EXACTLY?
I...
LET ME *ENLIGHTEN* YOU. FIRST TRADE STATION, I'M CASHING BOTH OF YOU IN. YOU'LL GET SOLD ON AGAIN AND AGAIN 'TIL YOU REACH THE WEST COAST WHERE THE QUEEN'S ROUNDING UP EVERY LAST ONE OF YOU.
I'LL TAKE THAT PROFIT, HIRE ME SOME HANDS AND BACKS AND GO ROUND UP ALL YOUR FRIENDS AND FAMILY. I'LL DRAG EVERY LAST MAN, WOMAN AND CHILD OUT OF THAT CITY IN CHAINS IF I HAVE TO!
WHY? WHAT'VE WE EVER DONE TO YOU?
EVERYTHING!
YOU'VE *NEVER* BEEN GOOD AT ACCEPTING ANYTHING OTHER THAN YOURSELVES. YOU EVEN TURN ON EACH OTHER--BLACK, GAY, JEW, MUSLIM. YOU LOOK FOR ANY EXCUSE TO GRIND SOMEONE ELSE UNDER YOUR BOOT HEEL!
WE WERE A CIVILIZATION ONCE, A UNION OF RACES--THE HINTERKIND--WHILE YOUR ANCESTORS HAD BARELY LEARNT TO WALK UPRIGHT.
WE PAID YOU LITTLE MIND, AND THAT WAS *OUR* FAILING. YOU BRED FAST AND SMART, THE WAY VERMIN DO!
INSTEAD OF CULLING YOU WHILE WE HAD THE CHANCE, WE RETREATED INTO *MYTH*, HIDING IN THE FORESTS AND MOUNTAINS, THE LAST *LOST* CORNERS OF THE EARTH.

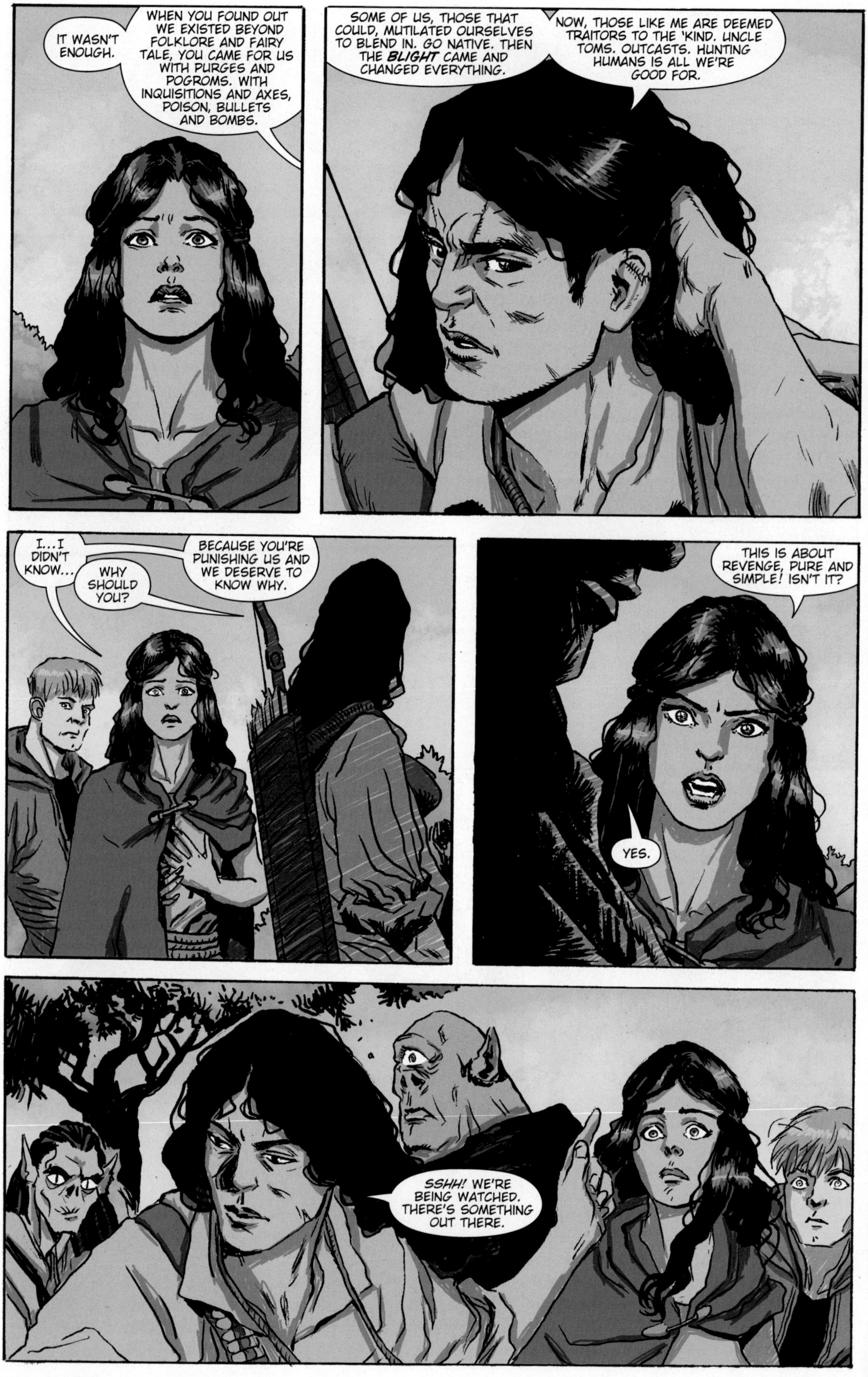
IT WASN'T ENOUGH.
WHEN YOU FOUND OUT WE EXISTED BEYOND FOLKLORE AND FAIRY TALE, YOU CAME FOR US WITH PURGES AND POGROMS. WITH INQUISITIONS AND AXES, POISON, BULLETS AND BOMBS.
SOME OF US, THOSE THAT COULD, MUTILATED OURSELVES TO BLEND IN. GO NATIVE. THEN THE BLIGHT CAME AND CHANGED EVERYTHING.
NOW, THOSE LIKE ME ARE DEEMED TRAITORS TO THE 'KIND. UNCLE TOMS. OUTCASTS. HUNTING HUMANS IS ALL WE'RE GOOD FOR.
I...I DIDN'T KNOW...
WHY SHOULD YOU?
BECAUSE YOU'RE PUNISHING US AND WE DESERVE TO KNOW WHY.
THIS IS ABOUT REVENGE, PURE AND SIMPLE! ISN'T IT?
YES.
SSHH! WE'RE BEING WATCHED. THERE'S SOMETHING OUT THERE.

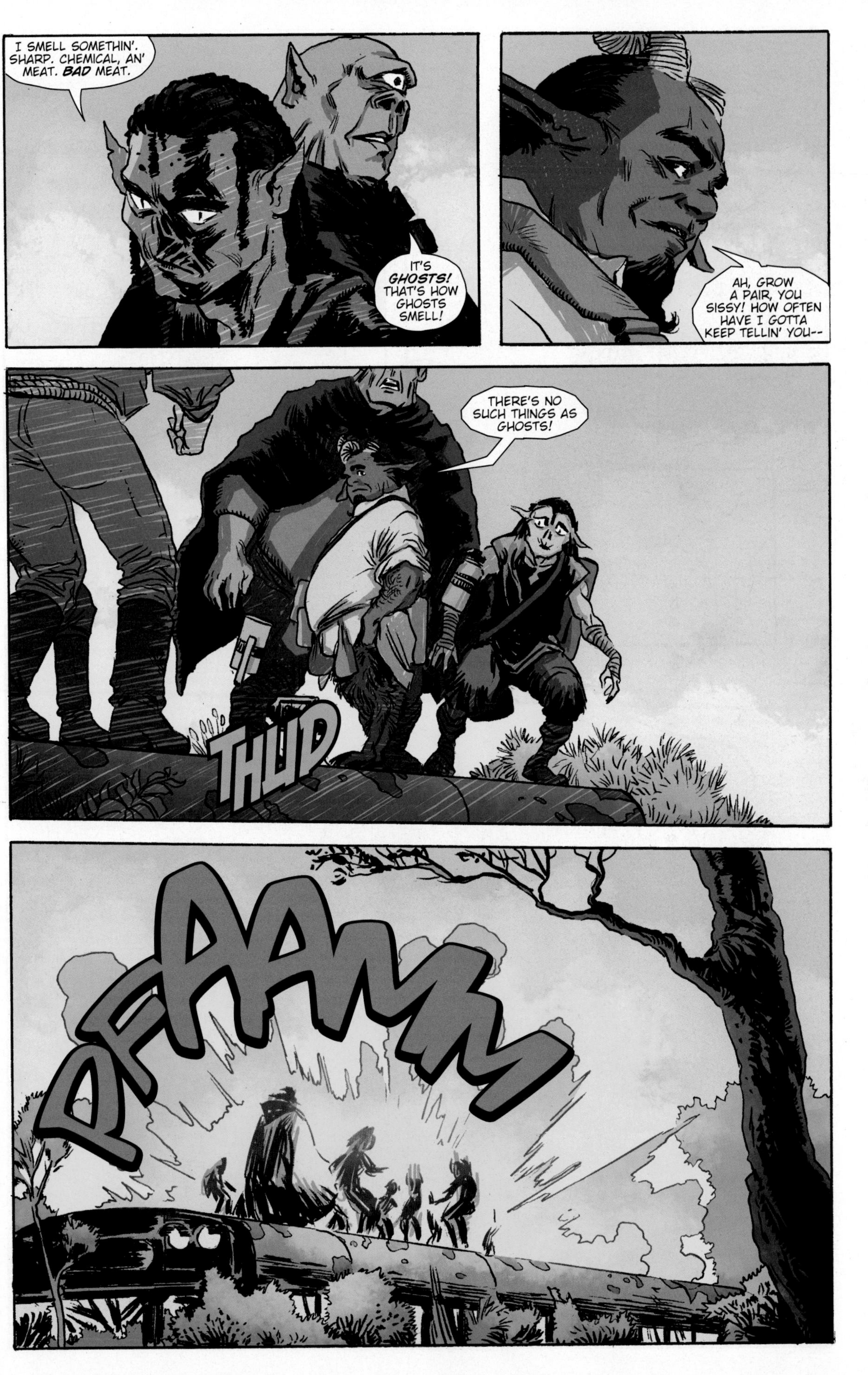
I SMELL SOMETHIN'. SHARP. CHEMICAL, AN' MEAT. *BAD* MEAT.
IT'S *GHOSTS!* THAT'S HOW GHOSTS SMELL!
AH, GROW A PAIR, YOU SISSY! HOW OFTEN HAVE I GOTTA KEEP TELLIN' YOU--
THERE'S NO SUCH THINGS AS GHOSTS!
THUD
PFAAM

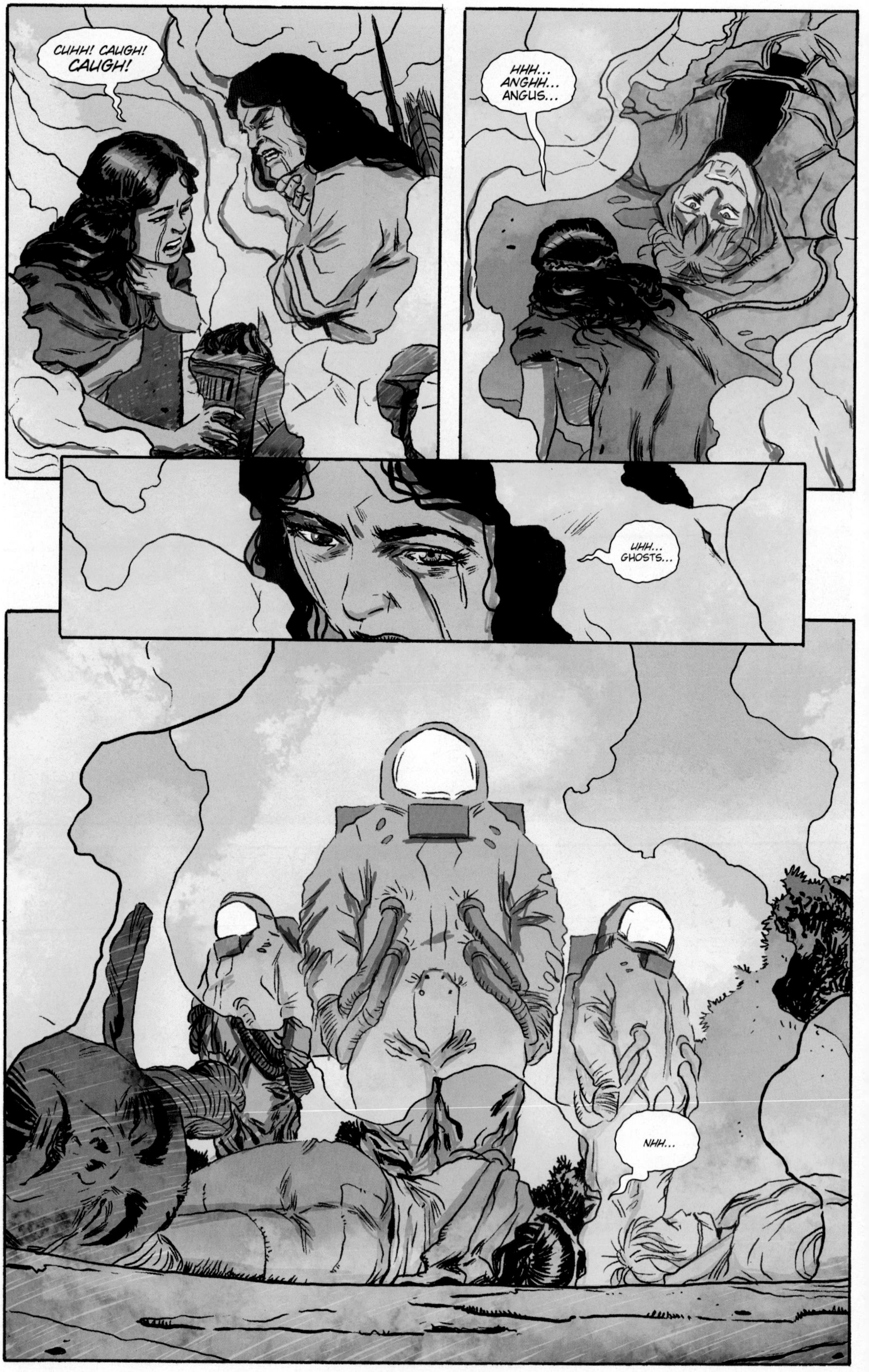
CUHH! CAUGH! CAUGH!
HHH... ANGHH... ANGUS...
UHH... GHOSTS...
NHH...

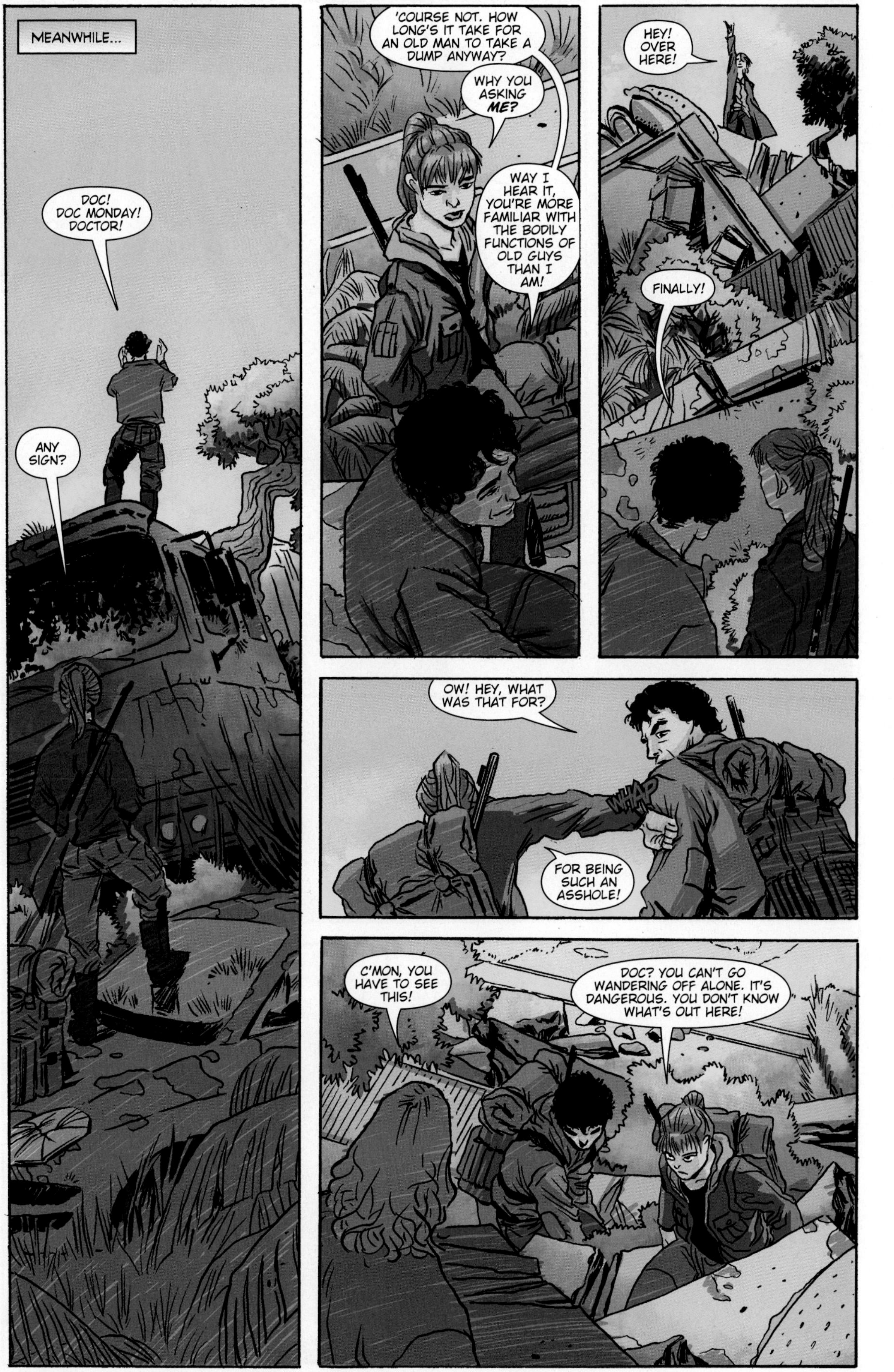
MEANWHILE...
DOC! DOC MONDAY! DOCTOR!
ANY SIGN?
'COURSE NOT. HOW LONG'S IT TAKE FOR AN OLD MAN TO TAKE A DUMP ANYWAY?
WHY YOU ASKING ME?
WAY I HEAR IT, YOU'RE MORE FAMILIAR WITH THE BODILY FUNCTIONS OF OLD GUYS THAN I AM!
HEY! OVER HERE!
FINALLY!
OW! HEY, WHAT WAS THAT FOR?
WHAP
FOR BEING SUCH AN ASSHOLE!
C'MON, YOU HAVE TO SEE THIS!
DOC? YOU CAN'T GO WANDERING OFF ALONE. IT'S DANGEROUS. YOU DON'T KNOW WHAT'S OUT HERE!

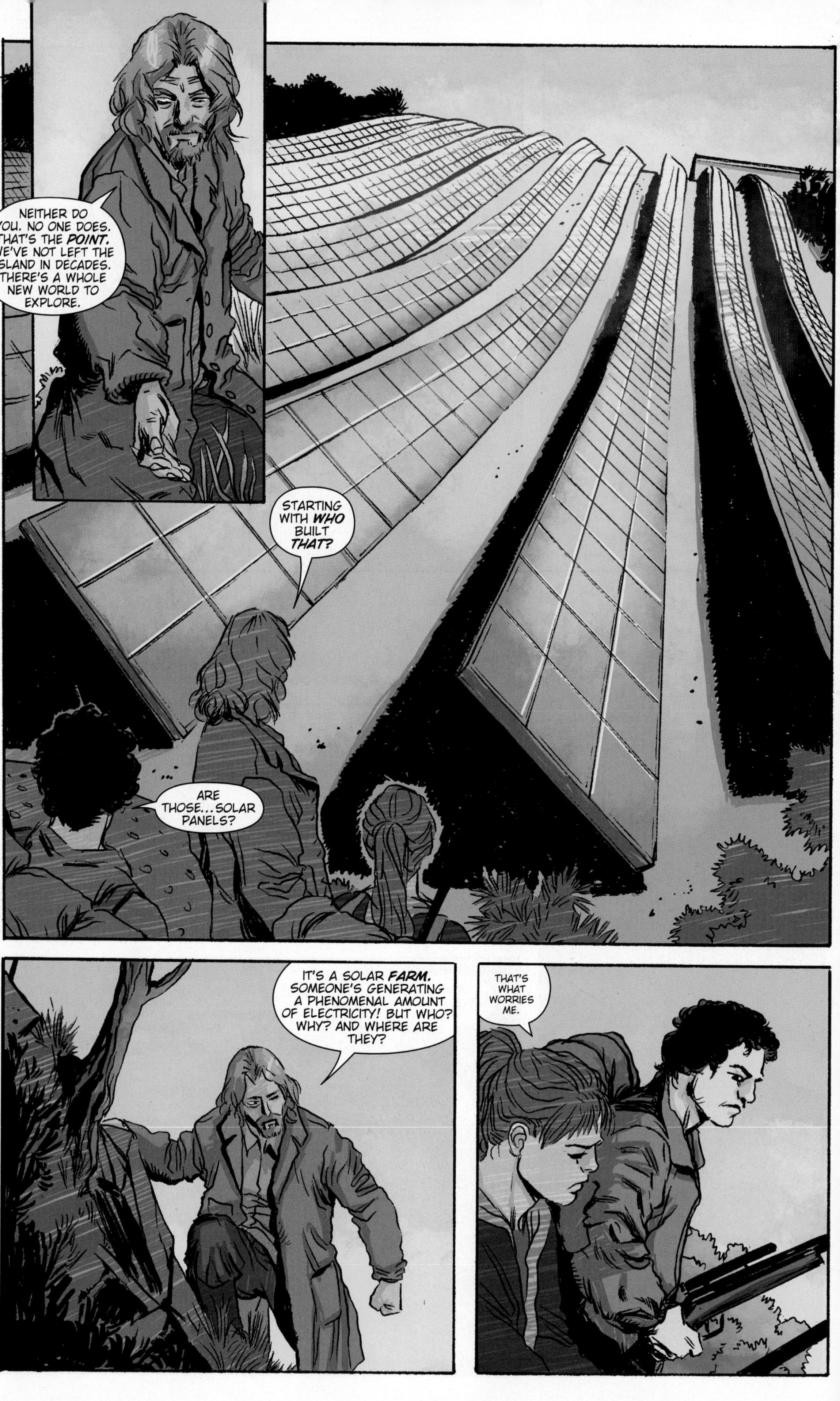
NEITHER DO YOU. NO ONE DOES. THAT'S THE POINT. WE'VE NOT LEFT THE ISLAND IN DECADES. THERE'S A WHOLE NEW WORLD TO EXPLORE.
STARTING WITH WHO BUILT THAT?
ARE THOSE...SOLAR PANELS?
IT'S A SOLAR FARM. SOMEONE'S GENERATING A PHENOMENAL AMOUNT OF ELECTRICITY! BUT WHO? WHY? AND WHERE ARE THEY?
THAT'S WHAT WORRIES ME.

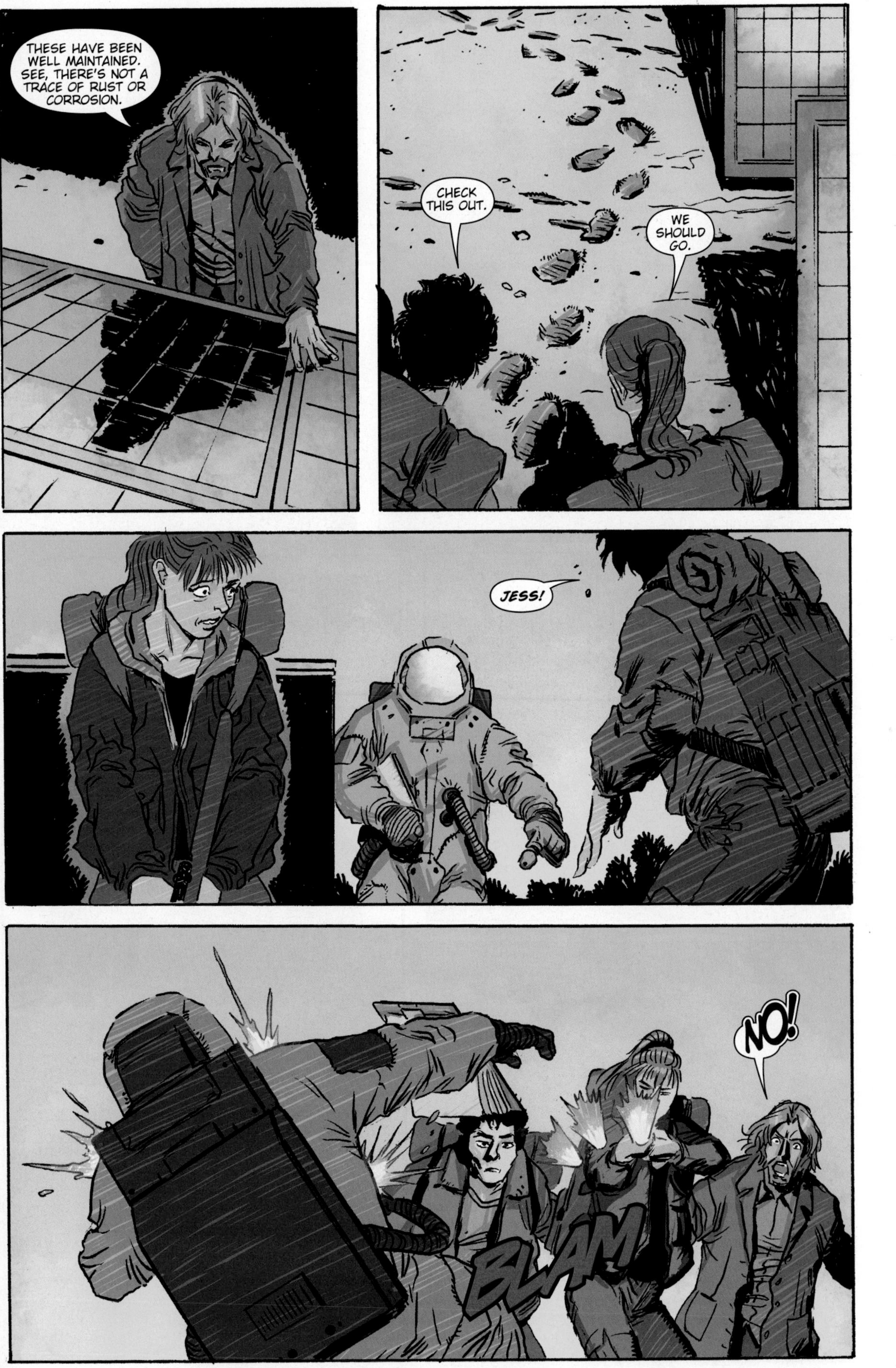
THESE HAVE BEEN WELL MAINTAINED. SEE, THERE'S NOT A TRACE OF RUST OR CORROSION.
CHECK THIS OUT.
WE SHOULD GO.
JESS!
NO!
BLAM

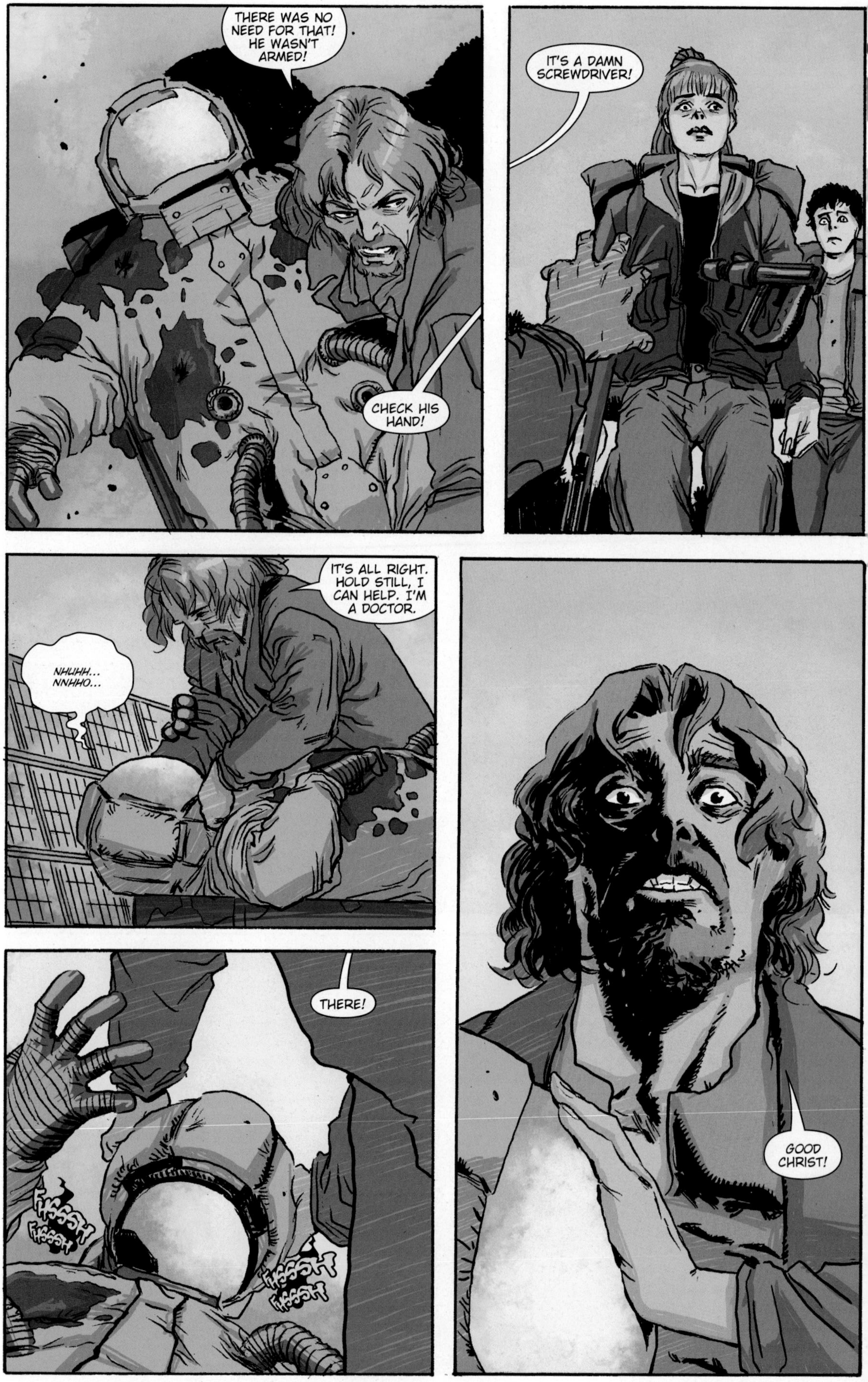
THERE WAS NO NEED FOR THAT! HE WASN'T ARMED!
CHECK HIS HAND!
IT'S A DAMN SCREWDRIVER!
IT'S ALL RIGHT. HOLD STILL, I CAN HELP. I'M A DOCTOR.
NHUHH... NNHHO...
THERE!
FHSSSH FHSSSH
FHSSSH FHSSSH
GOOD CHRIST!

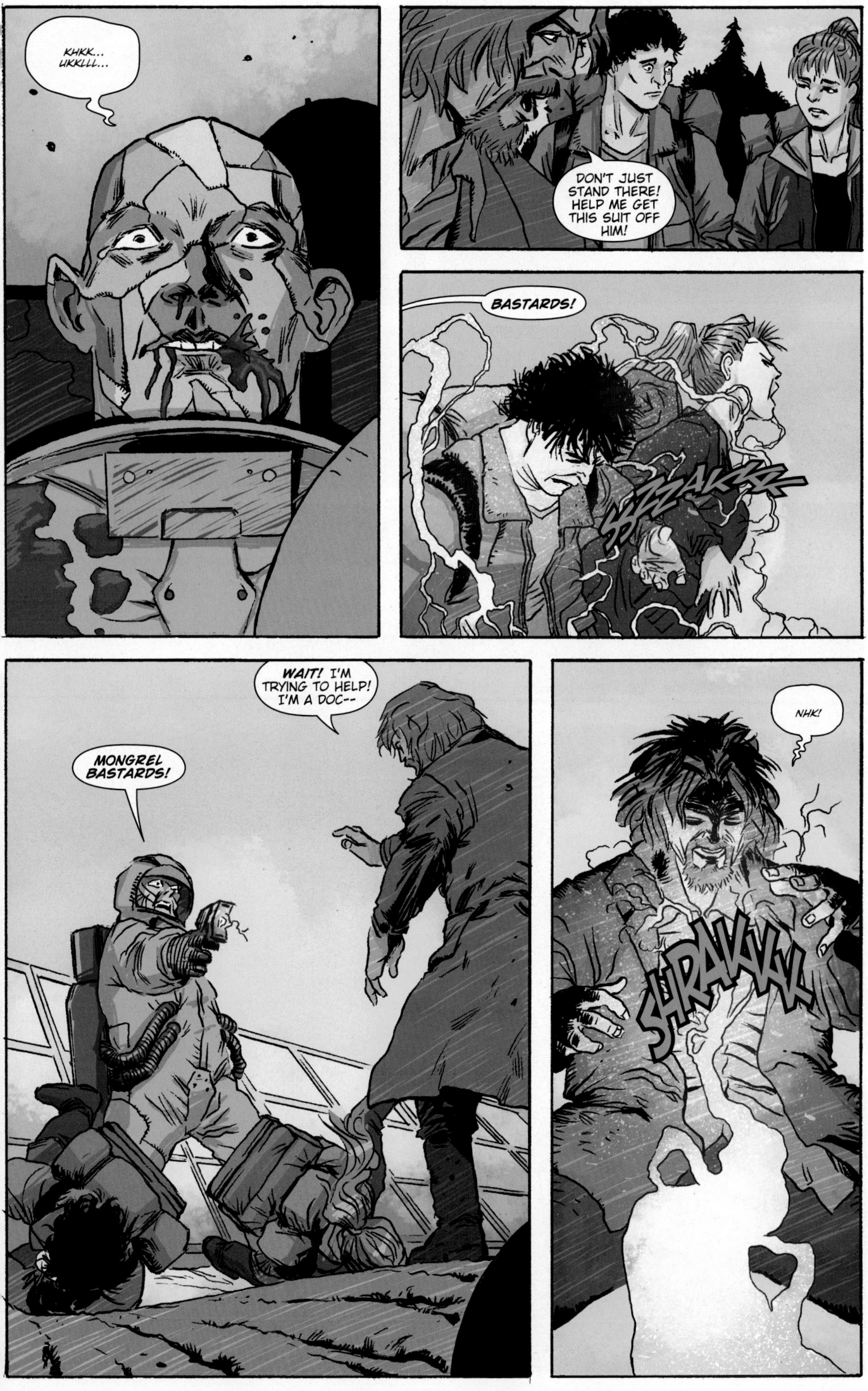
KHKK... UKKLLL...
DON'T JUST STAND THERE! HELP ME GET THIS SUIT OFF HIM!
BASTARDS!
SZZZAKKK
WAIT! I'M TRYING TO HELP! I'M A DOC--
MONGREL BASTARDS!
NHK!
SHRAKKK

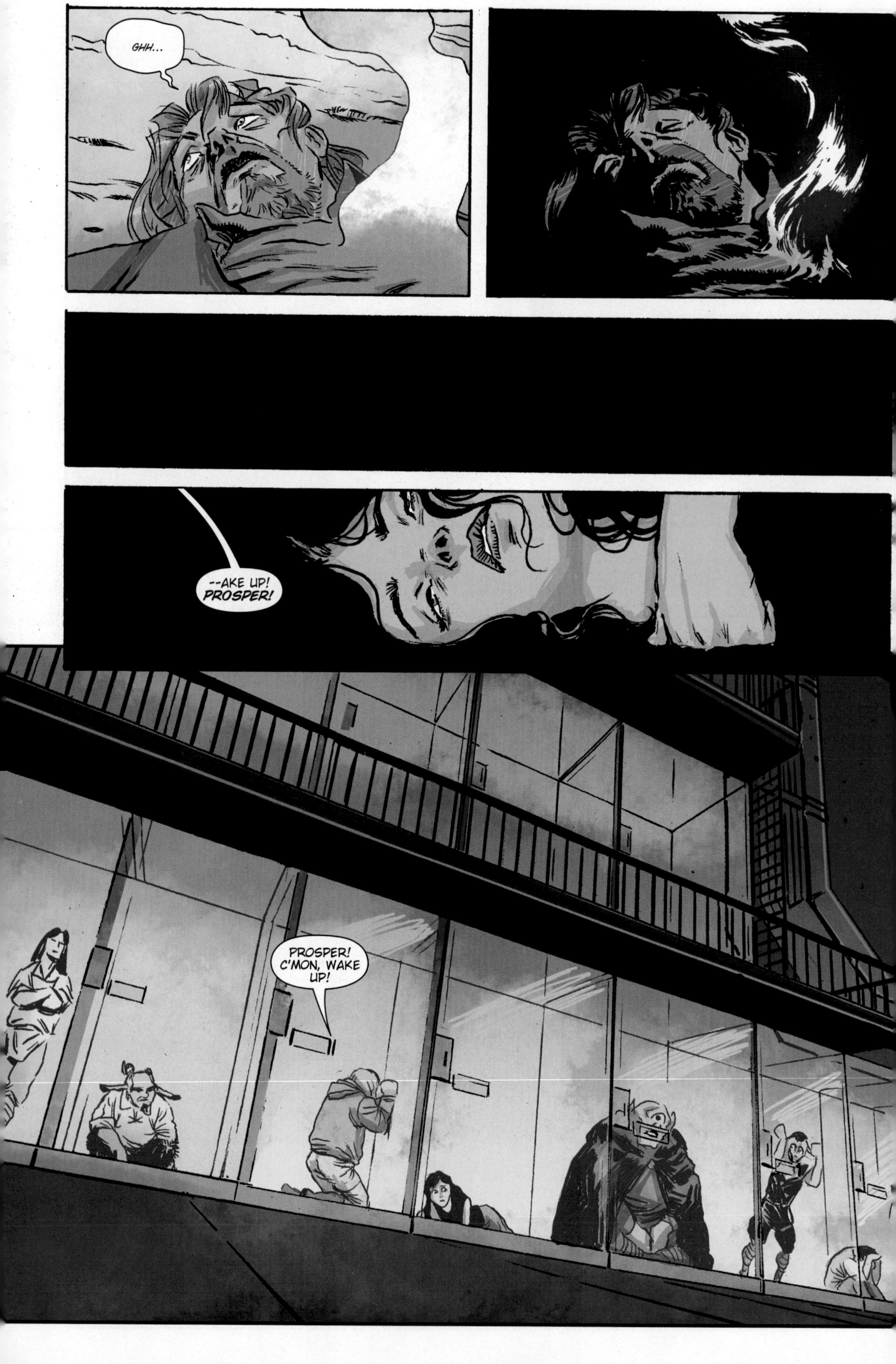
GHH...
--AKE UP! PROSPER!
PROSPER! C'MON, WAKE UP!

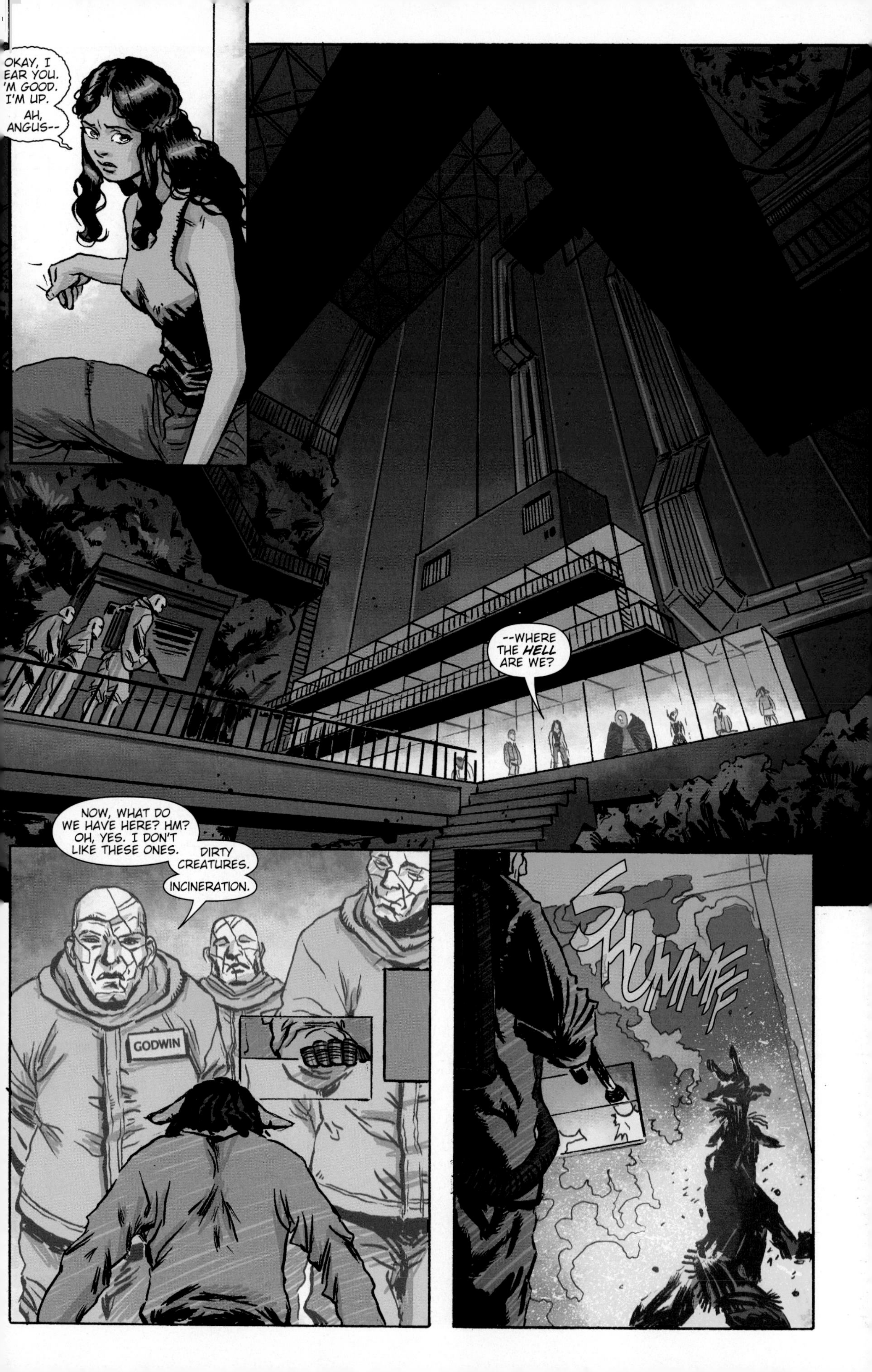
OKAY, I EAR YOU. 'M GOOD. I'M UP.
AH, ANGUS--
--WHERE THE HELL ARE WE?
NOW, WHAT DO WE HAVE HERE? HM? OH, YES. I DON'T LIKE THESE ONES.
DIRTY CREATURES.
INCINERATION.
GODWIN
SHUMMF

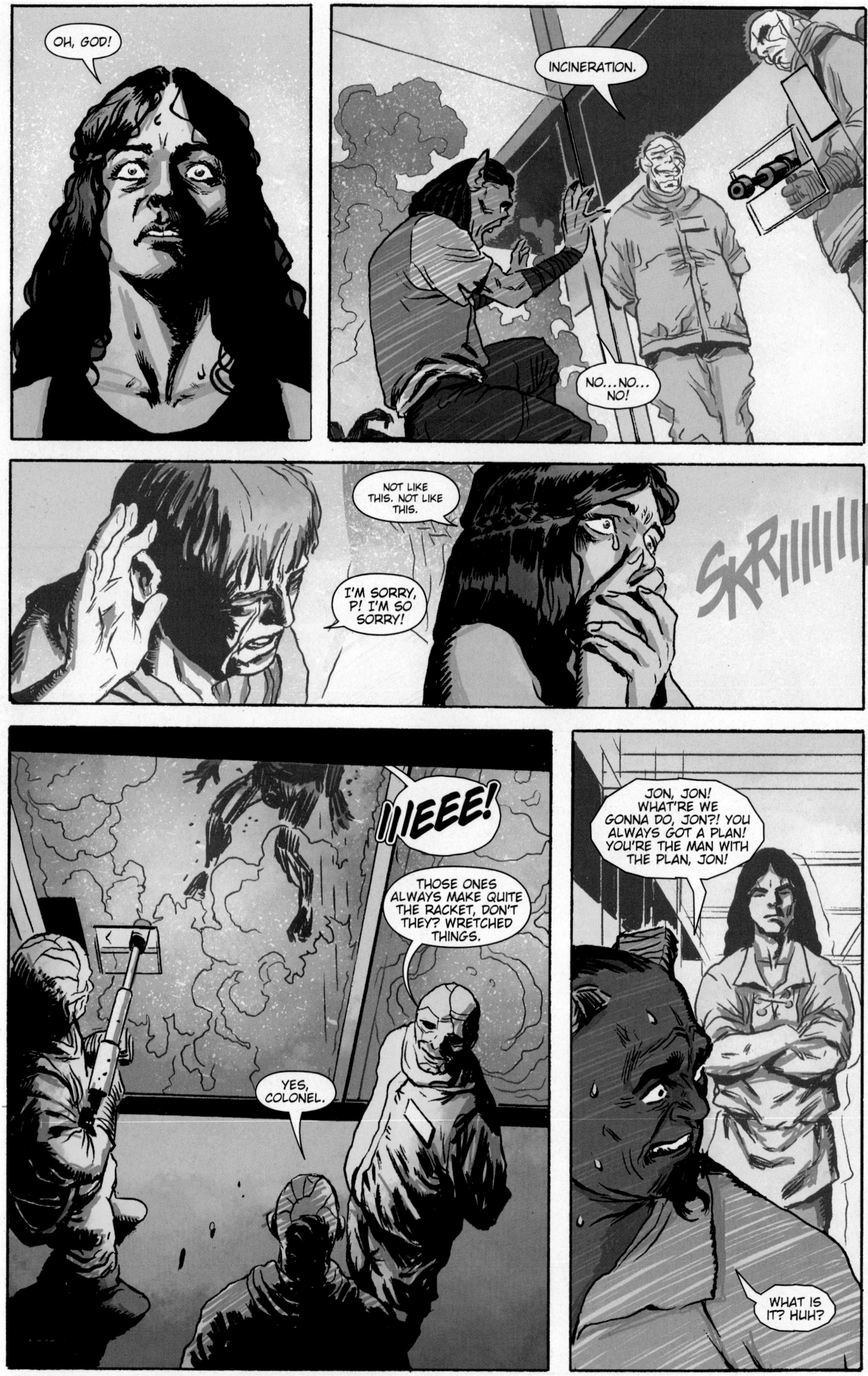
OH, GOD!
INCINERATION.
NO...NO... NO!
NOT LIKE THIS. NOT LIKE THIS.
I'M SORRY, P! I'M SO SORRY!
SKRIIIIIIII
IIIEEE!
THOSE ONES ALWAYS MAKE QUITE THE RACKET, DON'T THEY? WRETCHED THINGS.
YES, COLONEL.
JON, JON! WHAT'RE WE GONNA DO, JON?! YOU ALWAYS GOT A PLAN! YOU'RE THE MAN WITH THE PLAN, JON!
WHAT IS IT? HUH?

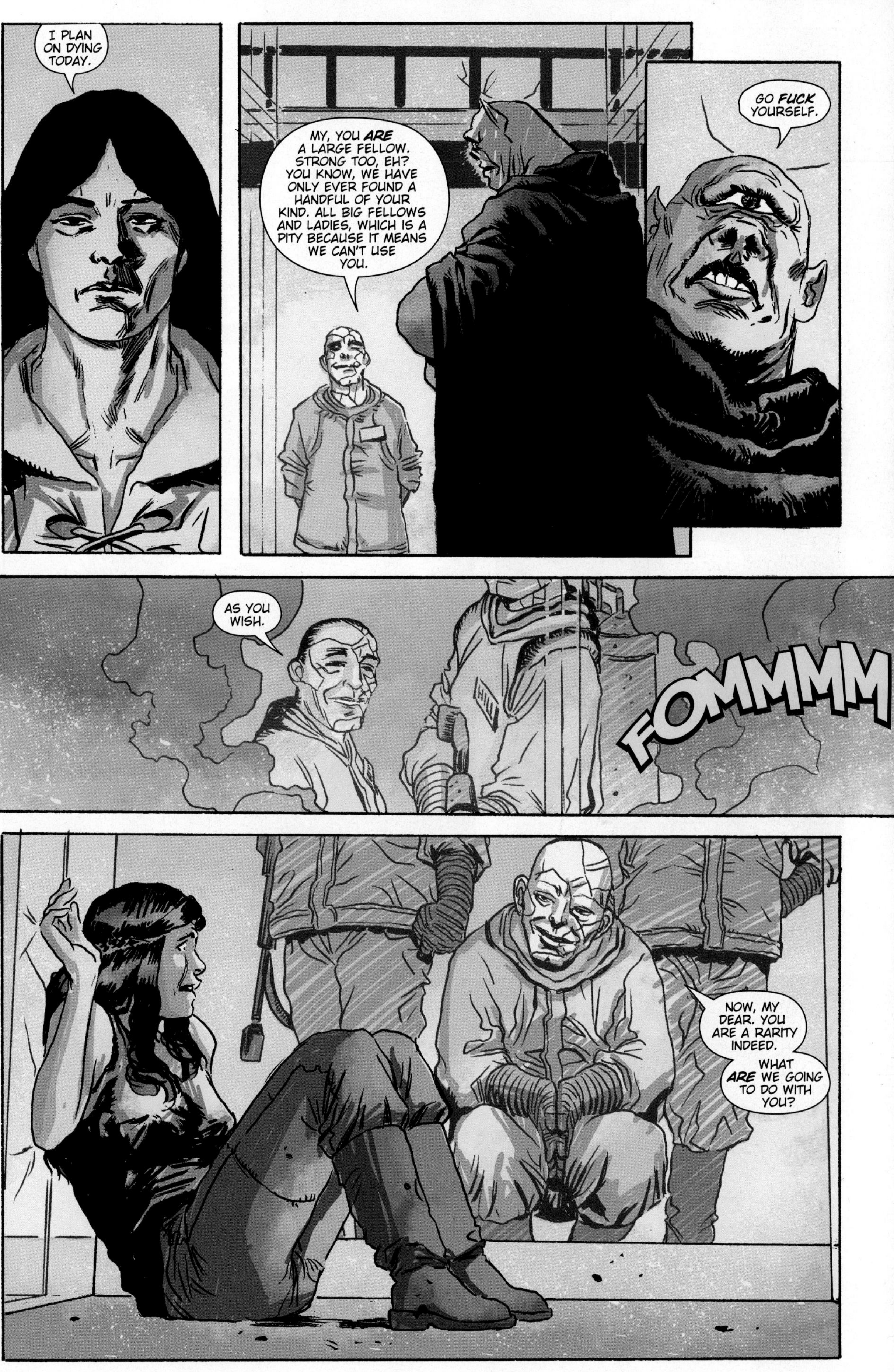
I PLAN ON DYING TODAY.
MY, YOU ARE A LARGE FELLOW. STRONG TOO, EH? YOU KNOW, WE HAVE ONLY EVER FOUND A HANDFUL OF YOUR KIND. ALL BIG FELLOWS AND LADIES, WHICH IS A PITY BECAUSE IT MEANS WE CAN'T USE YOU.
GO FUCK YOURSELF.
AS YOU WISH.
FOMMMM
NOW, MY DEAR. YOU ARE A RARITY INDEED.
WHAT ARE WE GOING TO DO WITH YOU?

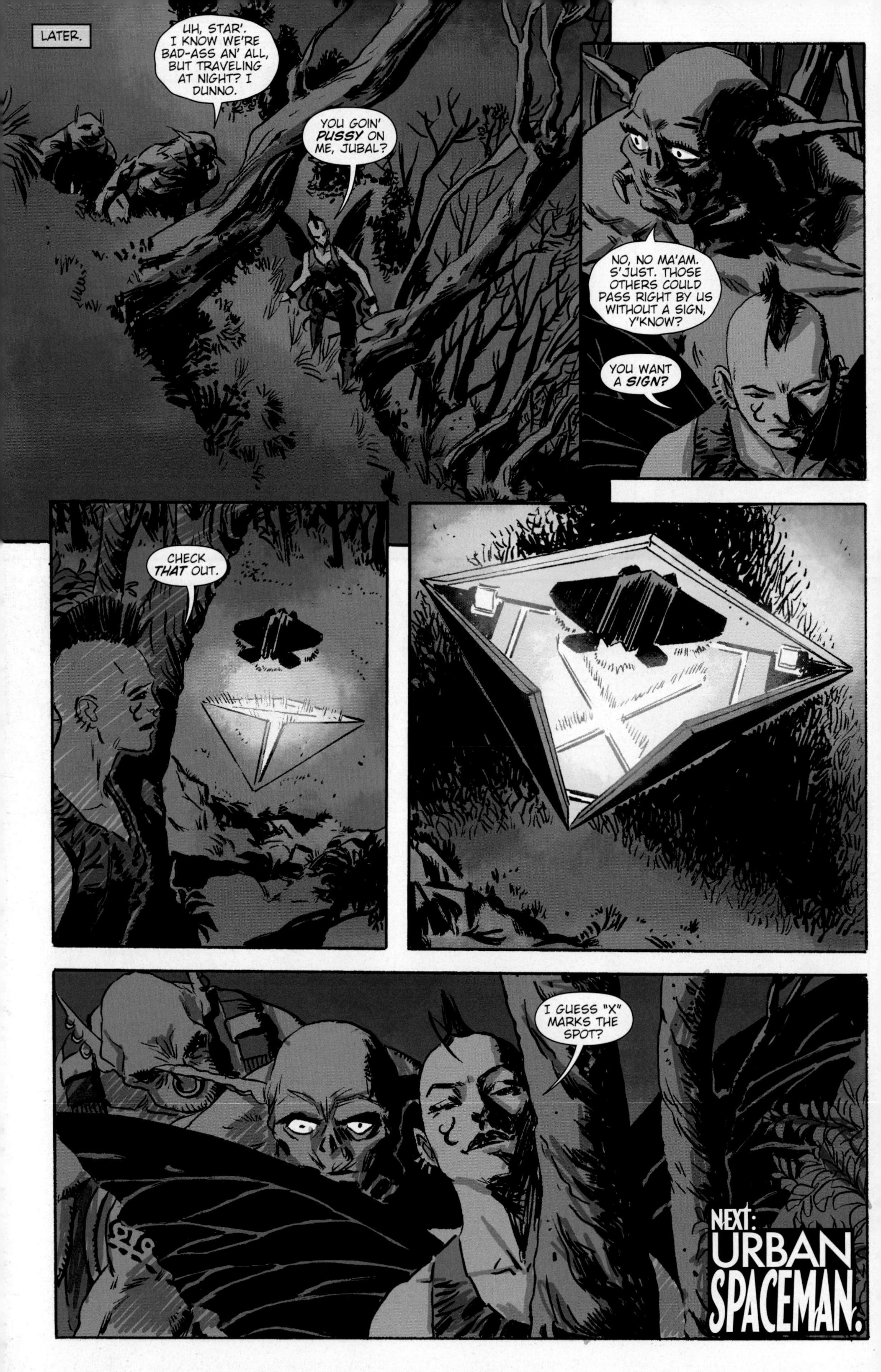
LATER.
UH, STAR'. I KNOW WE'RE BAD-ASS AN' ALL, BUT TRAVELING AT NIGHT? I DUNNO.
YOU GOIN' PUSSY ON ME, JUBAL?
NO, NO MA'AM. S'JUST. THOSE OTHERS COULD PASS RIGHT BY US WITHOUT A SIGN, Y'KNOW?
YOU WANT A SIGN?
CHECK THAT OUT.
I GUESS "X" MARKS THE SPOT?
NEXT: URBAN SPACEMAN.

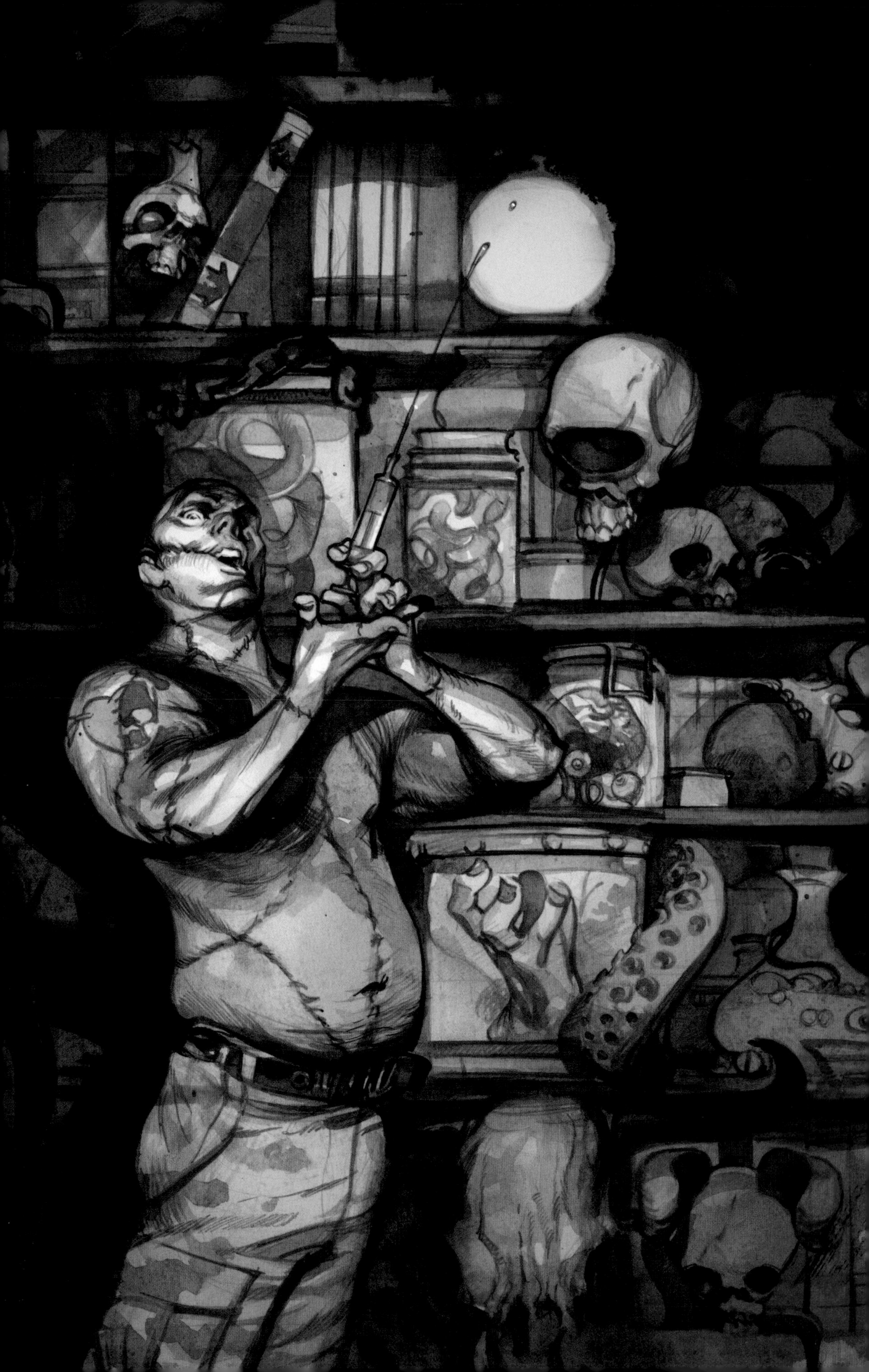

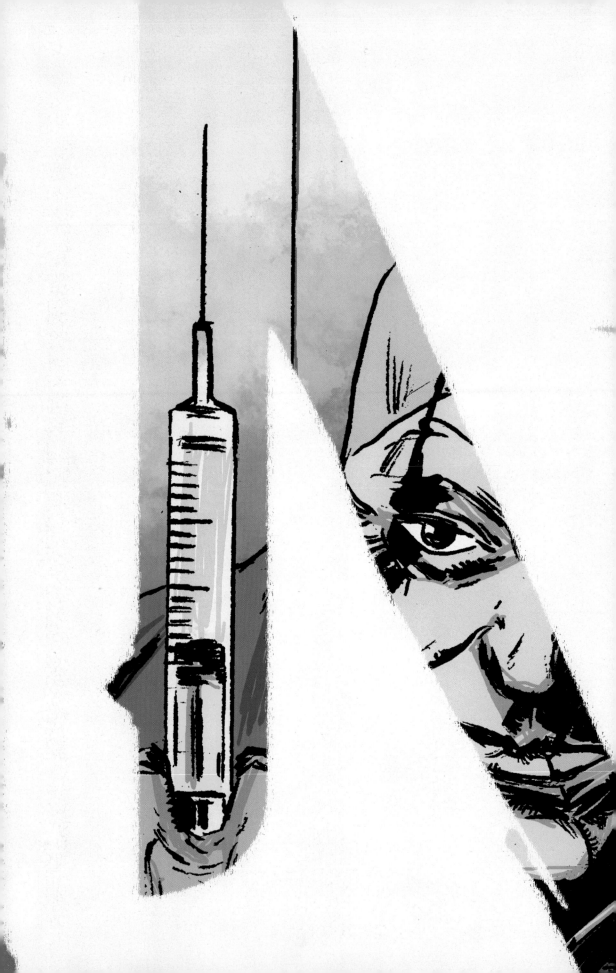

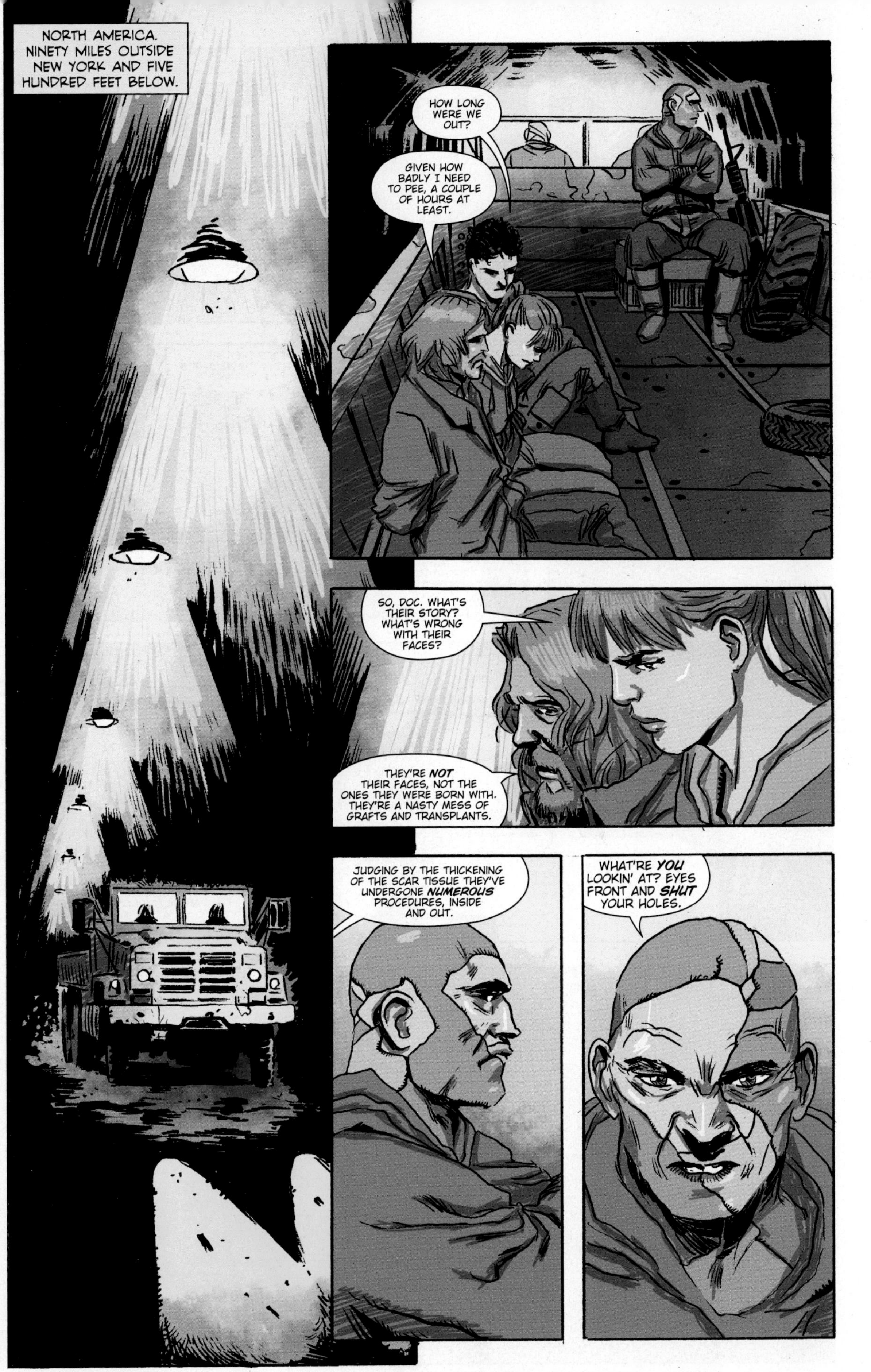
NORTH AMERICA. NINETY MILES OUTSIDE NEW YORK AND FIVE HUNDRED FEET BELOW.
HOW LONG WERE WE OUT?
GIVEN HOW BADLY I NEED TO PEE, A COUPLE OF HOURS AT LEAST.
SO, DOC. WHAT'S THEIR STORY? WHAT'S WRONG WITH THEIR FACES?
THEY'RE NOT THEIR FACES, NOT THE ONES THEY WERE BORN WITH. THEY'RE A NASTY MESS OF GRAFTS AND TRANSPLANTS.
JUDGING BY THE THICKENING OF THE SCAR TISSUE THEY'VE UNDERGONE NUMEROUS PROCEDURES, INSIDE AND OUT.
WHAT'RE YOU LOOKIN' AT? EYES FRONT AND SHUT YOUR HOLES.

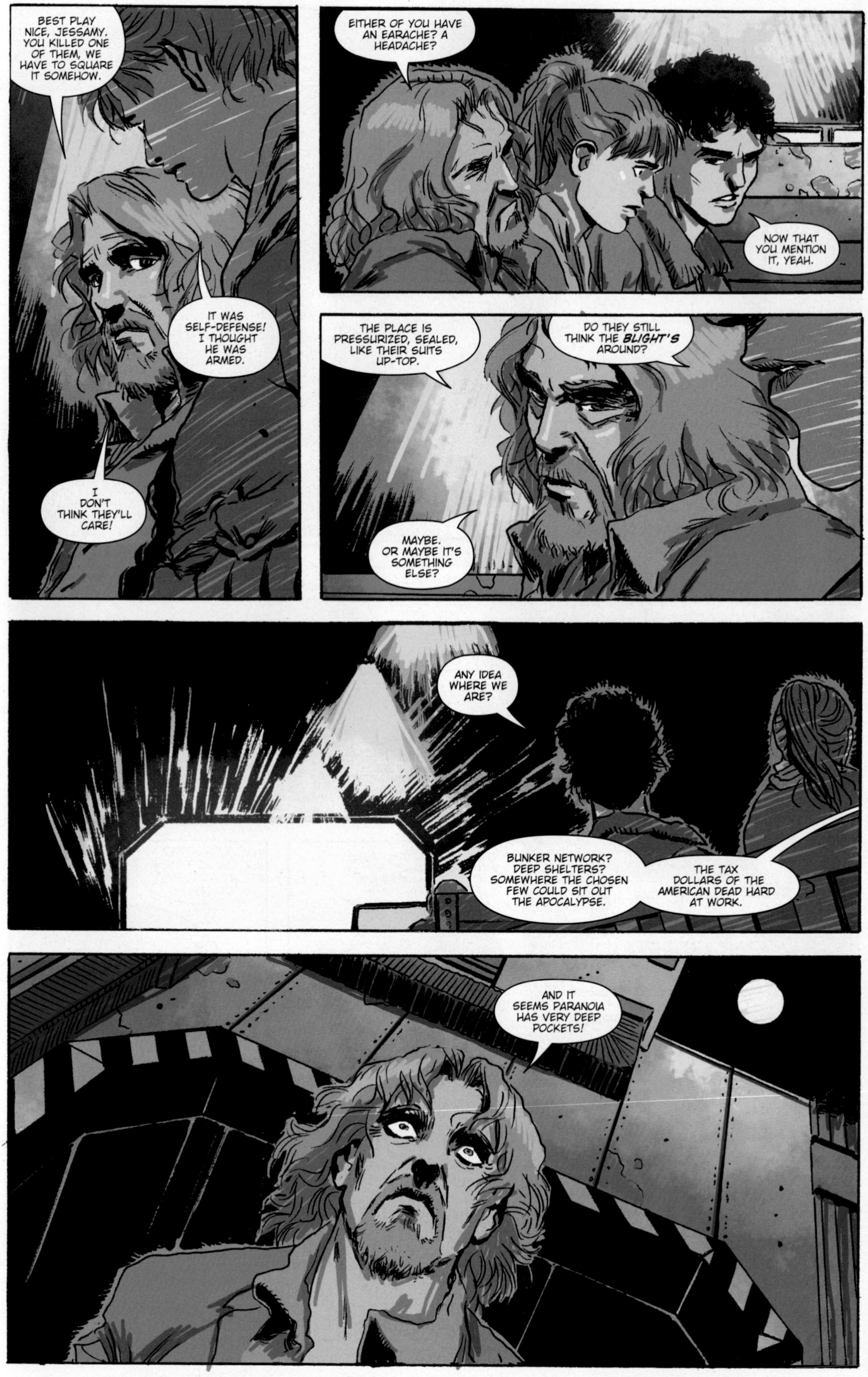
BEST PLAY NICE, JESSAMY. YOU KILLED ONE OF THEM, WE HAVE TO SQUARE IT SOMEHOW.
IT WAS SELF-DEFENSE! I THOUGHT HE WAS ARMED.
I DON'T THINK THEY'LL CARE!
EITHER OF YOU HAVE AN EARACHE? A HEADACHE?
NOW THAT YOU MENTION IT, YEAH.
THE PLACE IS PRESSURIZED, SEALED, LIKE THEIR SUITS UP-TOP.
DO THEY STILL THINK THE BLIGHT'S AROUND?
MAYBE. OR MAYBE IT'S SOMETHING ELSE?
ANY IDEA WHERE WE ARE?
BUNKER NETWORK? DEEP SHELTERS? SOMEWHERE THE CHOSEN FEW COULD SIT OUT THE APOCALYPSE.
THE TAX DOLLARS OF THE AMERICAN DEAD HARD AT WORK.
AND IT SEEMS PARANOIA HAS VERY DEEP POCKETS!

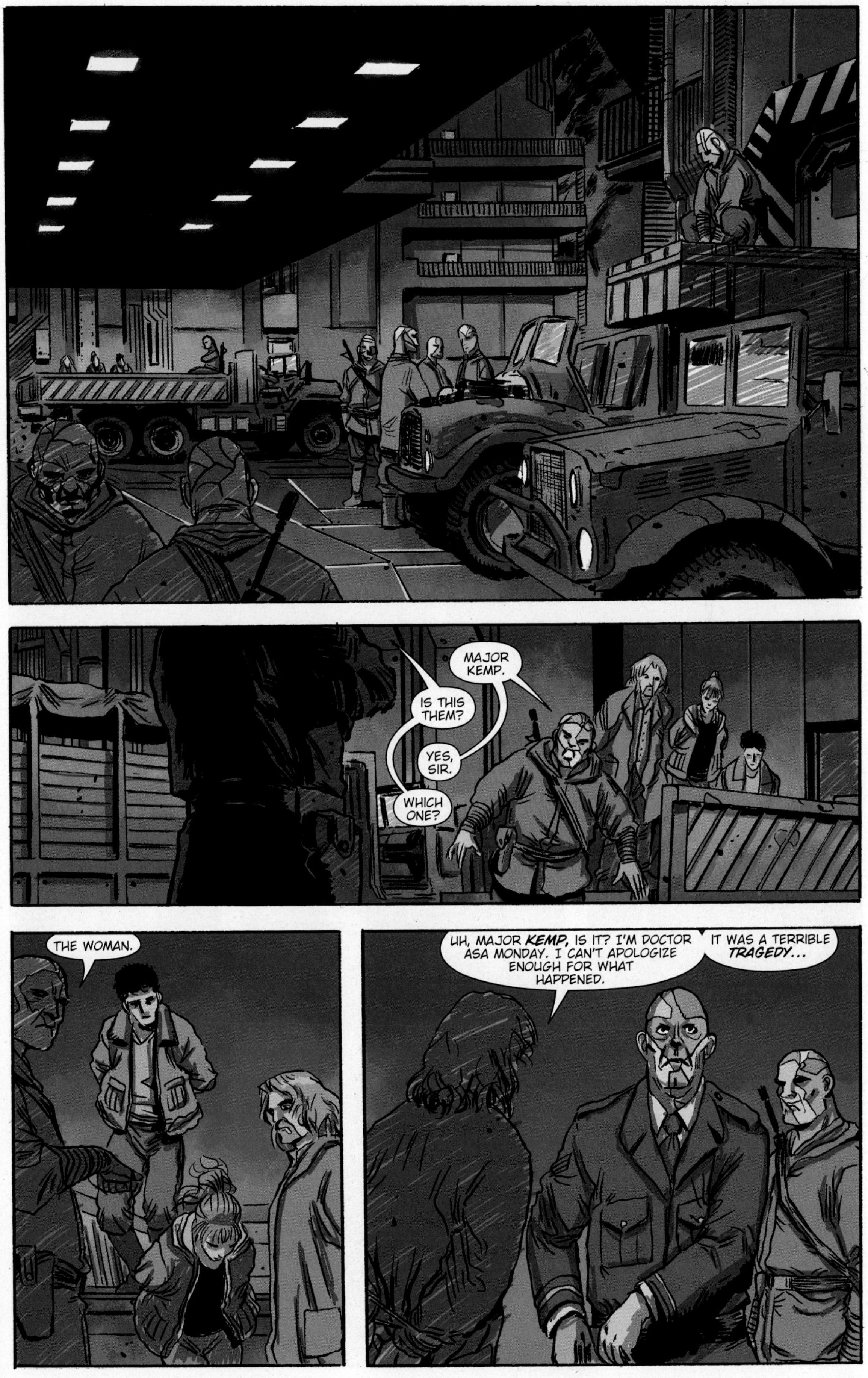
MAJOR KEMP.
IS THIS THEM?
YES, SIR.
WHICH ONE?
THE WOMAN.
UH, MAJOR *KEMP,* IS IT? I'M DOCTOR ASA MONDAY. I CAN'T APOLOGIZE ENOUGH FOR WHAT HAPPENED.
IT WAS A TERRIBLE *TRAGEDY...*

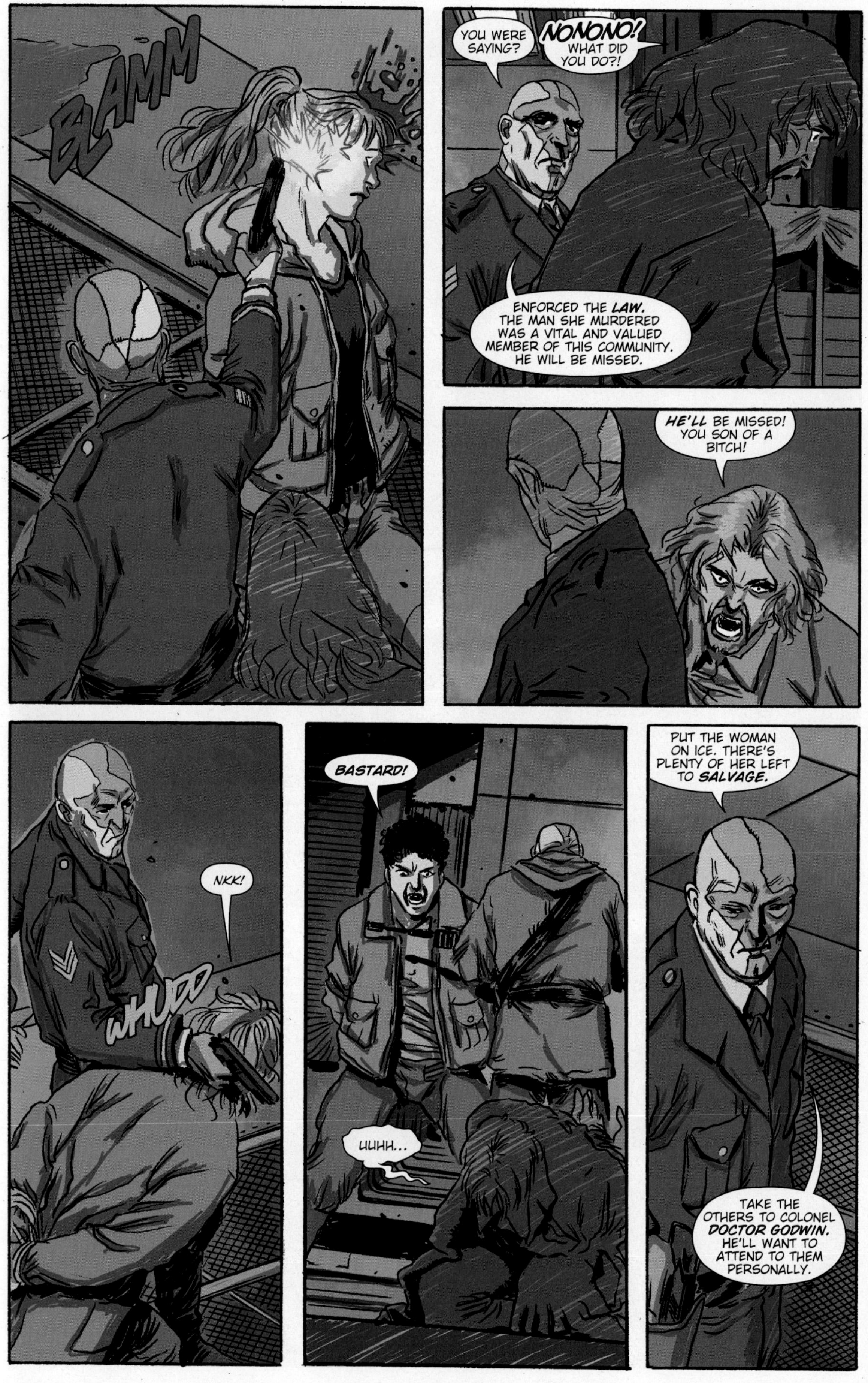
BLAMM
YOU WERE SAYING?
NONONO! WHAT DID YOU DO?!
ENFORCED THE LAW. THE MAN SHE MURDERED WAS A VITAL AND VALUED MEMBER OF THIS COMMUNITY. HE WILL BE MISSED.
HE'LL BE MISSED! YOU SON OF A BITCH!
NKK!
WHUDD
BASTARD!
UUHH...
PUT THE WOMAN ON ICE. THERE'S PLENTY OF HER LEFT TO SALVAGE.
TAKE THE OTHERS TO COLONEL DOCTOR GODWIN. HE'LL WANT TO ATTEND TO THEM PERSONALLY.

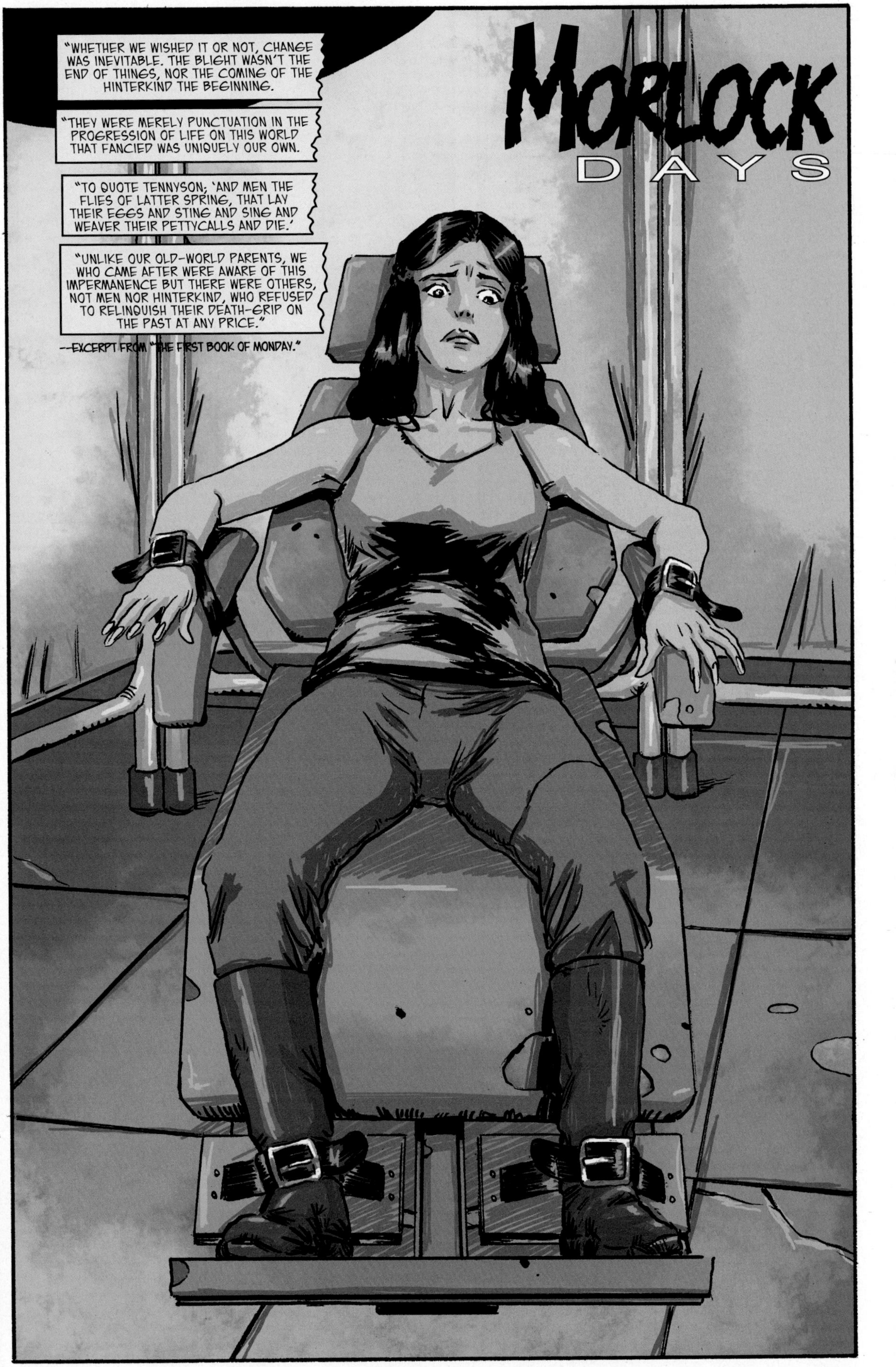
MORLOCK DAYS
"WHETHER WE WISHED IT OR NOT, CHANGE WAS INEVITABLE. THE BLIGHT WASN'T THE END OF THINGS, NOR THE COMING OF THE HINTERKIND THE BEGINNING.
"THEY WERE MERELY PUNCTUATION IN THE PROGRESSION OF LIFE ON THIS WORLD THAT FANCIED WAS UNIQUELY OUR OWN.
"TO QUOTE TENNYSON; 'AND MEN THE FLIES OF LATTER SPRING, THAT LAY THEIR EGGS AND STING AND SING AND WEAVER THEIR PETTYCALLS AND DIE.'
"UNLIKE OUR OLD-WORLD PARENTS, WE WHO CAME AFTER WERE AWARE OF THIS IMPERMANENCE BUT THERE WERE OTHERS, NOT MEN NOR HINTERKIND, WHO REFUSED TO RELINQUISH THEIR DEATH-GRIP ON THE PAST AT ANY PRICE."
--EXCERPT FROM "THE FIRST BOOK OF MONDAY."

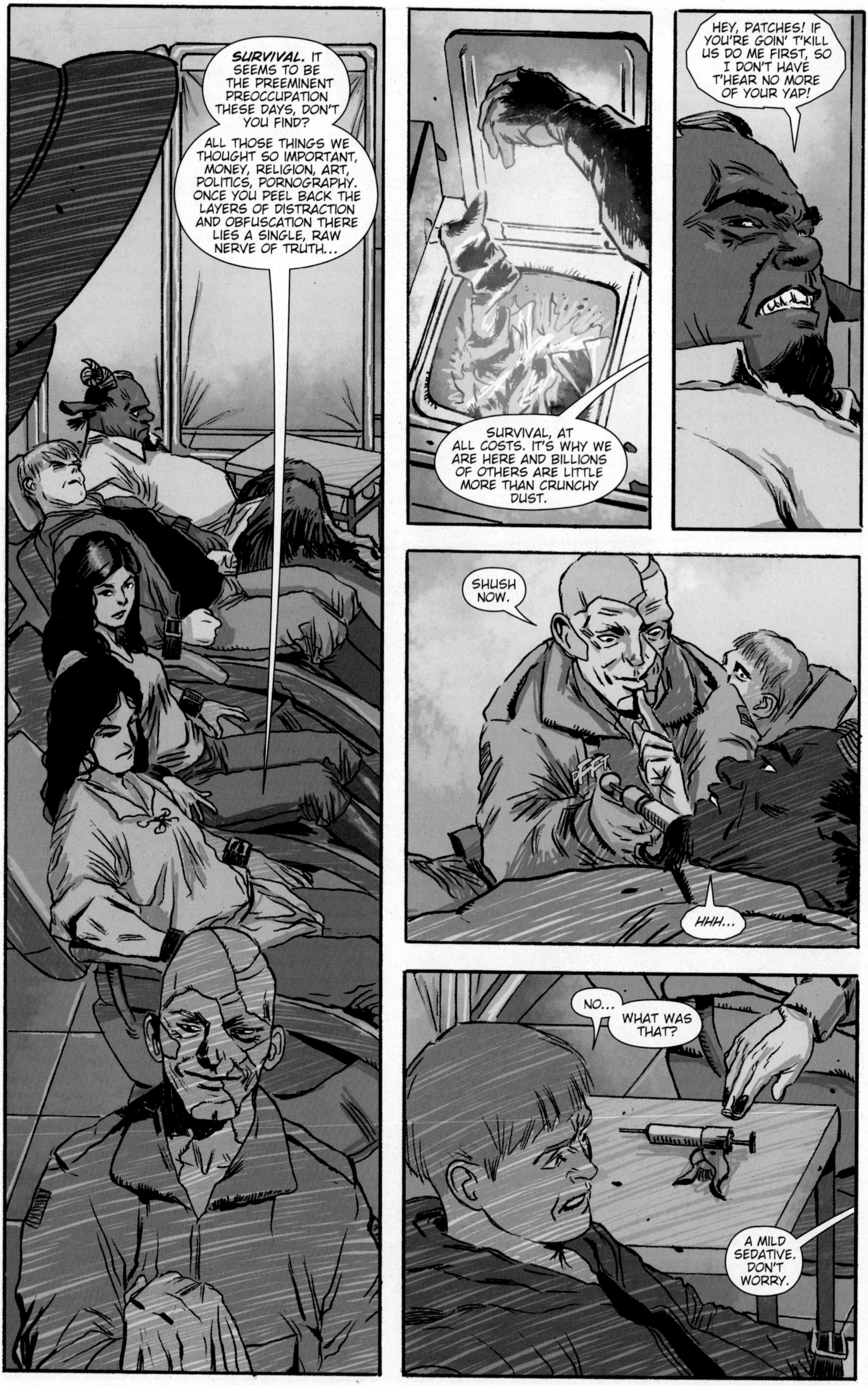
SURVIVAL. IT SEEMS TO BE THE PREEMINENT PREOCCUPATION THESE DAYS, DON'T YOU FIND?
ALL THOSE THINGS WE THOUGHT SO IMPORTANT, MONEY, RELIGION, ART, POLITICS, PORNOGRAPHY. ONCE YOU PEEL BACK THE LAYERS OF DISTRACTION AND OBFUSCATION THERE LIES A SINGLE, RAW NERVE OF TRUTH...
SURVIVAL, AT ALL COSTS. IT'S WHY WE ARE HERE AND BILLIONS OF OTHERS ARE LITTLE MORE THAN CRUNCHY DUST.
HEY, PATCHES! IF YOU'RE GOIN' T'KILL US DO ME FIRST, SO I DON'T HAVE T'HEAR NO MORE OF YOUR YAP!
SHUSH NOW.
PFFT
HHH...
NO...
WHAT WAS THAT?
A MILD SEDATIVE. DON'T WORRY.

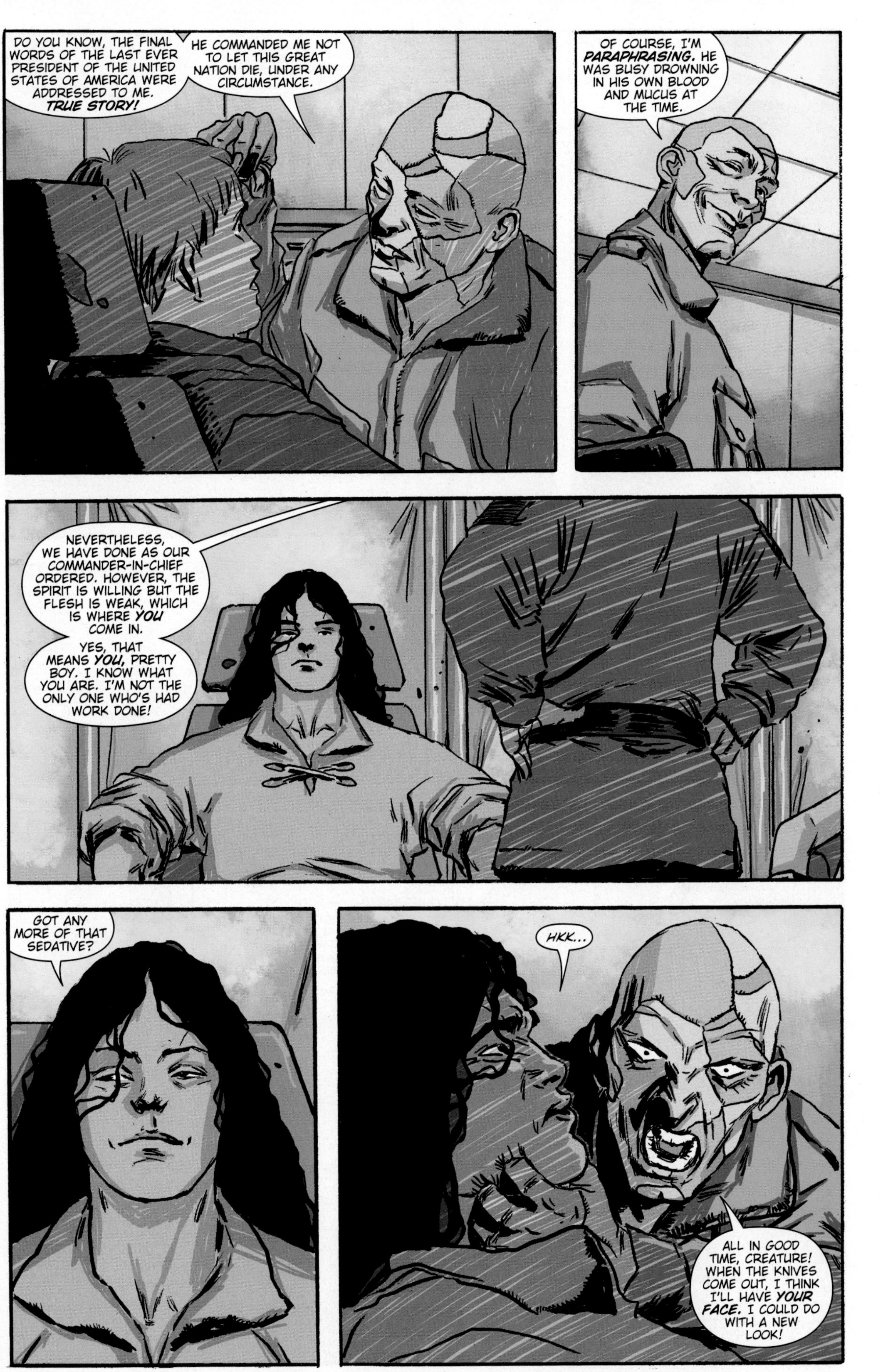
DO YOU KNOW, THE FINAL WORDS OF THE LAST EVER PRESIDENT OF THE UNITED STATES OF AMERICA WERE ADDRESSED TO ME. TRUE STORY!
HE COMMANDED ME NOT TO LET THIS GREAT NATION DIE, UNDER ANY CIRCUMSTANCE.
OF COURSE, I'M PARAPHRASING. HE WAS BUSY DROWNING IN HIS OWN BLOOD AND MUCUS AT THE TIME.
NEVERTHELESS, WE HAVE DONE AS OUR COMMANDER-IN-CHIEF ORDERED. HOWEVER, THE SPIRIT IS WILLING BUT THE FLESH IS WEAK, WHICH IS WHERE YOU COME IN.
YES, THAT MEANS YOU, PRETTY BOY. I KNOW WHAT YOU ARE. I'M NOT THE ONLY ONE WHO'S HAD WORK DONE!
GOT ANY MORE OF THAT SEDATIVE?
HKK...
ALL IN GOOD TIME, CREATURE! WHEN THE KNIVES COME OUT, I THINK I'LL HAVE YOUR FACE. I COULD DO WITH A NEW LOOK!

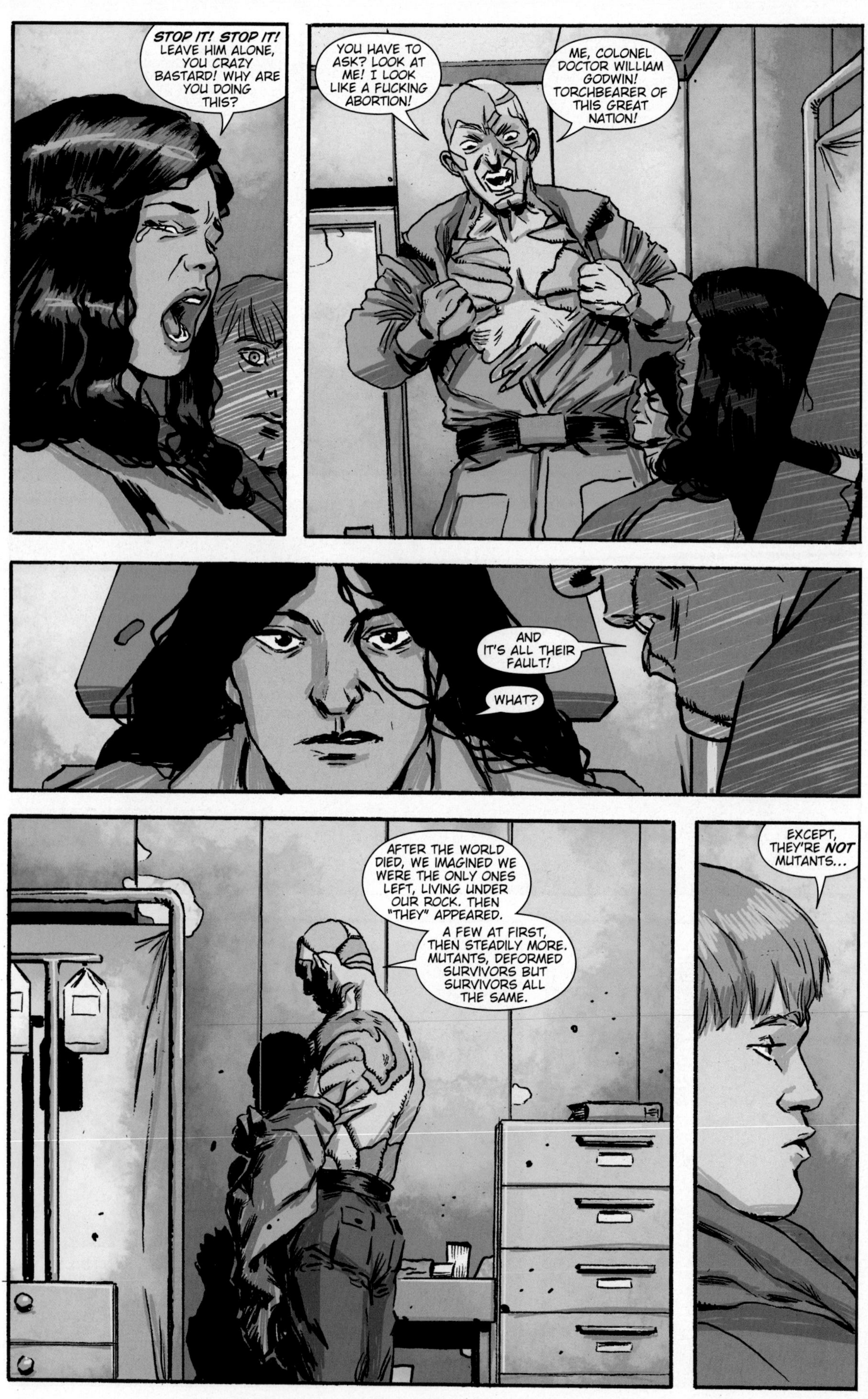
STOP IT! STOP IT! LEAVE HIM ALONE, YOU CRAZY BASTARD! WHY ARE YOU DOING THIS?
YOU HAVE TO ASK? LOOK AT ME! I LOOK LIKE A FUCKING ABORTION!
ME, COLONEL DOCTOR WILLIAM GODWIN! TORCHBEARER OF THIS GREAT NATION!
AND IT'S ALL THEIR FAULT!
WHAT?
AFTER THE WORLD DIED, WE IMAGINED WE WERE THE ONLY ONES LEFT, LIVING UNDER OUR ROCK. THEN "THEY" APPEARED.
A FEW AT FIRST, THEN STEADILY MORE. MUTANTS, DEFORMED SURVIVORS BUT SURVIVORS ALL THE SAME.
EXCEPT, THEY'RE NOT MUTANTS...

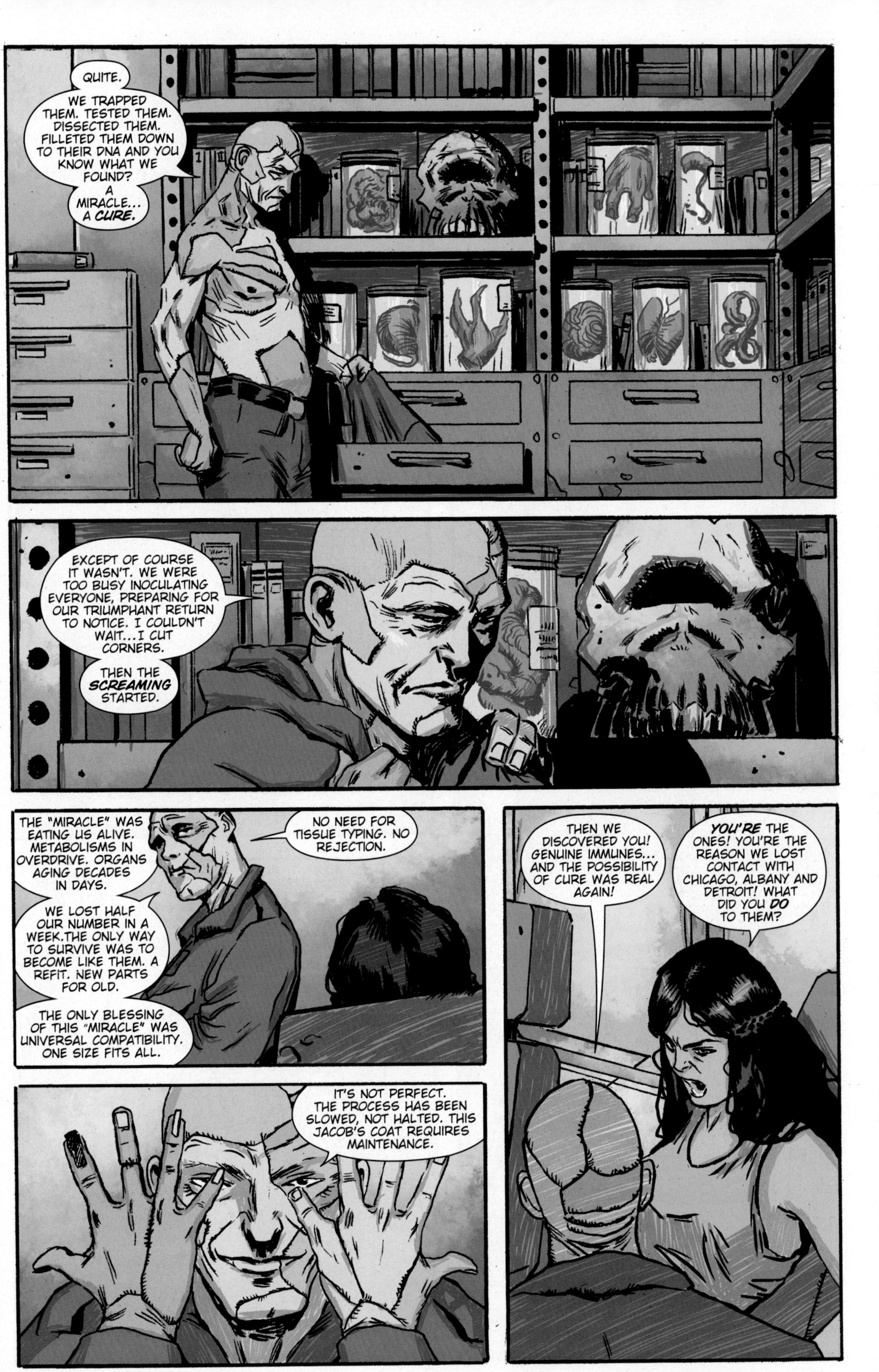
QUITE.
WE TRAPPED THEM. TESTED THEM. DISSECTED THEM. FILLETED THEM DOWN TO THEIR DNA AND YOU KNOW WHAT WE FOUND?
A MIRACLE... A CURE.
EXCEPT OF COURSE IT WASN'T. WE WERE TOO BUSY INOCULATING EVERYONE, PREPARING FOR OUR TRIUMPHANT RETURN TO NOTICE. I COULDN'T WAIT...I CUT CORNERS.
THEN THE SCREAMING STARTED.
THE "MIRACLE" WAS EATING US ALIVE. METABOLISMS IN OVERDRIVE. ORGANS AGING DECADES IN DAYS.
WE LOST HALF OUR NUMBER IN A WEEK.THE ONLY WAY TO SURVIVE WAS TO BECOME LIKE THEM. A REFIT. NEW PARTS FOR OLD.
THE ONLY BLESSING OF THIS "MIRACLE" WAS UNIVERSAL COMPATIBILITY. ONE SIZE FITS ALL.
NO NEED FOR TISSUE TYPING. NO REJECTION.
IT'S NOT PERFECT. THE PROCESS HAS BEEN SLOWED, NOT HALTED. THIS JACOB'S COAT REQUIRES MAINTENANCE.
THEN WE DISCOVERED YOU! GENUINE IMMUNES... AND THE POSSIBILITY OF CURE WAS REAL AGAIN!
YOU'RE THE ONES! YOU'RE THE REASON WE LOST CONTACT WITH CHICAGO, ALBANY AND DETROIT! WHAT DID YOU DO TO THEM?

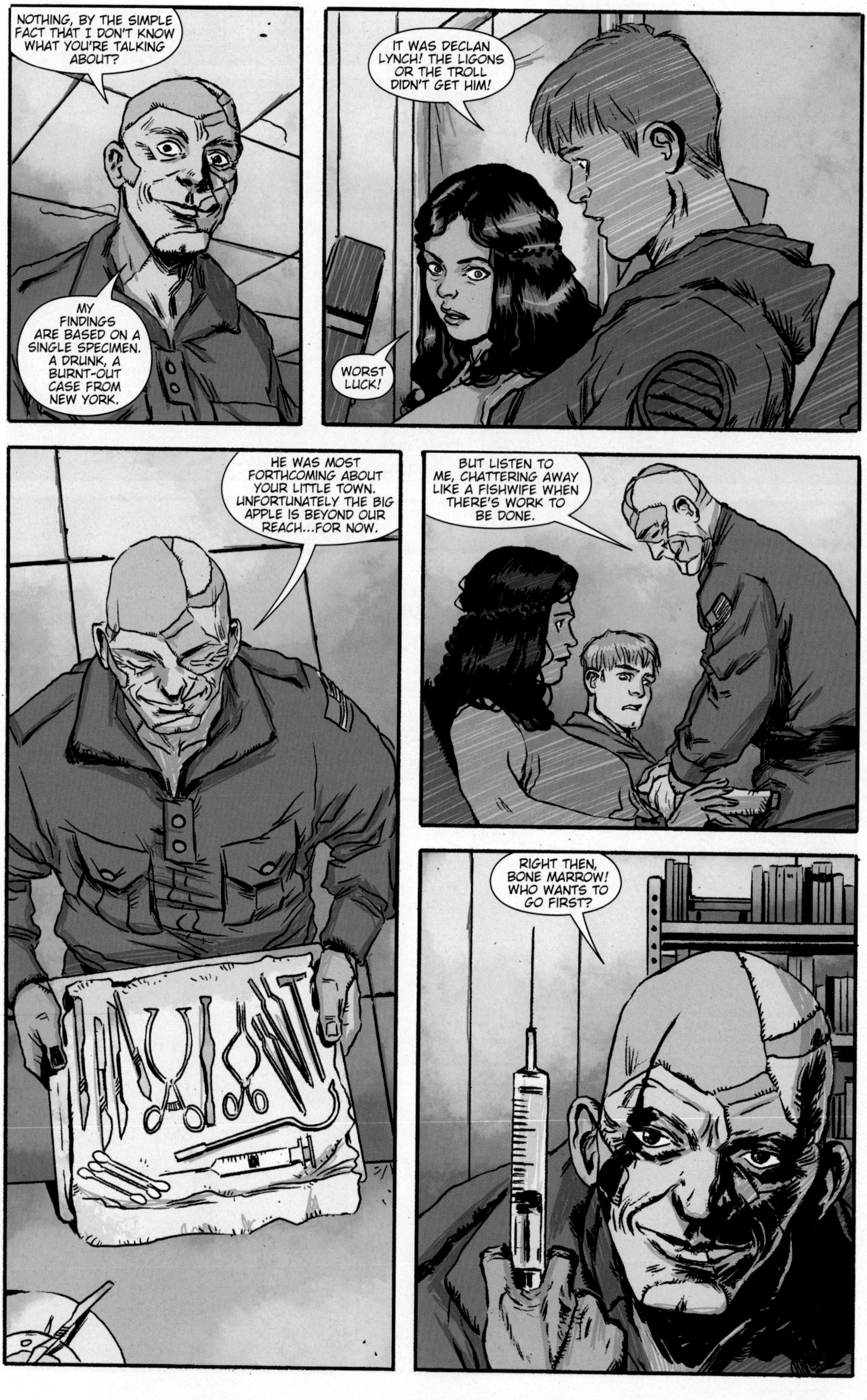
NOTHING, BY THE SIMPLE FACT THAT I DON'T KNOW WHAT YOU'RE TALKING ABOUT?
MY FINDINGS ARE BASED ON A SINGLE SPECIMEN. A DRUNK, A BURNT-OUT CASE FROM NEW YORK.
IT WAS DECLAN LYNCH! THE LIGONS OR THE TROLL DIDN'T GET HIM!
WORST LUCK!
HE WAS MOST FORTHCOMING ABOUT YOUR LITTLE TOWN. UNFORTUNATELY THE BIG APPLE IS BEYOND OUR REACH...FOR NOW.
BUT LISTEN TO ME, CHATTERING AWAY LIKE A FISHWIFE WHEN THERE'S WORK TO BE DONE.
RIGHT THEN, BONE MARROW! WHO WANTS TO GO FIRST?

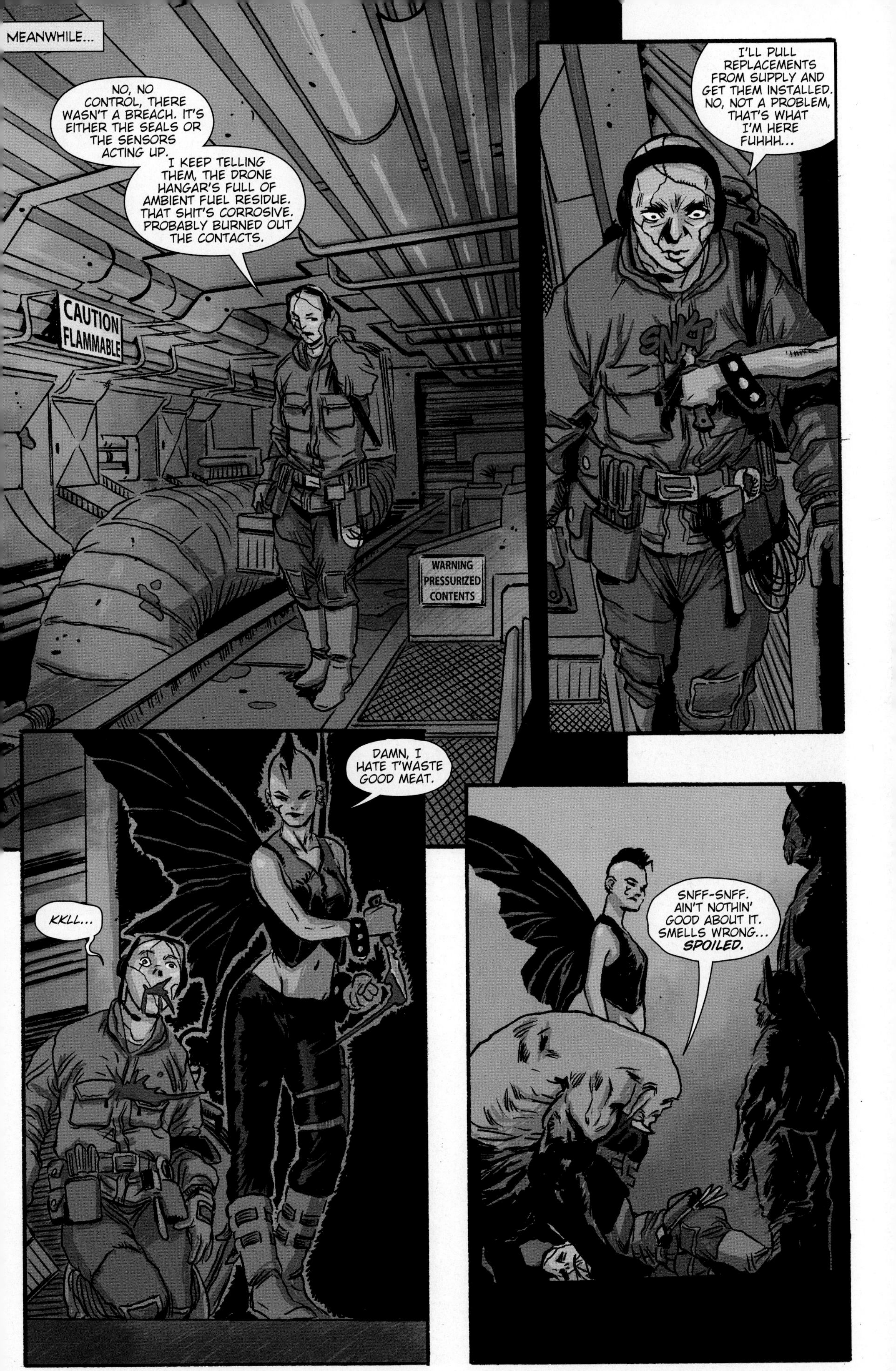
MEANWHILE...
NO, NO CONTROL, THERE WASN'T A BREACH. IT'S EITHER THE SEALS OR THE SENSORS ACTING UP.
I KEEP TELLING THEM, THE DRONE HANGAR'S FULL OF AMBIENT FUEL RESIDUE. THAT SHIT'S CORROSIVE. PROBABLY BURNED OUT THE CONTACTS.
CAUTION FLAMMABLE
WARNING PRESSURIZED CONTENTS
I'LL PULL REPLACEMENTS FROM SUPPLY AND GET THEM INSTALLED. NO, NOT A PROBLEM, THAT'S WHAT I'M HERE FUHHH...
DAMN, I HATE T'WASTE GOOD MEAT.
KKLL...
SNFF-SNFF. AIN'T NOTHIN' GOOD ABOUT IT. SMELLS WRONG... SPOILED.

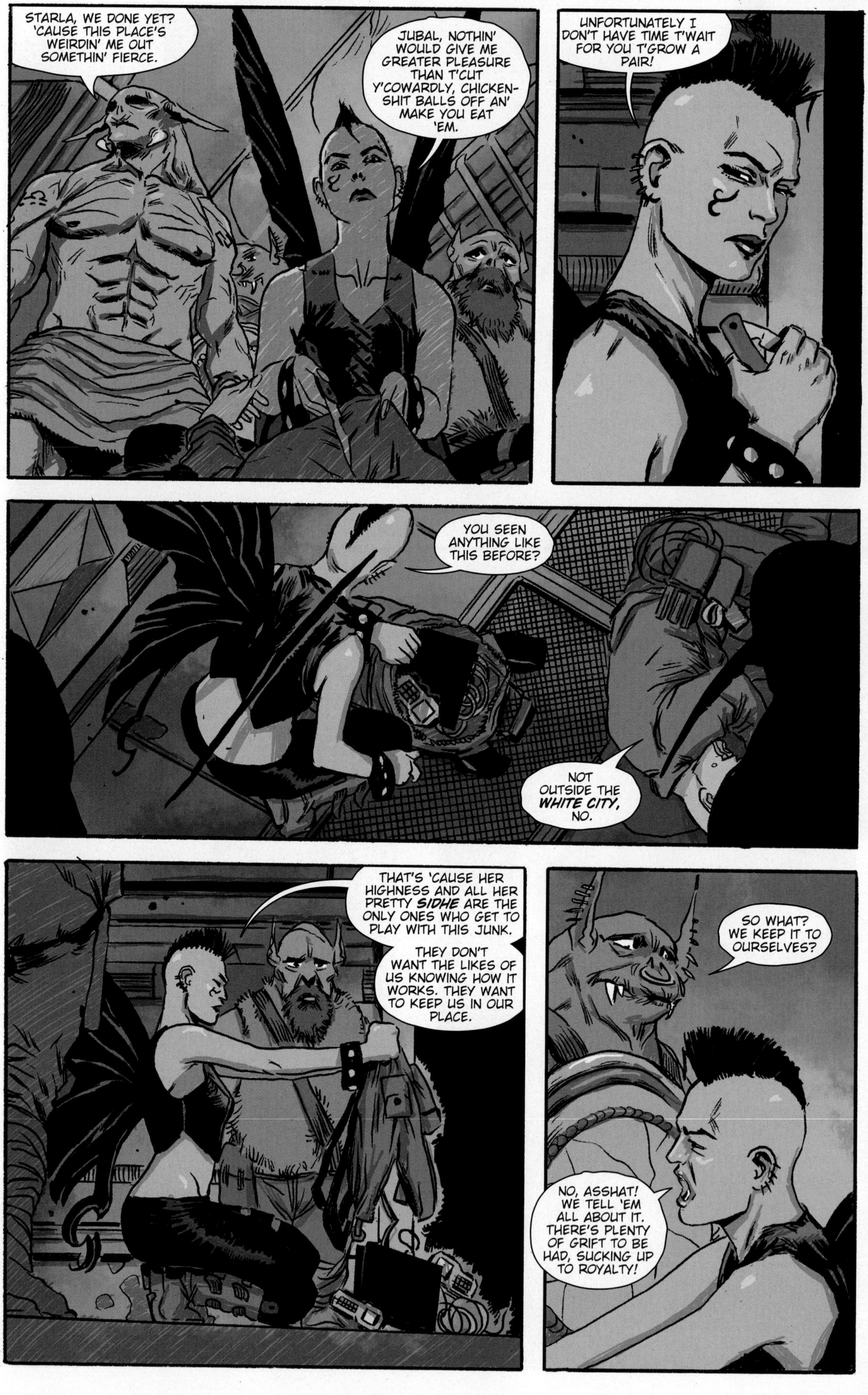
STARLA, WE DONE YET? 'CAUSE THIS PLACE'S WEIRDIN' ME OUT SOMETHIN' FIERCE.
JUBAL, NOTHIN' WOULD GIVE ME GREATER PLEASURE THAN T'CUT Y'COWARDLY, CHICKEN-SHIT BALLS OFF AN' MAKE YOU EAT 'EM.
UNFORTUNATELY I DON'T HAVE TIME T'WAIT FOR YOU T'GROW A PAIR!
YOU SEEN ANYTHING LIKE THIS BEFORE?
NOT OUTSIDE THE ***WHITE CITY***, NO.
THAT'S 'CAUSE HER HIGHNESS AND ALL HER PRETTY ***SIDHE*** ARE THE ONLY ONES WHO GET TO PLAY WITH THIS JUNK.
THEY DON'T WANT THE LIKES OF US KNOWING HOW IT WORKS. THEY WANT TO KEEP US IN OUR PLACE.
SO WHAT? WE KEEP IT TO OURSELVES?
NO, ASSHAT! WE TELL 'EM ALL ABOUT IT. THERE'S PLENTY OF GRIFT TO BE HAD, SUCKING UP TO ROYALTY!

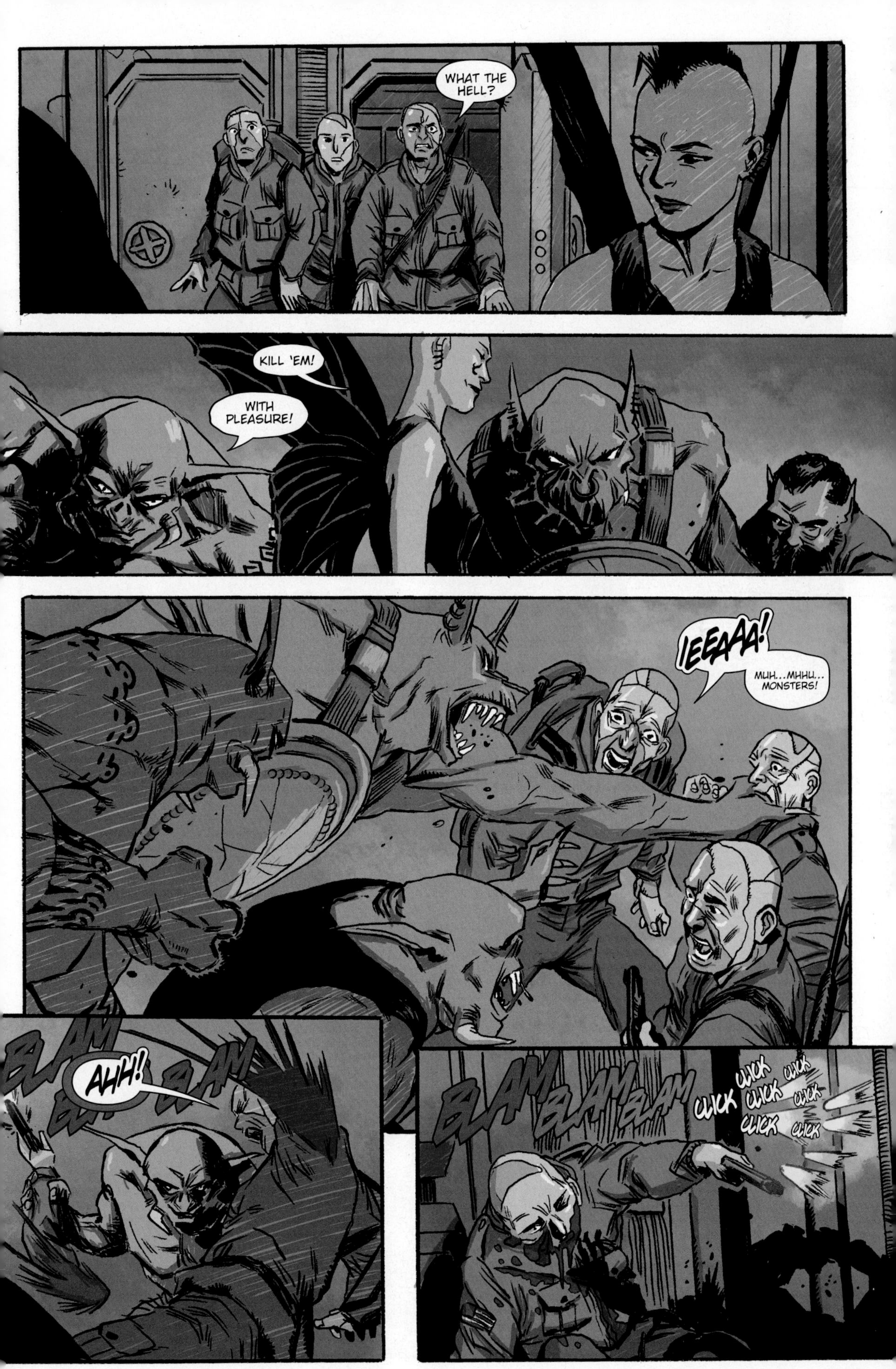
WHAT THE HELL?
KILL 'EM!
WITH PLEASURE!
IEEAAA!
MUH...MHHU... MONSTERS!
BLAM BLAM BLAM
AHH!
BLAM BLAMBLAM
CLICK CLICK CLICK CLICK CLICK CLICK CLICK CLICK

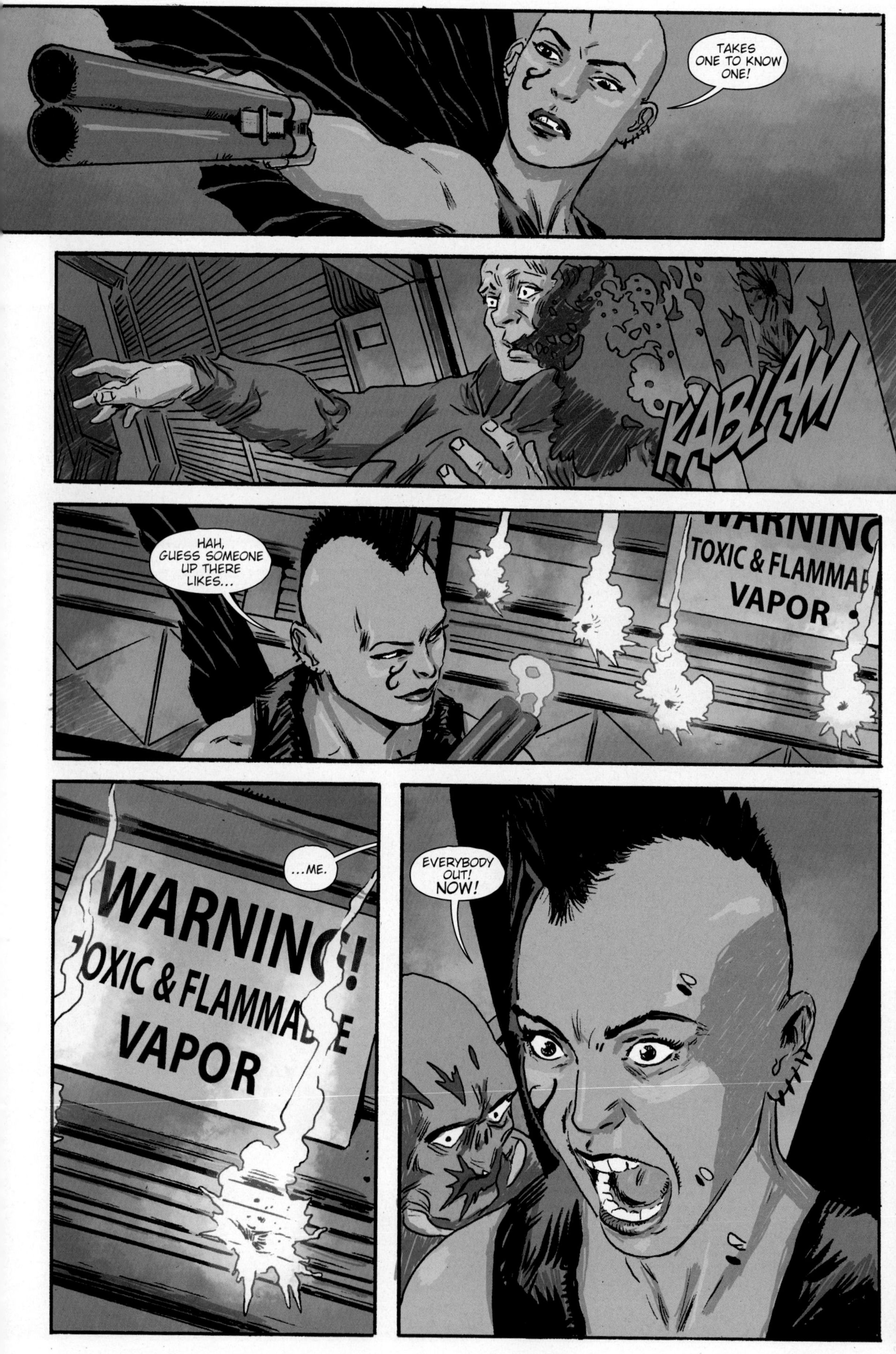

TAKES ONE TO KNOW ONE!
KABLAM
HAH, GUESS SOMEONE UP THERE LIKES...
WARNING TOXIC & FLAMMAB VAPOR
...ME.
WARNING! TOXIC & FLAMMABLE VAPOR
EVERYBODY OUT! NOW!

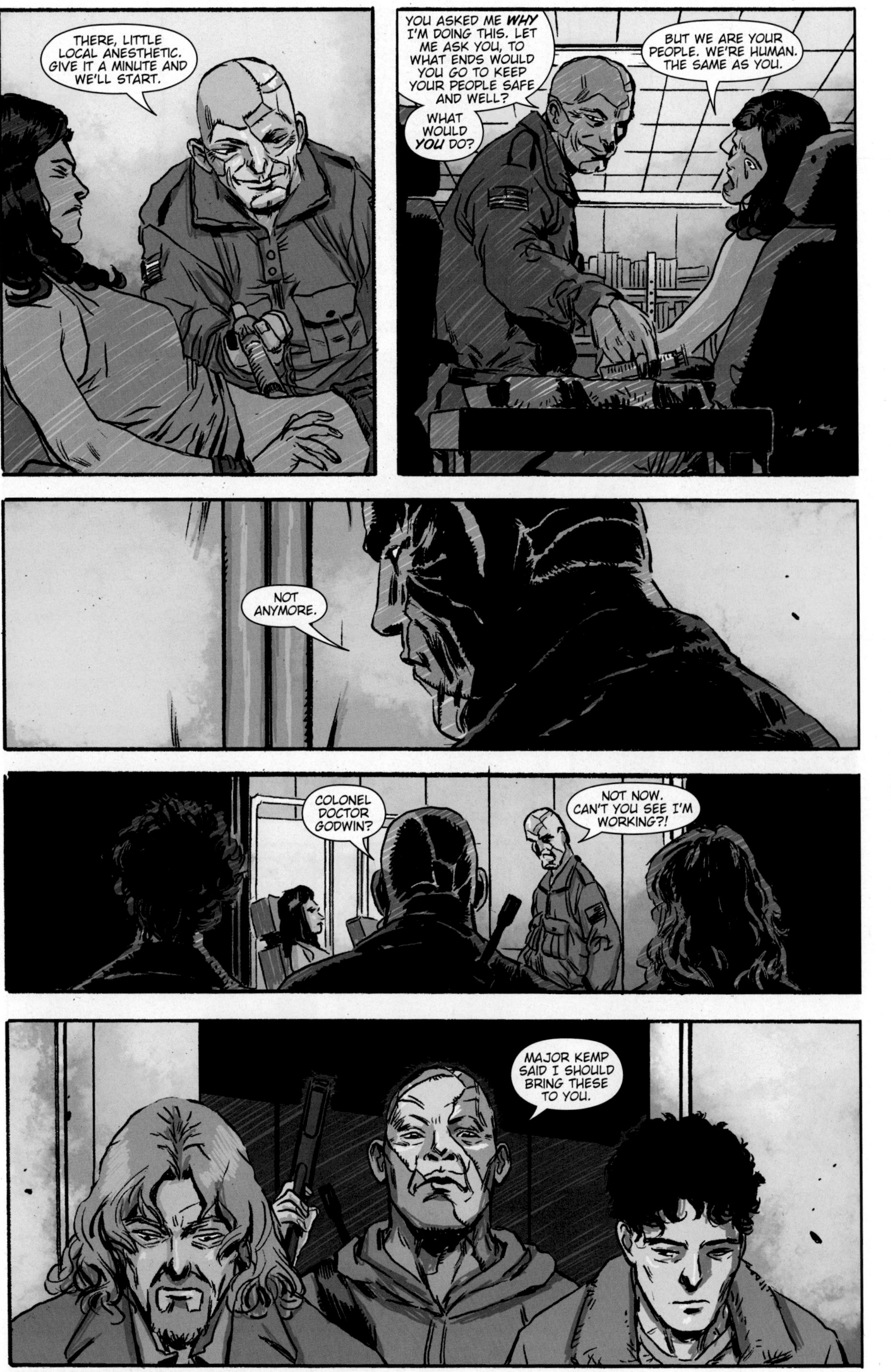
THERE, LITTLE LOCAL ANESTHETIC. GIVE IT A MINUTE AND WE'LL START.
YOU ASKED ME WHY I'M DOING THIS. LET ME ASK YOU, TO WHAT ENDS WOULD YOU GO TO KEEP YOUR PEOPLE SAFE AND WELL?
WHAT WOULD YOU DO?
BUT WE ARE YOUR PEOPLE. WE'RE HUMAN. THE SAME AS YOU.
NOT ANYMORE.
COLONEL DOCTOR GODWIN?
NOT NOW. CAN'T YOU SEE I'M WORKING?!
MAJOR KEMP SAID I SHOULD BRING THESE TO YOU.

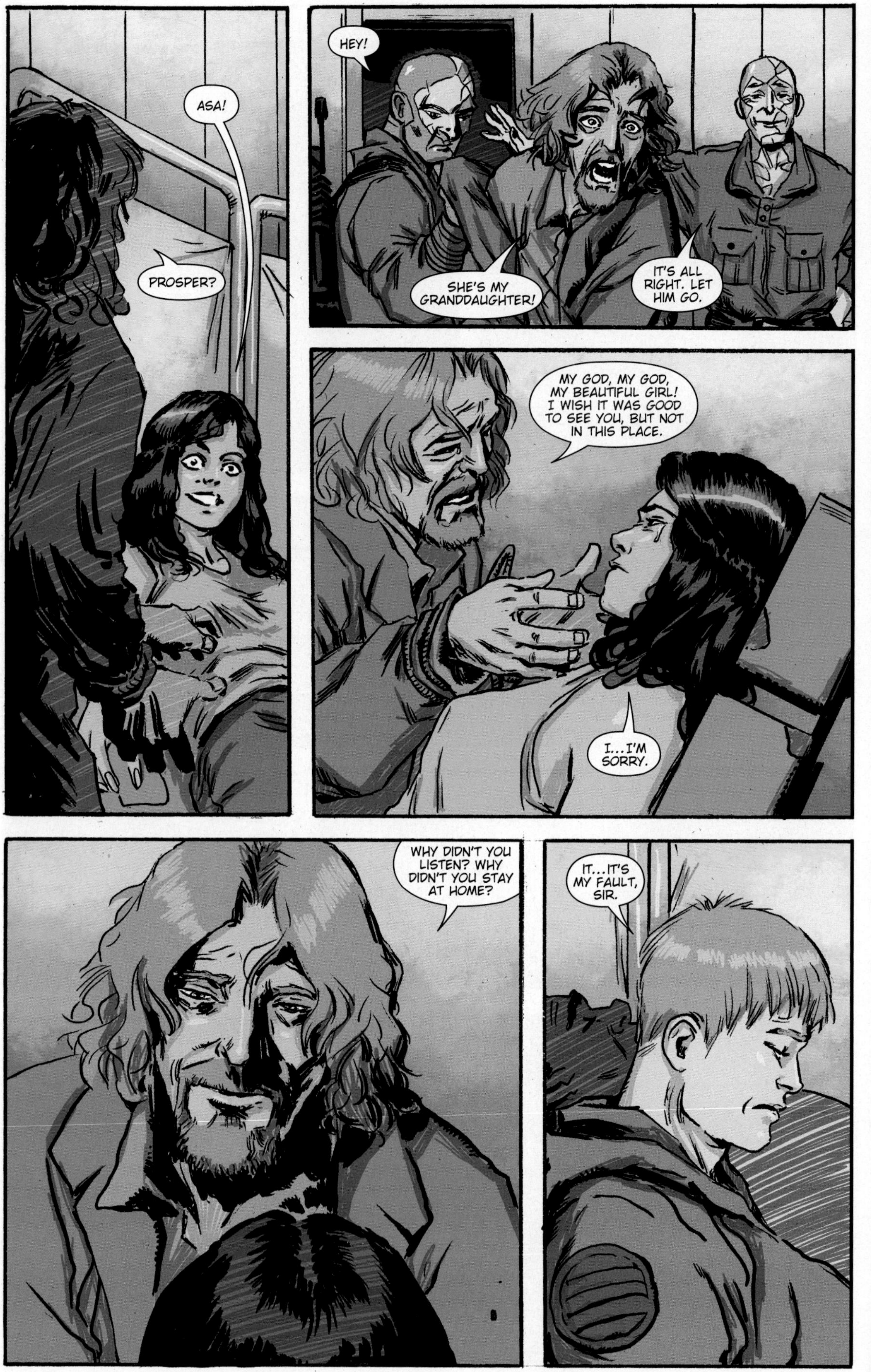
ASA!
PROSPER?
HEY!
SHE'S MY GRANDDAUGHTER!
IT'S ALL RIGHT. LET HIM GO.
MY GOD, MY GOD, MY BEAUTIFUL GIRL! I WISH IT WAS GOOD TO SEE YOU, BUT NOT IN THIS PLACE.
I...I'M SORRY.
WHY DIDN'T YOU LISTEN? WHY DIDN'T YOU STAY AT HOME?
IT...IT'S MY FAULT, SIR.

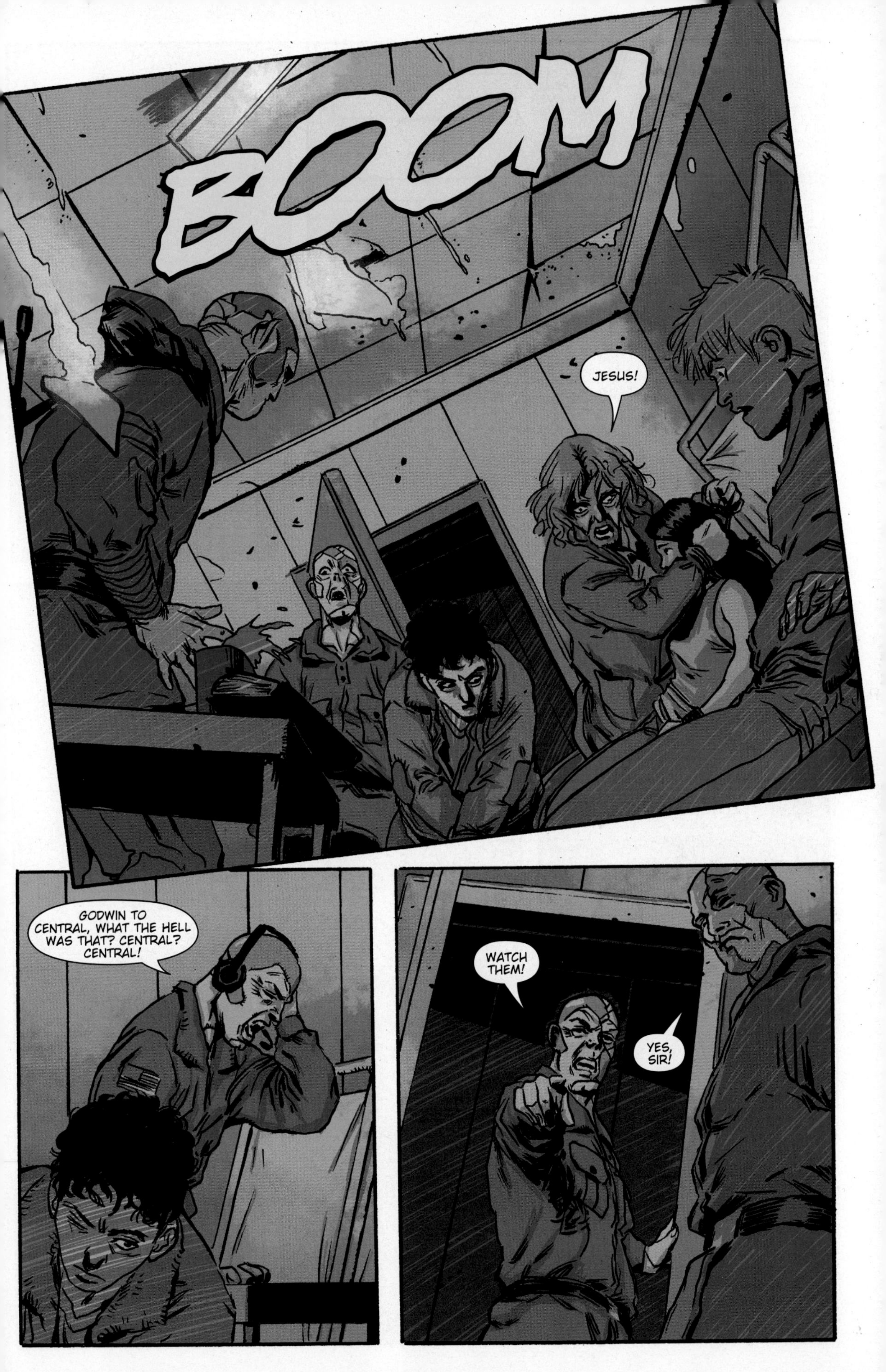
BOOM
JESUS!
GODWIN TO CENTRAL, WHAT THE HELL WAS THAT? CENTRAL? CENTRAL!
WATCH THEM!
YES, SIR!

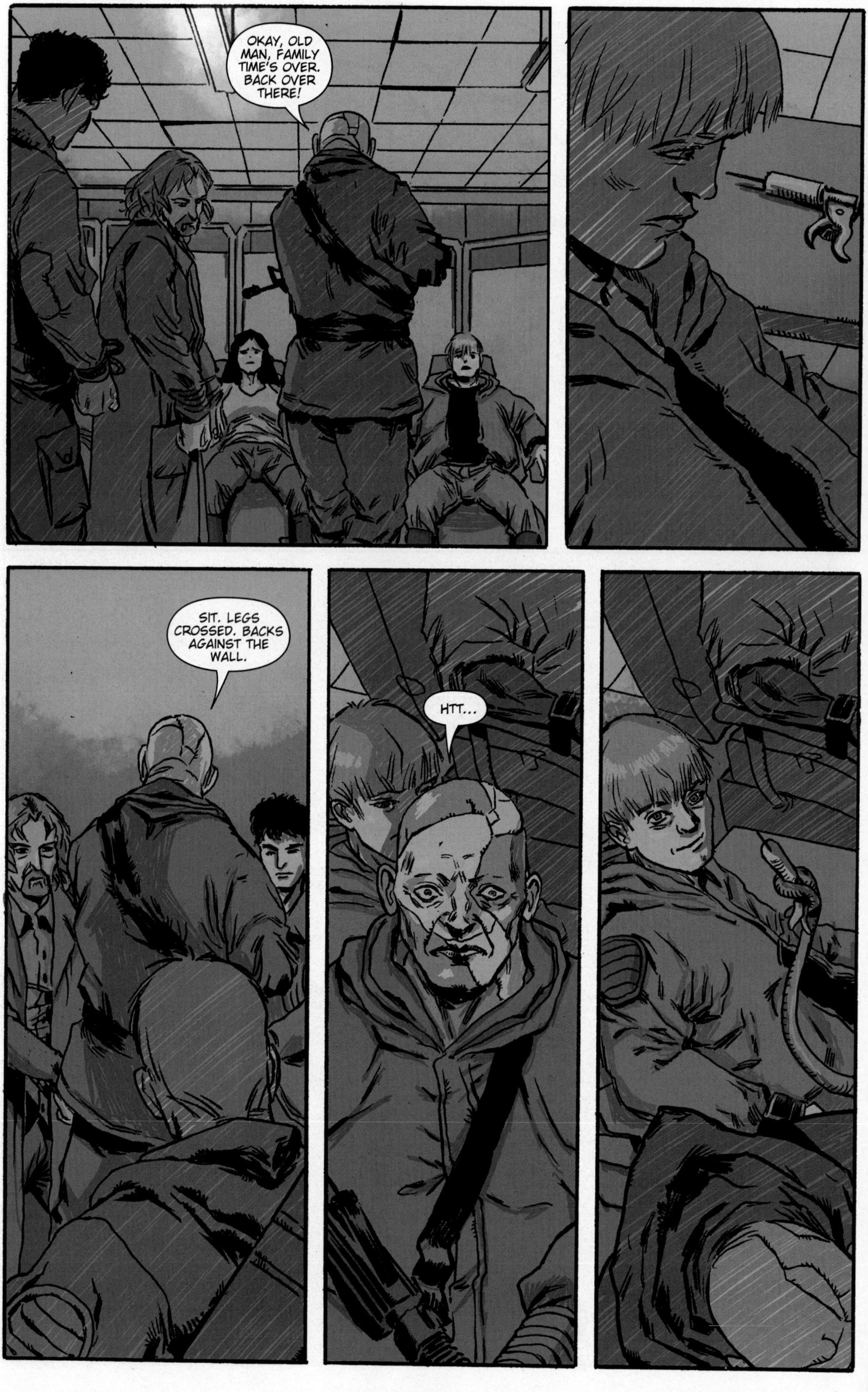
OKAY, OLD MAN, FAMILY TIME'S OVER. BACK OVER THERE!
SIT. LEGS CROSSED. BACKS AGAINST THE WALL.
HTT...

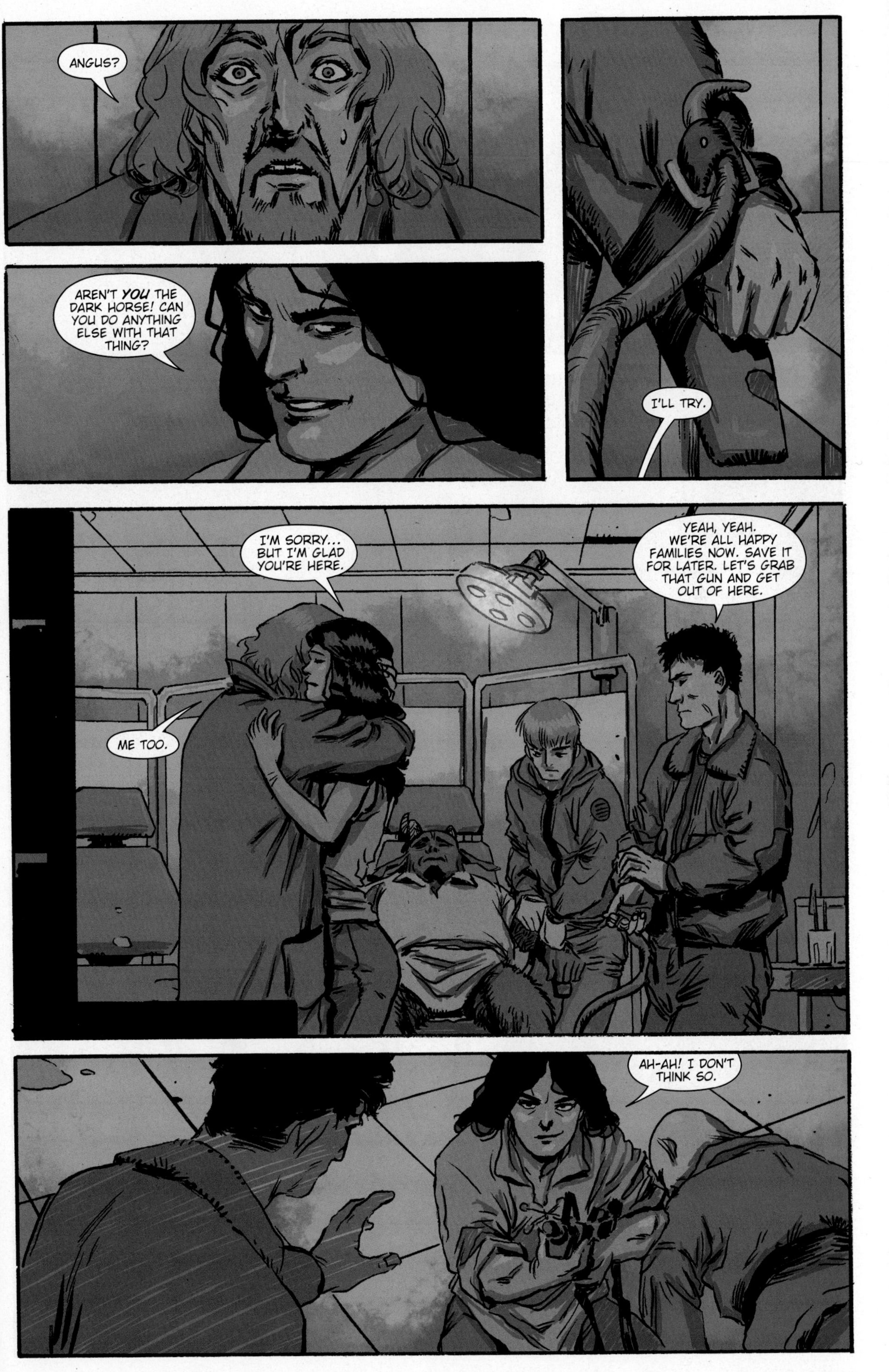
ANGUS?
I'LL TRY.
AREN'T *YOU* THE DARK HORSE! CAN YOU DO ANYTHING ELSE WITH THAT THING?
I'M SORRY... BUT I'M GLAD YOU'RE HERE.
ME TOO.
YEAH, YEAH. WE'RE ALL HAPPY FAMILIES NOW. SAVE IT FOR LATER. LET'S GRAB THAT GUN AND GET OUT OF HERE.
AH-AH! I DON'T THINK SO.

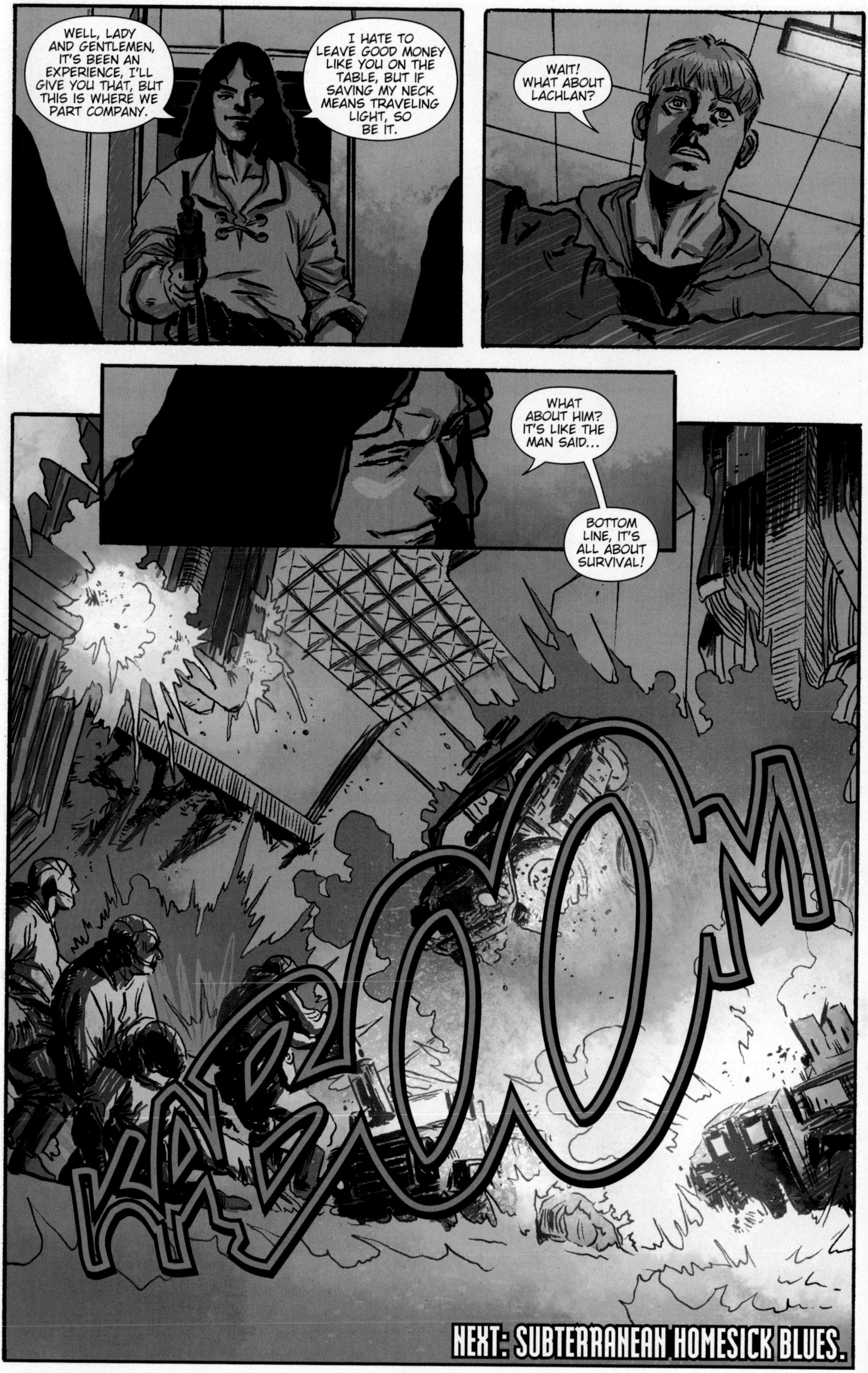
WELL, LADY AND GENTLEMEN, IT'S BEEN AN EXPERIENCE, I'LL GIVE YOU THAT, BUT THIS IS WHERE WE PART COMPANY.
I HATE TO LEAVE GOOD MONEY LIKE YOU ON THE TABLE, BUT IF SAVING MY NECK MEANS TRAVELING LIGHT, SO BE IT.
WAIT! WHAT ABOUT LACHLAN?
WHAT ABOUT HIM? IT'S LIKE THE MAN SAID...
BOTTOM LINE, IT'S ALL ABOUT SURVIVAL!
KABOOOM
NEXT: SUBTERRANEAN HOMESICK BLUES.

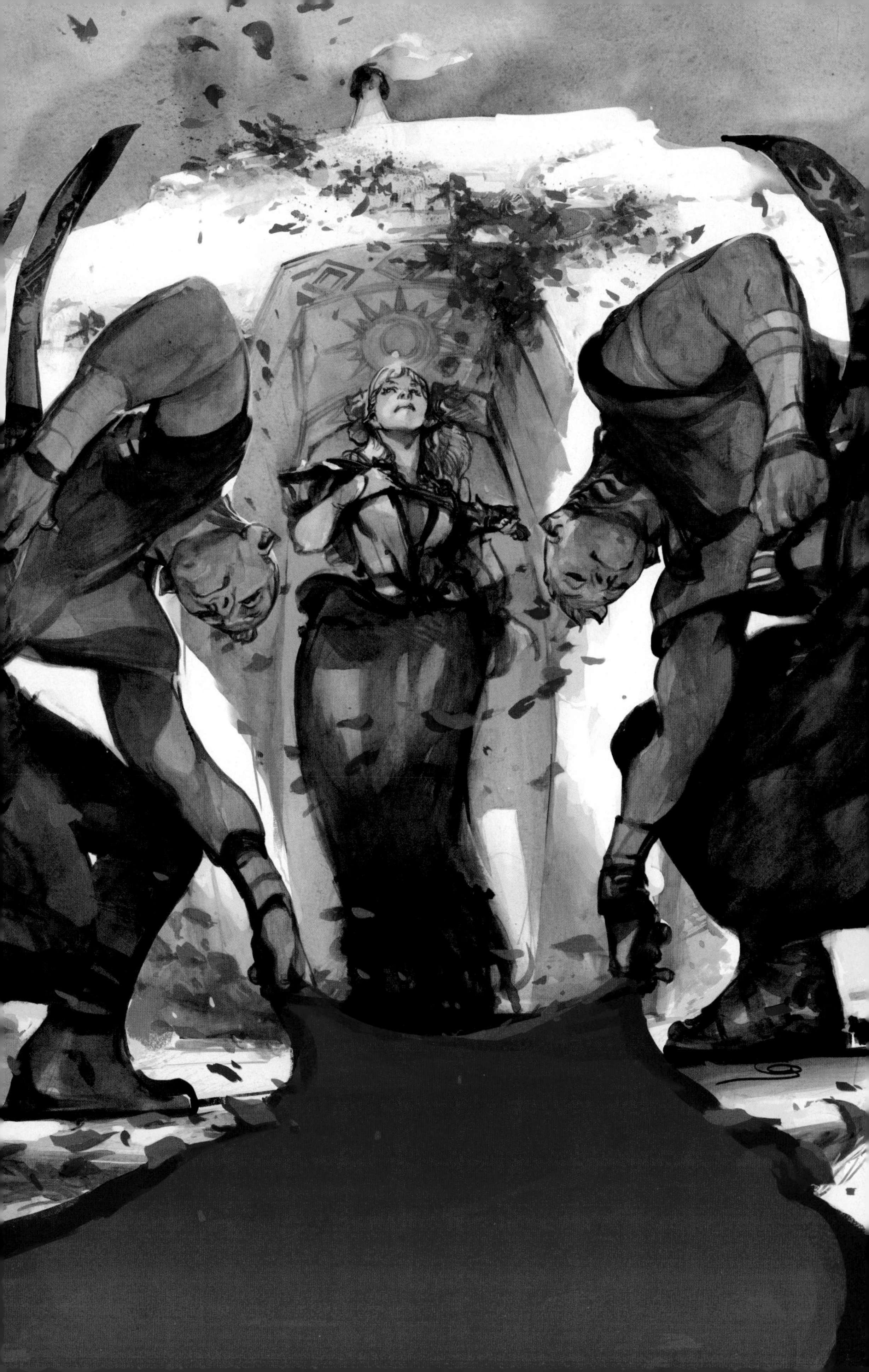

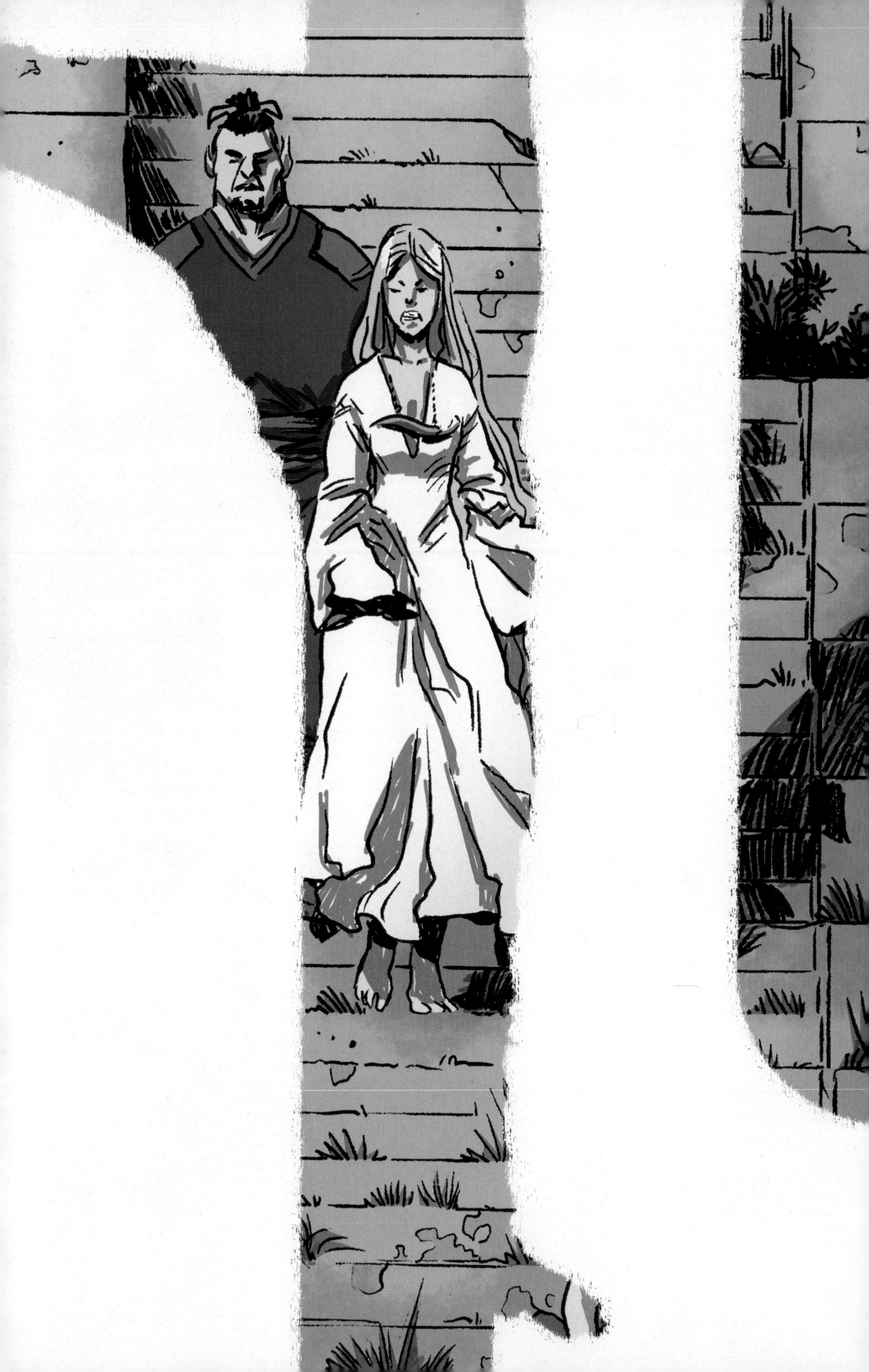

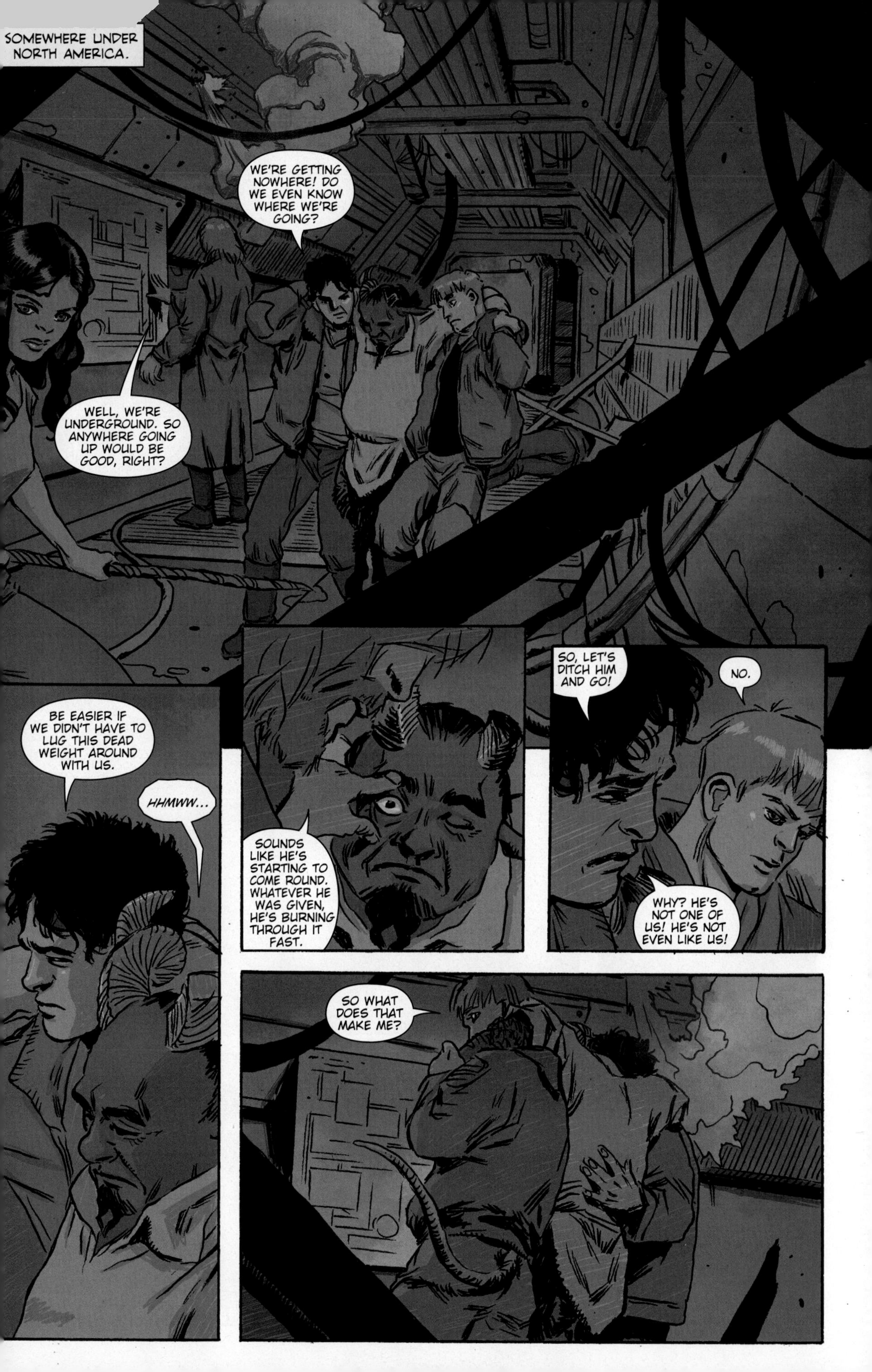
SOMEWHERE UNDER NORTH AMERICA.
WE'RE GETTING NOWHERE! DO WE EVEN KNOW WHERE WE'RE GOING?
WELL, WE'RE UNDERGROUND. SO ANYWHERE GOING UP WOULD BE GOOD, RIGHT?
BE EASIER IF WE DIDN'T HAVE TO LUG THIS DEAD WEIGHT AROUND WITH US.
HHMWW...
SOUNDS LIKE HE'S STARTING TO COME ROUND. WHATEVER HE WAS GIVEN, HE'S BURNING THROUGH IT FAST.
SO, LET'S DITCH HIM AND GO!
NO.
WHY? HE'S NOT ONE OF US! HE'S NOT EVEN LIKE US!
SO WHAT DOES THAT MAKE ME?

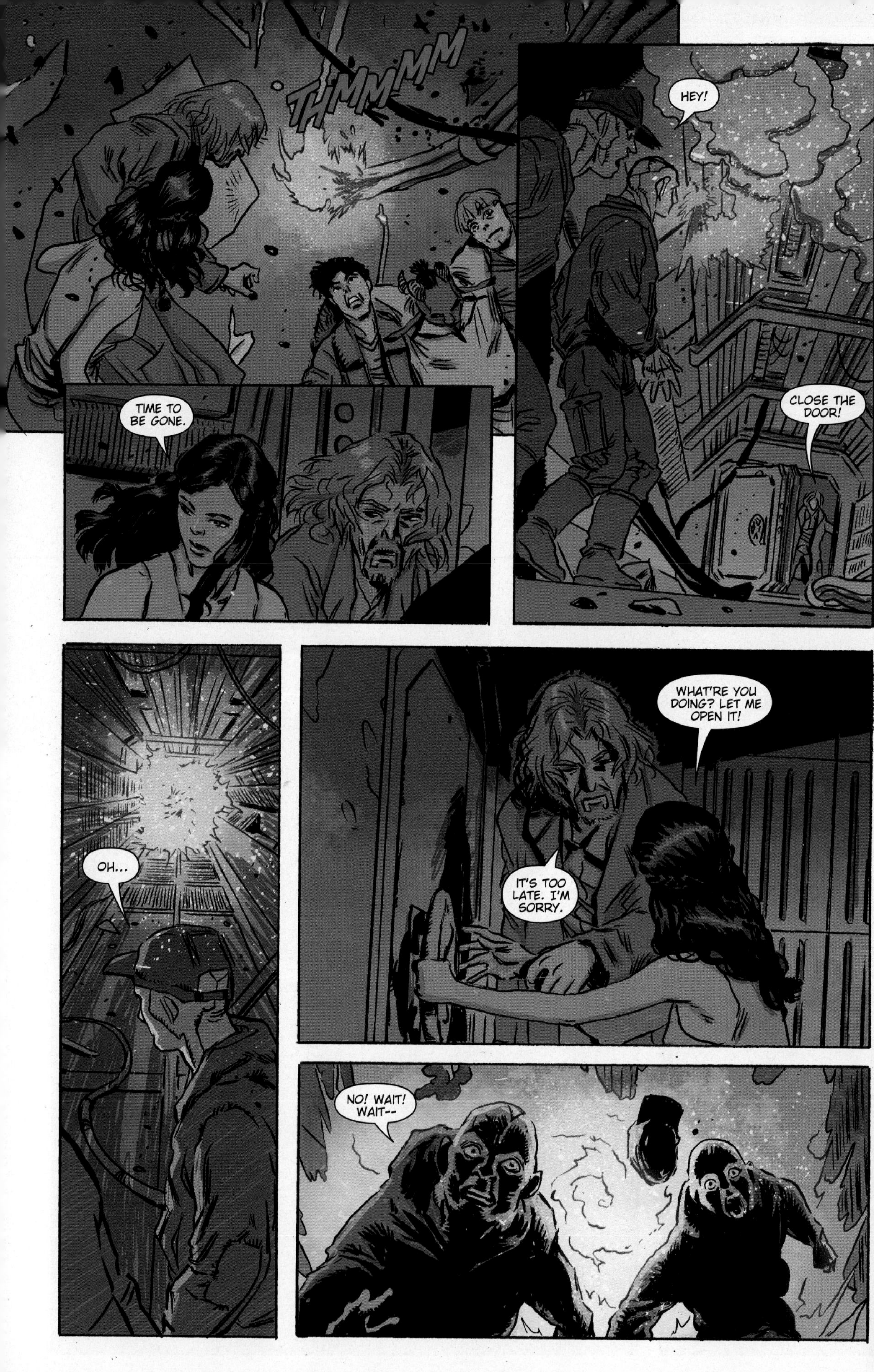
THMMMM
HEY!
TIME TO BE GONE.
CLOSE THE DOOR!
OH...
WHAT'RE YOU DOING? LET ME OPEN IT!
IT'S TOO LATE. I'M SORRY.
NO! WAIT! WAIT--

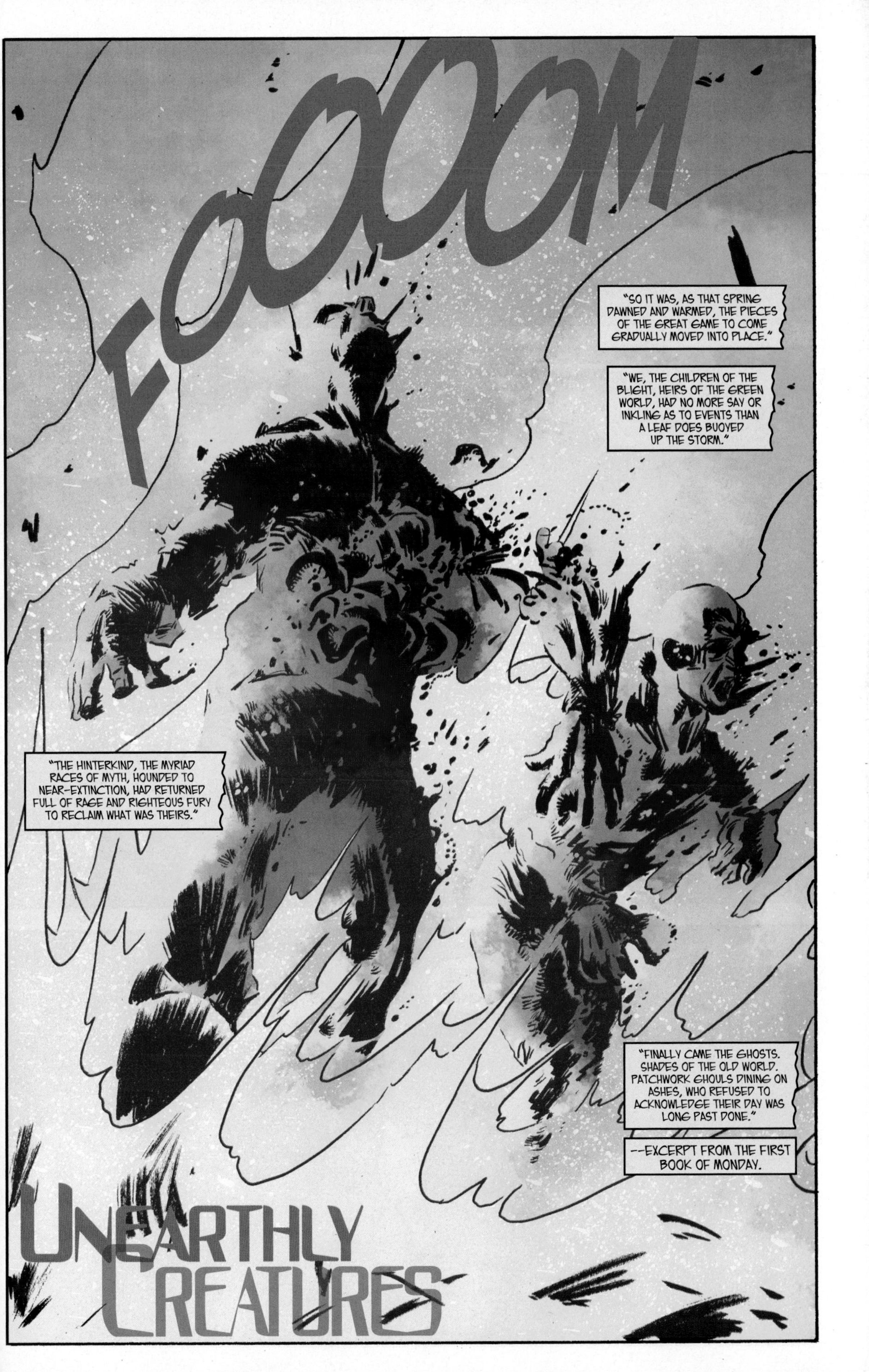
FOOOOM
"SO IT WAS, AS THAT SPRING DAWNED AND WARMED, THE PIECES OF THE GREAT GAME TO COME GRADUALLY MOVED INTO PLACE."
"WE, THE CHILDREN OF THE BLIGHT, HEIRS OF THE GREEN WORLD, HAD NO MORE SAY OR INKLING AS TO EVENTS THAN A LEAF DOES BUOYED UP THE STORM."
"THE HINTERKIND, THE MYRIAD RACES OF MYTH, HOUNDED TO NEAR-EXTINCTION, HAD RETURNED FULL OF RAGE AND RIGHTEOUS FURY TO RECLAIM WHAT WAS THEIRS."
"FINALLY CAME THE GHOSTS. SHADES OF THE OLD WORLD. PATCHWORK GHOULS DINING ON ASHES, WHO REFUSED TO ACKNOWLEDGE THEIR DAY WAS LONG PAST DONE."
--EXCERPT FROM THE FIRST BOOK OF MONDAY.
UNEARTHLY CREATURES

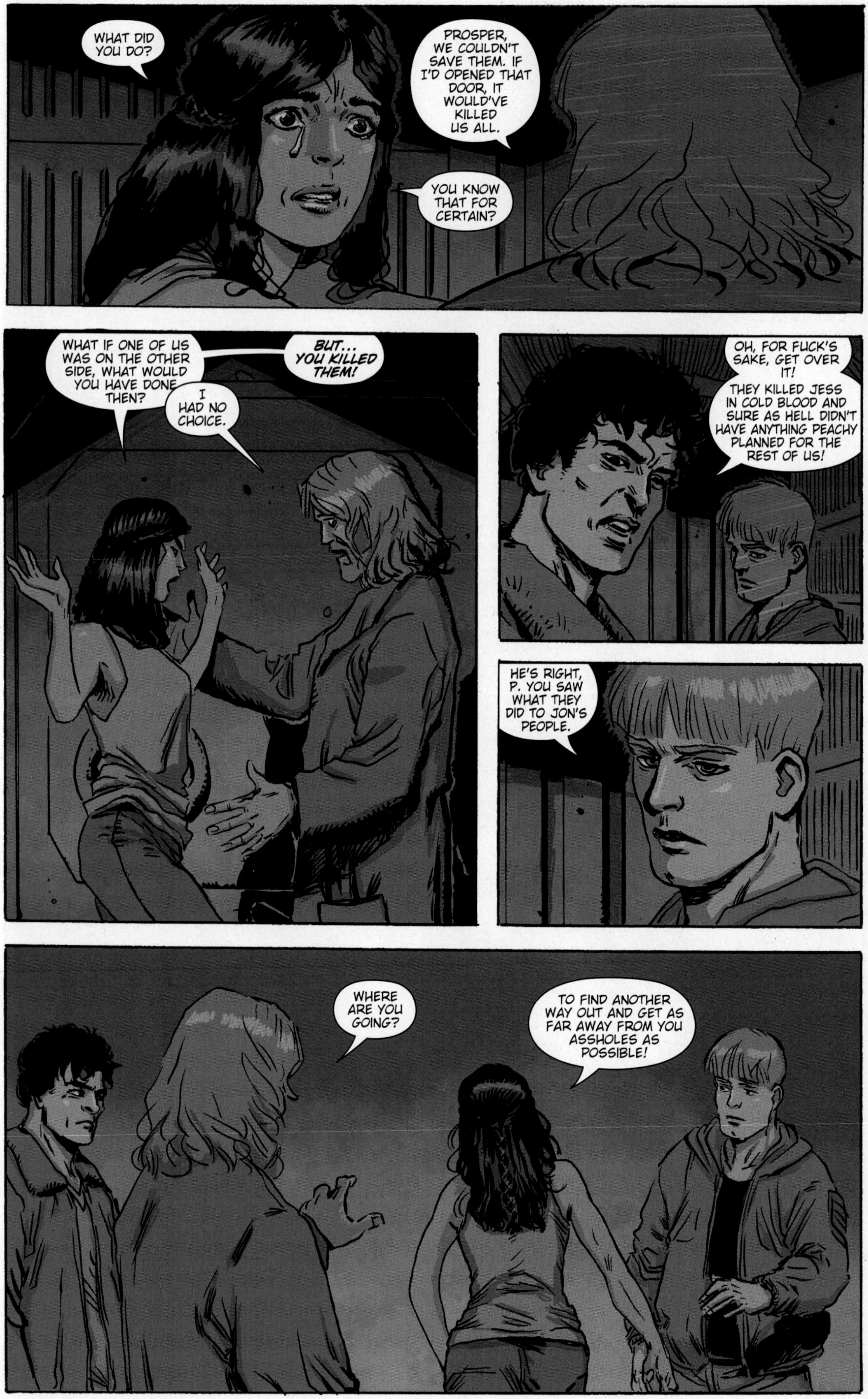
WHAT DID YOU DO?
PROSPER, WE COULDN'T SAVE THEM. IF I'D OPENED THAT DOOR, IT WOULD'VE KILLED US ALL.
YOU KNOW THAT FOR CERTAIN?
BUT... YOU KILLED THEM!
WHAT IF ONE OF US WAS ON THE OTHER SIDE, WHAT WOULD YOU HAVE DONE THEN?
I HAD NO CHOICE.
OH, FOR FUCK'S SAKE, GET OVER IT!
THEY KILLED JESS IN COLD BLOOD AND SURE AS HELL DIDN'T HAVE ANYTHING PEACHY PLANNED FOR THE REST OF US!
HE'S RIGHT, P. YOU SAW WHAT THEY DID TO JON'S PEOPLE.
WHERE ARE YOU GOING?
TO FIND ANOTHER WAY OUT AND GET AS FAR AWAY FROM YOU ASSHOLES AS POSSIBLE!

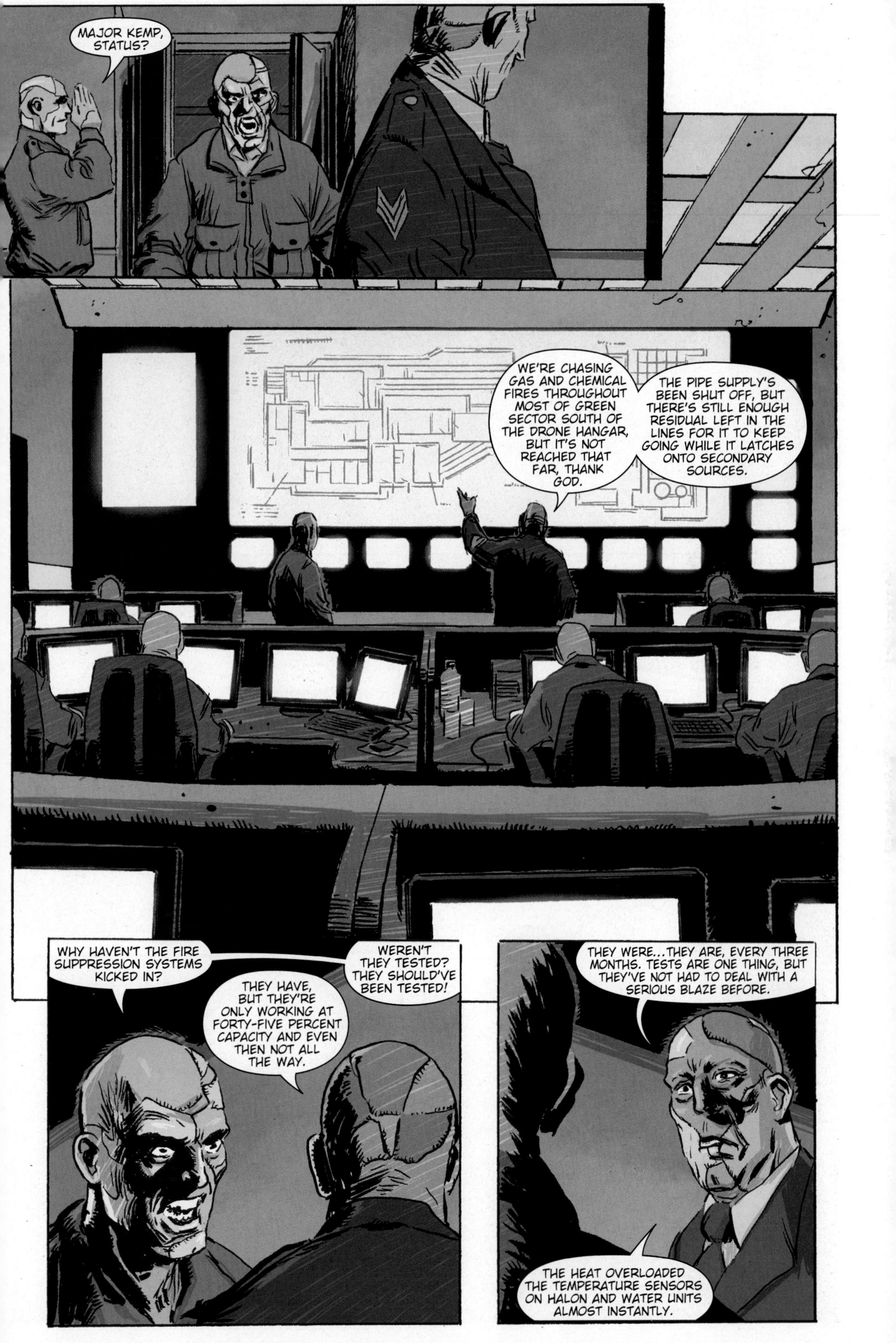
MAJOR KEMP, STATUS?
WE'RE CHASING GAS AND CHEMICAL FIRES THROUGHOUT MOST OF GREEN SECTOR SOUTH OF THE DRONE HANGAR, BUT IT'S NOT REACHED THAT FAR, THANK GOD.
THE PIPE SUPPLY'S BEEN SHUT OFF, BUT THERE'S STILL ENOUGH RESIDUAL LEFT IN THE LINES FOR IT TO KEEP GOING WHILE IT LATCHES ONTO SECONDARY SOURCES.
WHY HAVEN'T THE FIRE SUPPRESSION SYSTEMS KICKED IN?
THEY HAVE, BUT THEY'RE ONLY WORKING AT FORTY-FIVE PERCENT CAPACITY AND EVEN THEN NOT ALL THE WAY.
WEREN'T THEY TESTED? THEY SHOULD'VE BEEN TESTED!
THEY WERE...THEY ARE, EVERY THREE MONTHS. TESTS ARE ONE THING, BUT THEY'VE NOT HAD TO DEAL WITH A SERIOUS BLAZE BEFORE.
THE HEAT OVERLOADED THE TEMPERATURE SENSORS ON HALON AND WATER UNITS ALMOST INSTANTLY.

SEE, THIS IS WHAT HAPPENS WHEN THE CONSTRUCTION WORK'S PUT OUT TO THE LOWEST TENDER! WHAT EVER HAPPENED TO BUYING AMERICAN?

I...UH, THINK THEY WERE AMERICAN, SIR.

SHUT UP.

THUMMP

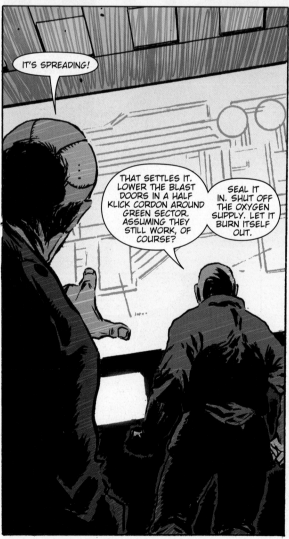

IT'S SPREADING!

THAT SETTLES IT. LOWER THE BLAST DOORS IN A HALF KLICK CORDON AROUND GREEN SECTOR. ASSUMING THEY STILL WORK, OF COURSE?

SEAL IT IN. SHUT OFF THE OXYGEN SUPPLY. LET IT BURN ITSELF OUT.

WE STILL HAVE MEN IN THERE, SIR. WE'D LOSE A LOT OF GOOD PEOPLE IF WE DO THAT.

WE'LL LOSE A DAMN SIGHT MORE IF WE DON'T. THOSE ARE MY ORDERS, MAJOR.

YES, SIR.

DO IT.

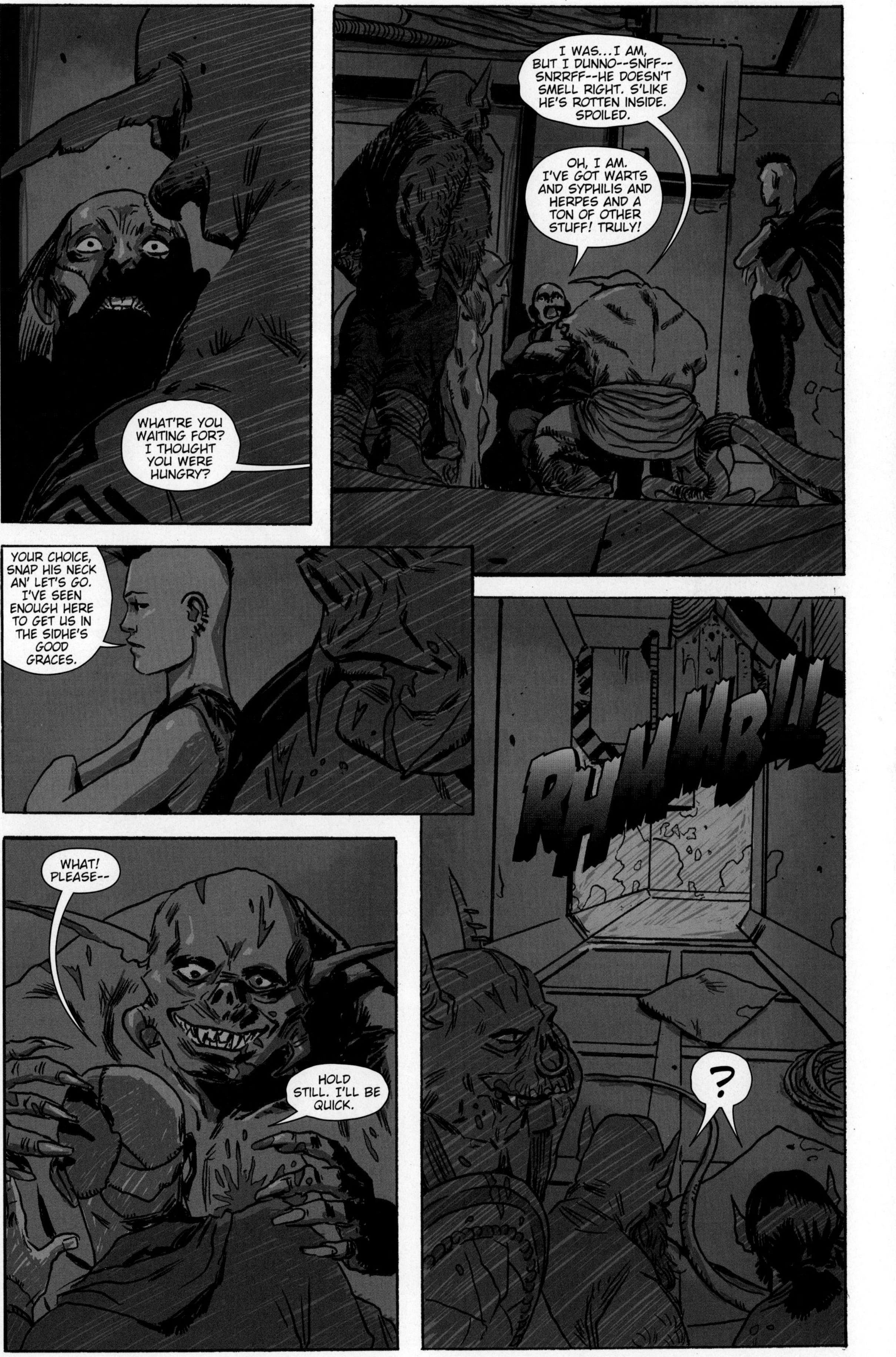
WHAT'RE YOU WAITING FOR? I THOUGHT YOU WERE HUNGRY?
I WAS...I AM, BUT I DUNNO--SNFF--SNRRFF--HE DOESN'T SMELL RIGHT. S'LIKE HE'S ROTTEN INSIDE. SPOILED.
OH, I AM. I'VE GOT WARTS AND SYPHILIS AND HERPES AND A TON OF OTHER STUFF! TRULY!
YOUR CHOICE, SNAP HIS NECK AN' LET'S GO. I'VE SEEN ENOUGH HERE TO GET US IN THE SIDHE'S GOOD GRACES.
WHAT! PLEASE--
HOLD STILL. I'LL BE QUICK.
RHMMB!!
?

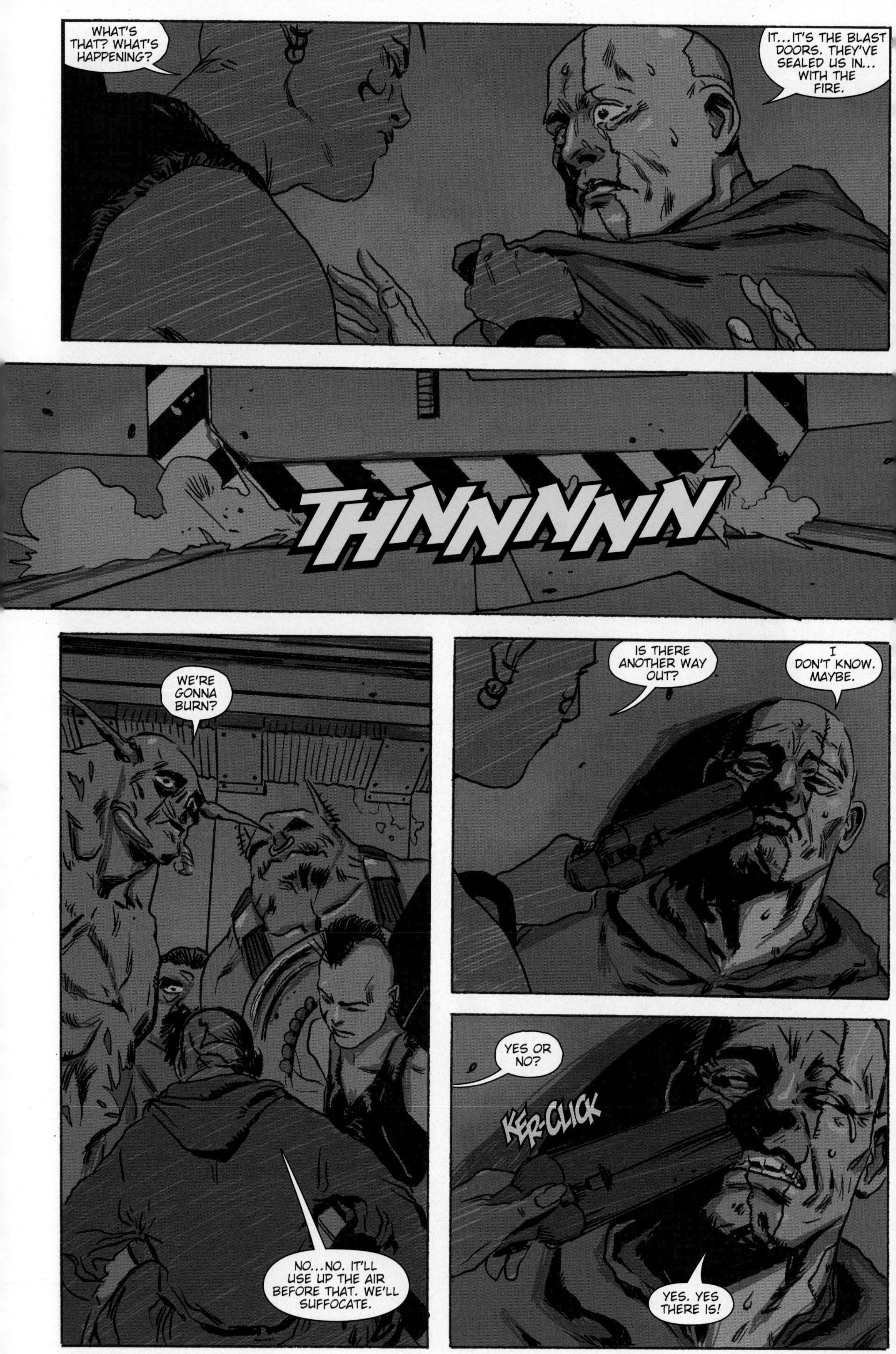
WHAT'S THAT? WHAT'S HAPPENING?
IT...IT'S THE BLAST DOORS. THEY'VE SEALED US IN... WITH THE FIRE.
THNNNNN
WE'RE GONNA BURN?
NO...NO. IT'LL USE UP THE AIR BEFORE THAT. WE'LL SUFFOCATE.
IS THERE ANOTHER WAY OUT?
I DON'T KNOW. MAYBE.
YES OR NO?
KER-CLICK
YES. YES THERE IS!

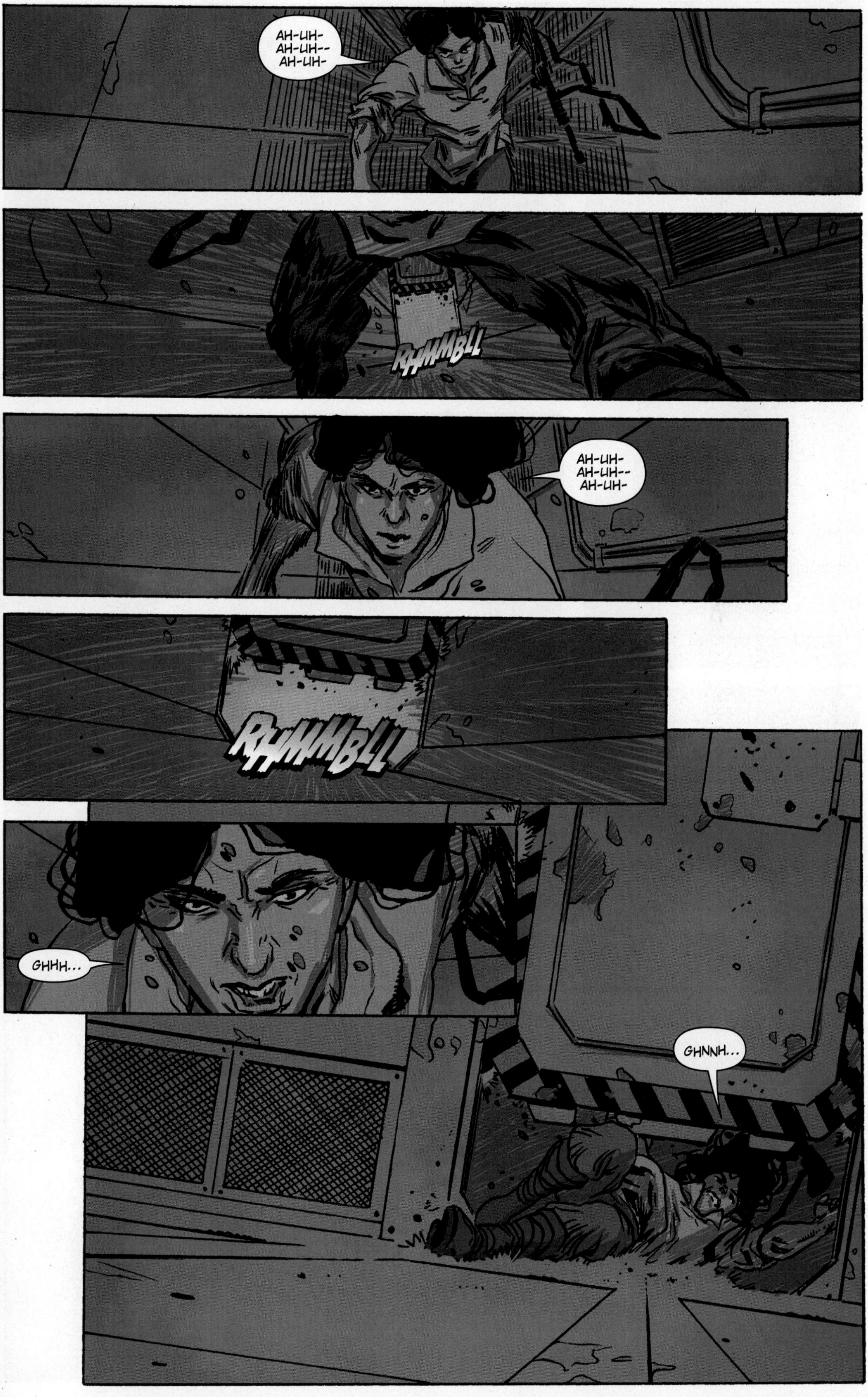
AH-UH-
AH-UH--
AH-UH-
RHMMBLL
AH-UH-
AH-UH--
AH-UH-
RHMMBLL
GHHH...
GHNNH...

UHH!

WWTHUNNNN

HI! I DON'T SUPPOSE ANY OF YOU UGLY SONS-OF-BITCHES KNOWS THE WAY OUT OF H HERE?

KLIK

KLIK

KLIK

KLIK

ON SECOND THOUGHT, DON'T BOTHER--

BRRAAPP RRAPP

--I'LL FIND MY OWN WAY OUT.

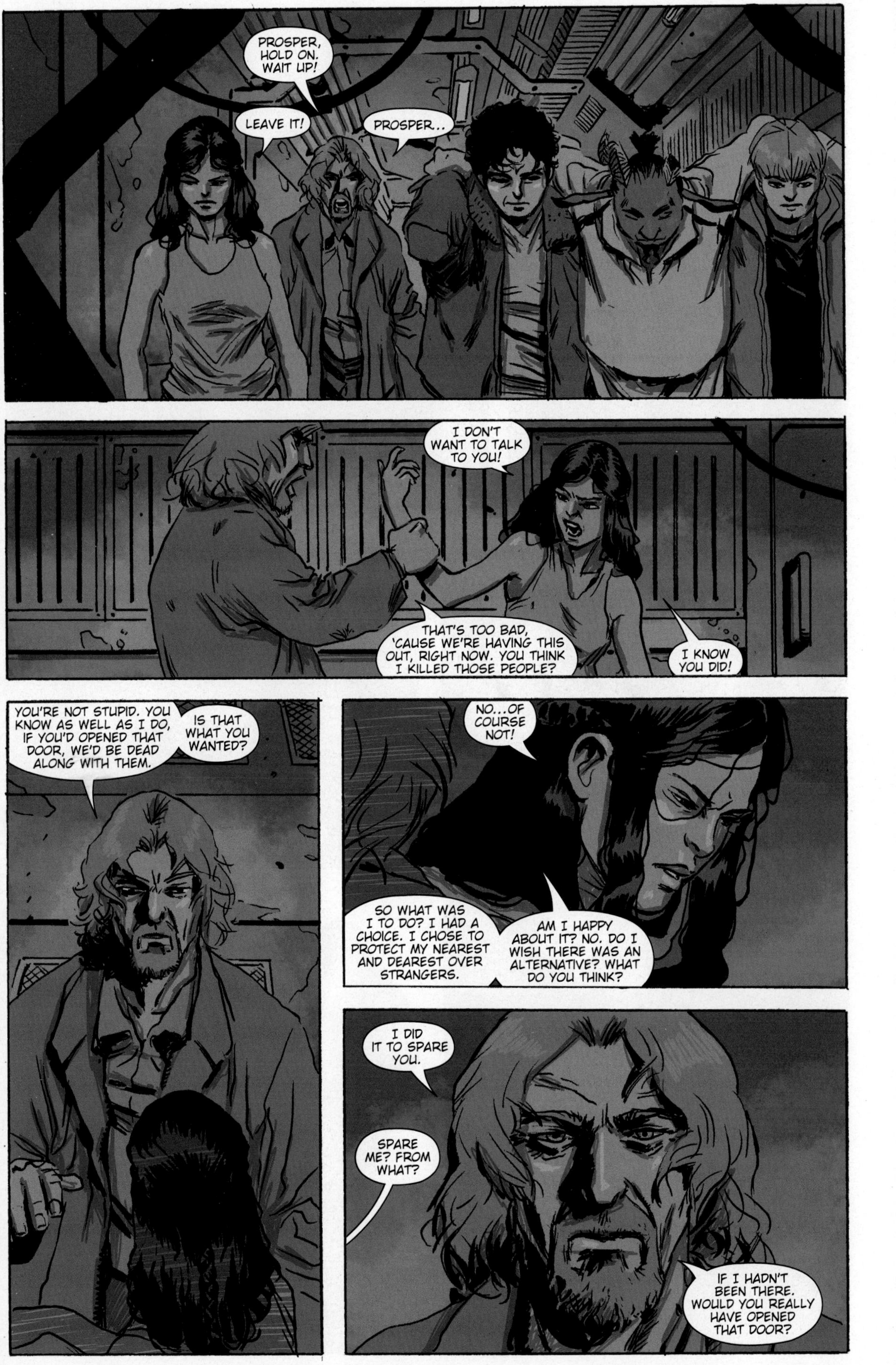
PROSPER, HOLD ON. WAIT UP!
LEAVE IT!
PROSPER...
I DON'T WANT TO TALK TO YOU!
THAT'S TOO BAD, 'CAUSE WE'RE HAVING THIS OUT, RIGHT NOW. YOU THINK I KILLED THOSE PEOPLE?
I KNOW YOU DID!
YOU'RE NOT STUPID. YOU KNOW AS WELL AS I DO, IF YOU'D OPENED THAT DOOR, WE'D BE DEAD ALONG WITH THEM.
IS THAT WHAT YOU WANTED?
NO...OF COURSE NOT!
SO WHAT WAS I TO DO? I HAD A CHOICE. I CHOSE TO PROTECT MY NEAREST AND DEAREST OVER STRANGERS.
AM I HAPPY ABOUT IT? NO. DO I WISH THERE WAS AN ALTERNATIVE? WHAT DO YOU THINK?
I DID IT TO SPARE YOU.
SPARE ME? FROM WHAT?
IF I HADN'T BEEN THERE, WOULD YOU REALLY HAVE OPENED THAT DOOR?

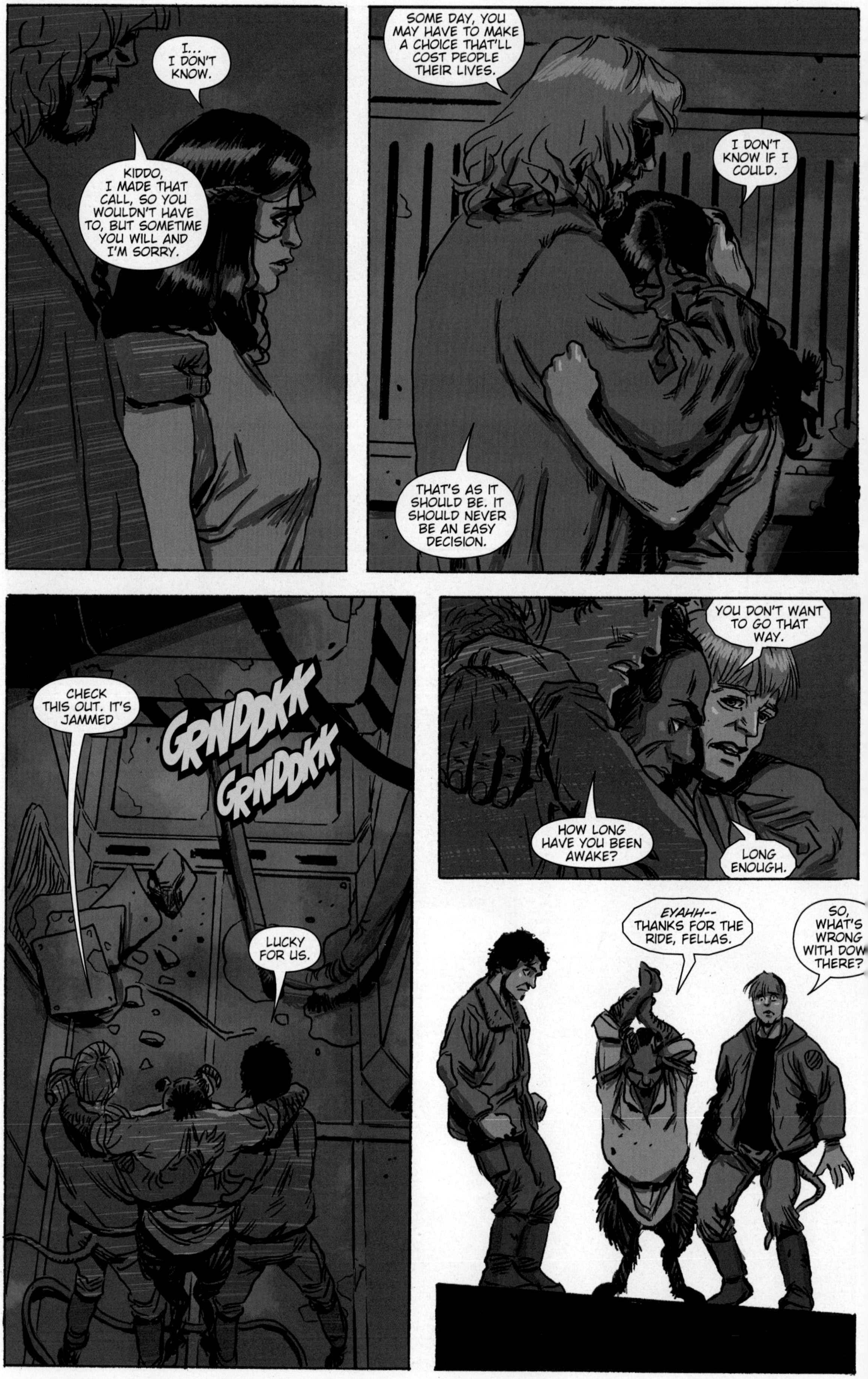
I... I DON'T KNOW.
KIDDO, I MADE THAT CALL, SO YOU WOULDN'T HAVE TO, BUT SOMETIME YOU WILL AND I'M SORRY.
SOME DAY, YOU MAY HAVE TO MAKE A CHOICE THAT'LL COST PEOPLE THEIR LIVES.
I DON'T KNOW IF I COULD.
THAT'S AS IT SHOULD BE. IT SHOULD NEVER BE AN EASY DECISION.
CHECK THIS OUT. IT'S JAMMED
GRNDDKK GRNDDKK
LUCKY FOR US.
YOU DON'T WANT TO GO THAT WAY.
HOW LONG HAVE YOU BEEN AWAKE?
LONG ENOUGH.
EYAHH-- THANKS FOR THE RIDE, FELLAS.
SO, WHAT'S WRONG WITH DOW THERE?

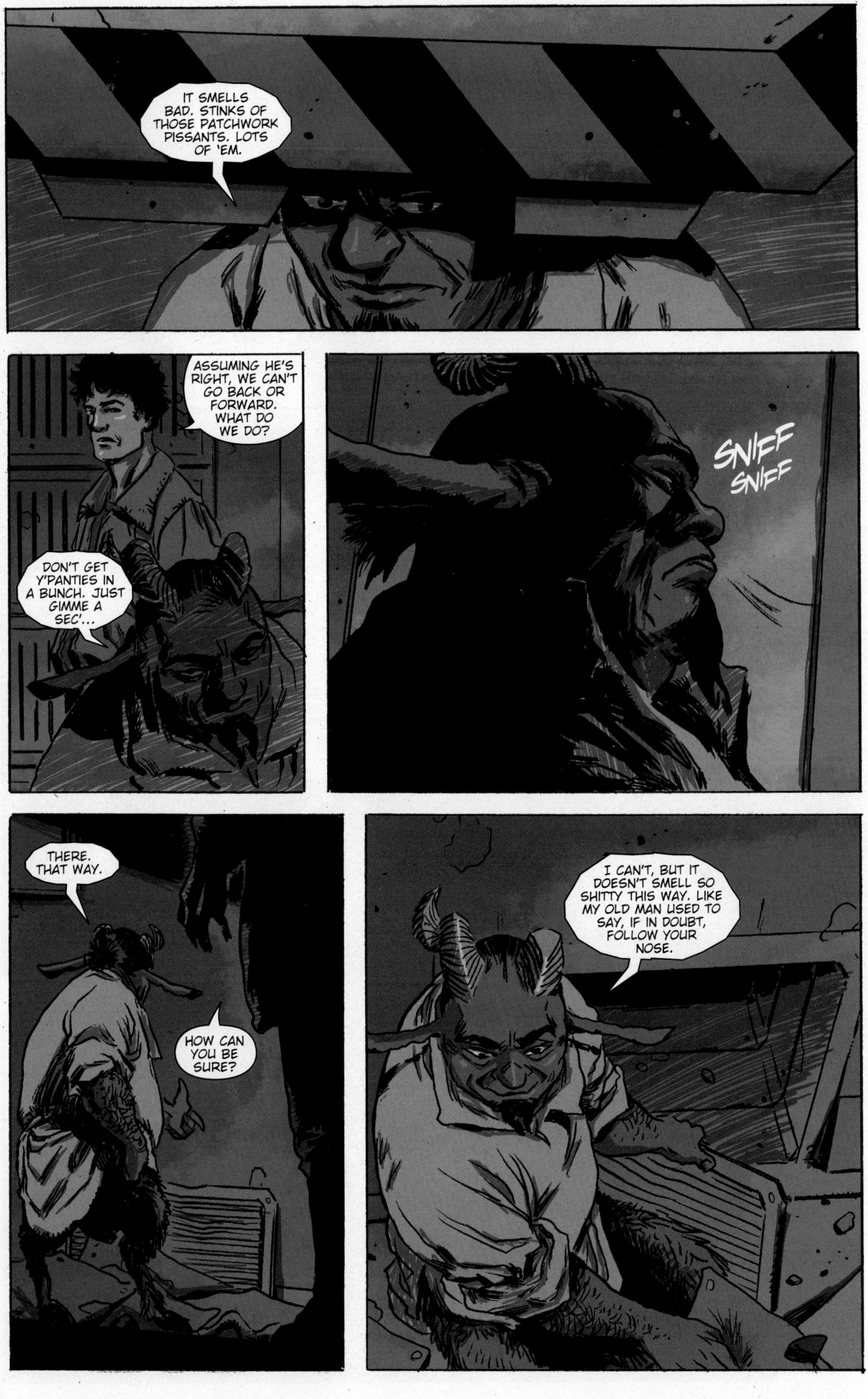
IT SMELLS BAD. STINKS OF THOSE PATCHWORK PISSANTS. LOTS OF 'EM.
ASSUMING HE'S RIGHT, WE CAN'T GO BACK OR FORWARD. WHAT DO WE DO?
DON'T GET Y'PANTIES IN A BUNCH. JUST GIMME A SEC'...
SNIFF SNIFF
THERE. THAT WAY.
HOW CAN YOU BE SURE?
I CAN'T, BUT IT DOESN'T SMELL SO SHITTY THIS WAY. LIKE MY OLD MAN USED TO SAY, IF IN DOUBT, FOLLOW YOUR NOSE.

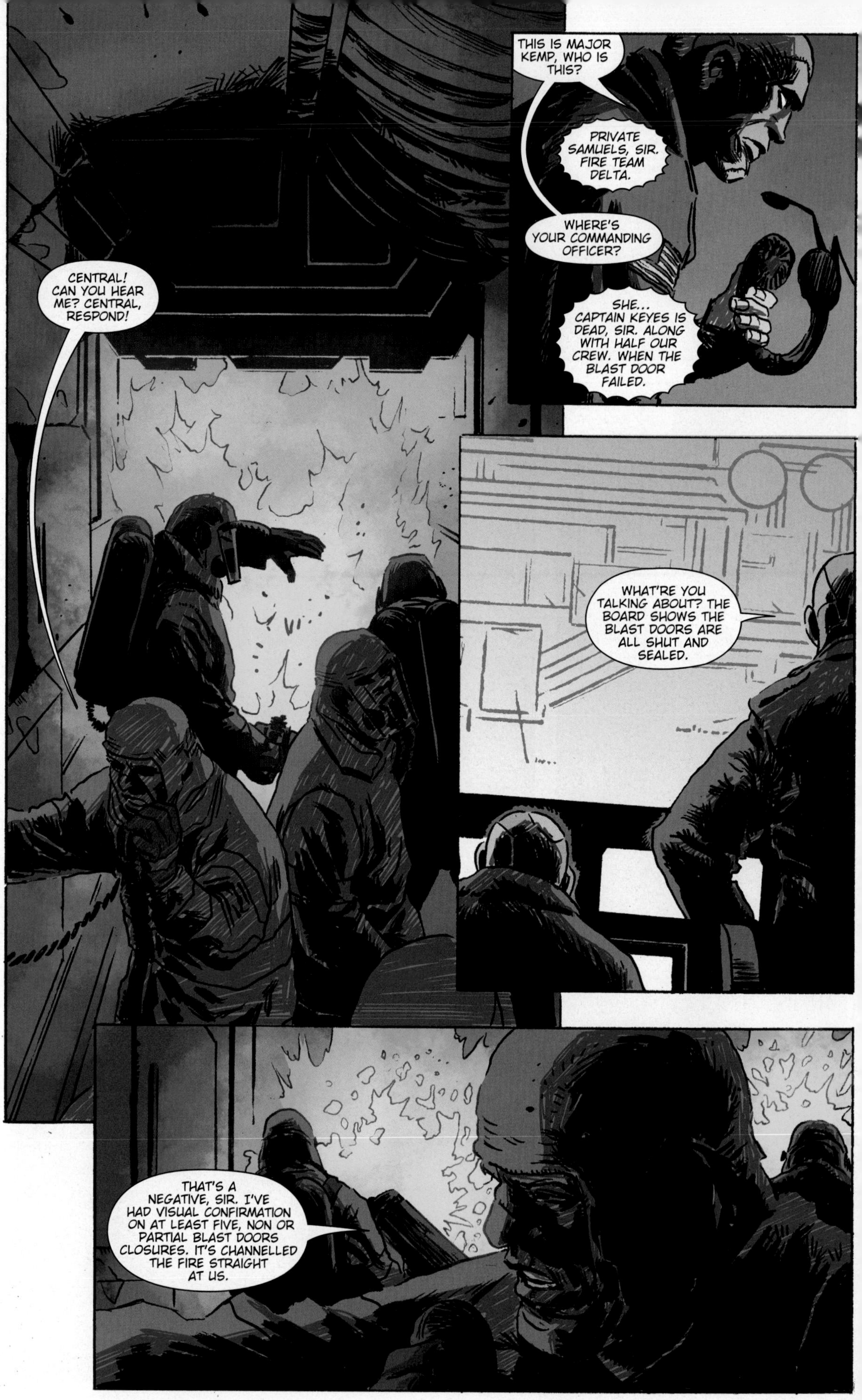
CENTRAL! CAN YOU HEAR ME? CENTRAL, RESPOND!
THIS IS MAJOR KEMP, WHO IS THIS?
PRIVATE SAMUELS, SIR. FIRE TEAM DELTA.
WHERE'S YOUR COMMANDING OFFICER?
SHE... CAPTAIN KEYES IS DEAD, SIR. ALONG WITH HALF OUR CREW. WHEN THE BLAST DOOR FAILED.
WHAT'RE YOU TALKING ABOUT? THE BOARD SHOWS THE BLAST DOORS ARE ALL SHUT AND SEALED.
THAT'S A NEGATIVE, SIR. I'VE HAD VISUAL CONFIRMATION ON AT LEAST FIVE, NON OR PARTIAL BLAST DOORS CLOSURES. IT'S CHANNELLED THE FIRE STRAIGHT AT US.

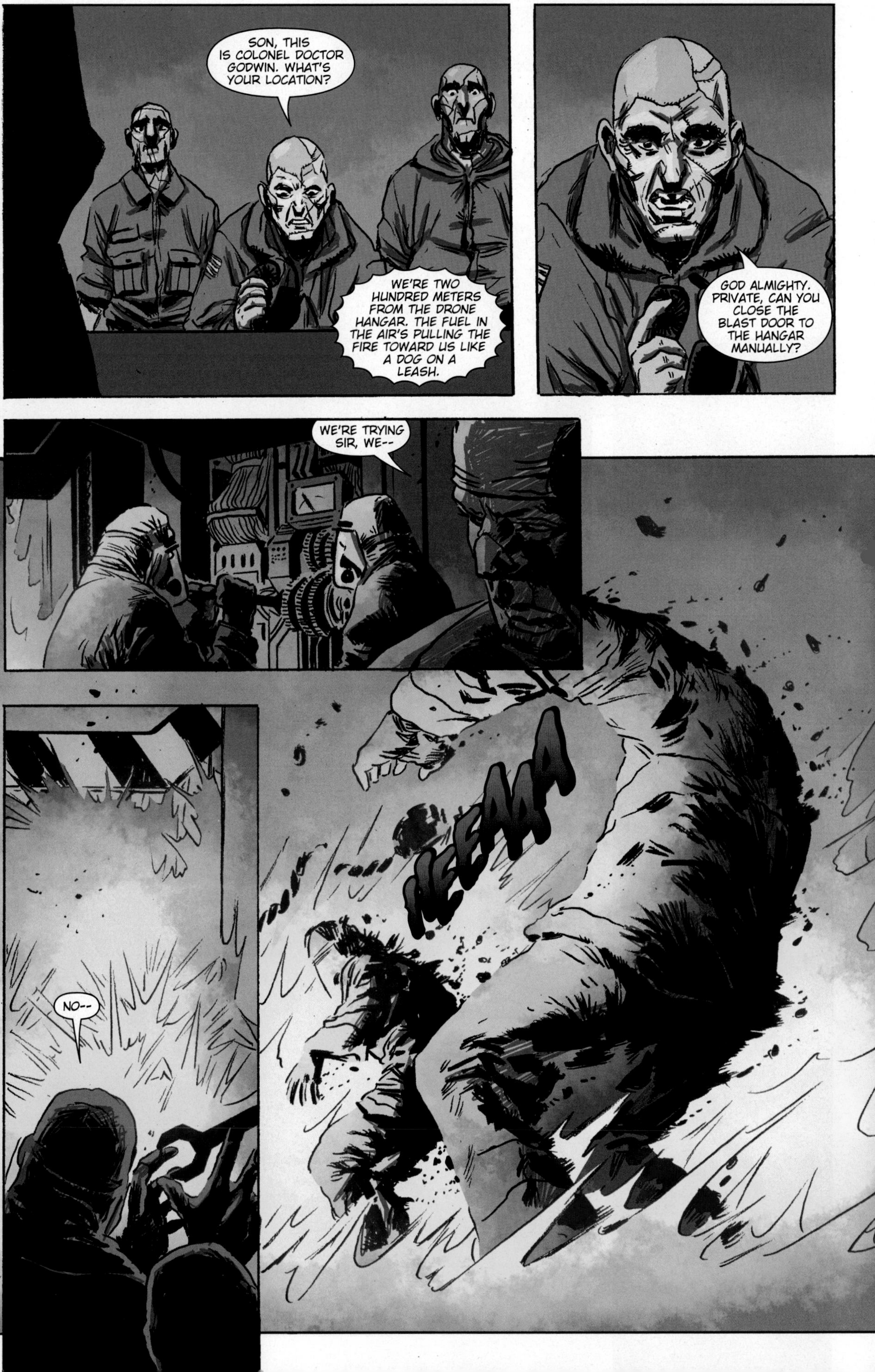
SON, THIS IS COLONEL DOCTOR GODWIN. WHAT'S YOUR LOCATION?
WE'RE TWO HUNDRED METERS FROM THE DRONE HANGAR. THE FUEL IN THE AIR'S PULLING THE FIRE TOWARD US LIKE A DOG ON A LEASH.
GOD ALMIGHTY. PRIVATE, CAN YOU CLOSE THE BLAST DOOR TO THE HANGAR MANUALLY?
WE'RE TRYING SIR, WE--
NO--
HEEAAA

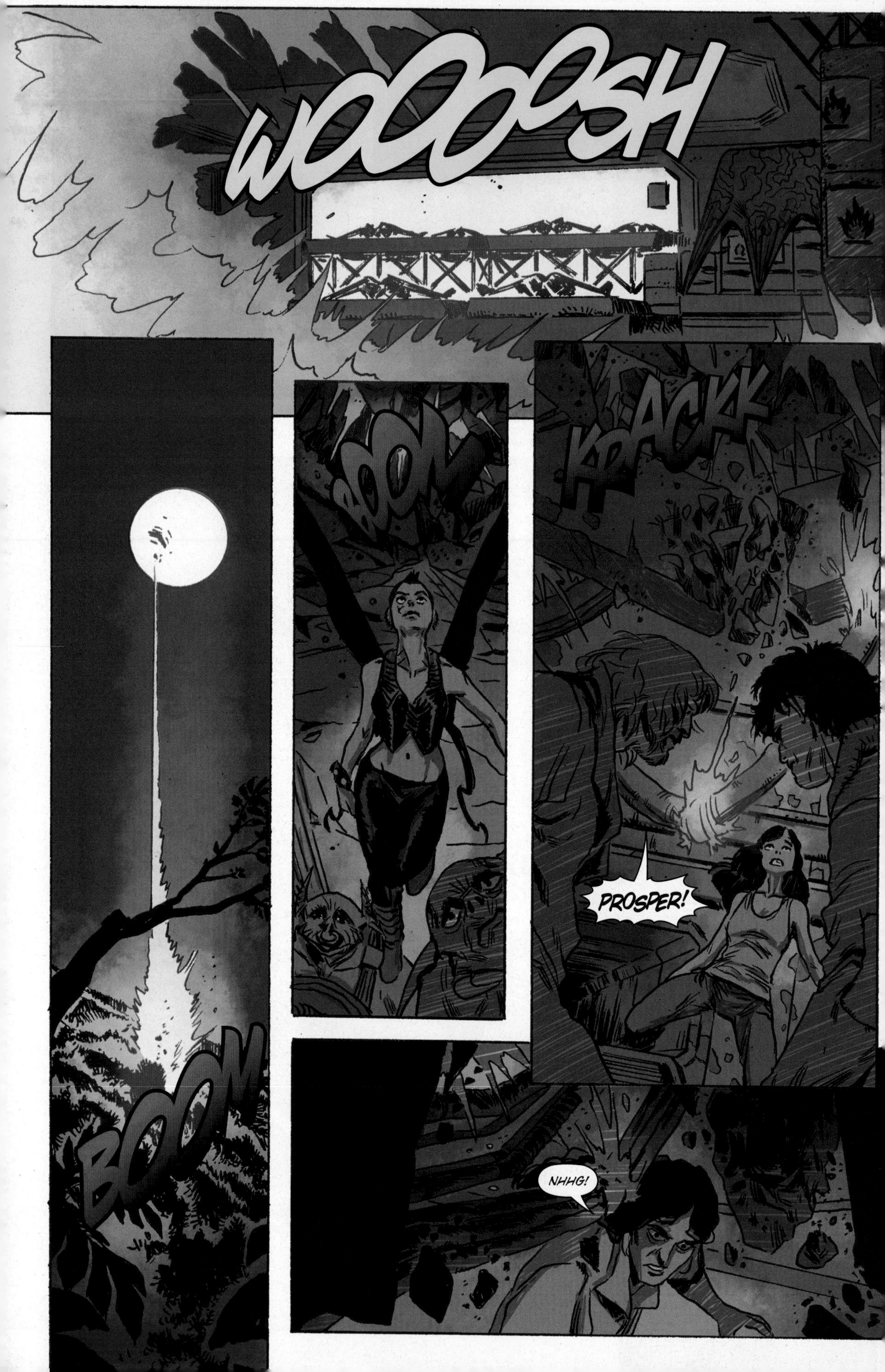
WOOOOSH
BOOM
BOOM
KRACKK
PROSPER!
NHHG!

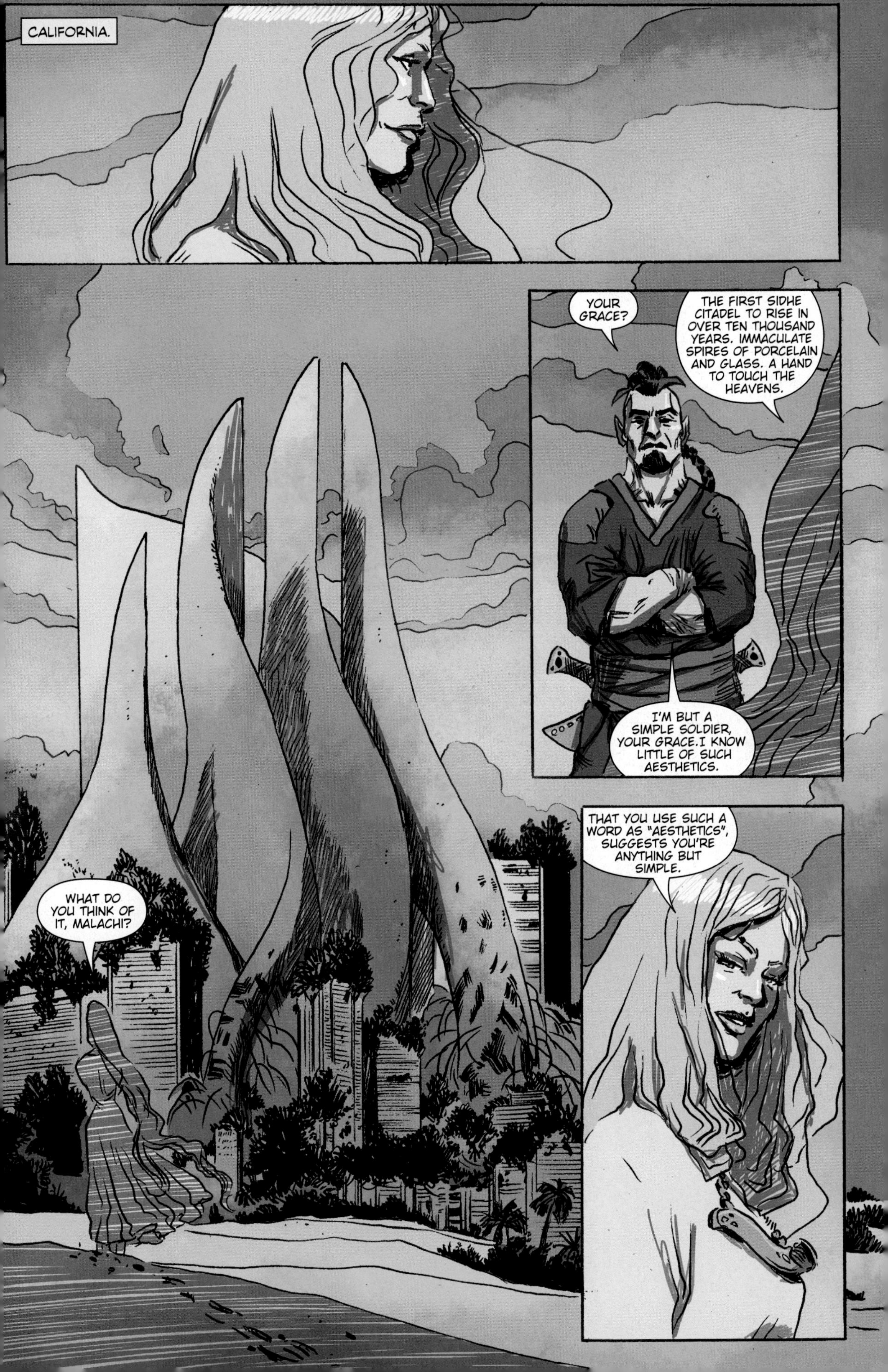
CALIFORNIA.
WHAT DO YOU THINK OF IT, MALACHI?
YOUR GRACE?
THE FIRST SIDHE CITADEL TO RISE IN OVER TEN THOUSAND YEARS. IMMACULATE SPIRES OF PORCELAIN AND GLASS. A HAND TO TOUCH THE HEAVENS.
I'M BUT A SIMPLE SOLDIER, YOUR GRACE.I KNOW LITTLE OF SUCH AESTHETICS.
THAT YOU USE SUCH A WORD AS "AESTHETICS", SUGGESTS YOU'RE ANYTHING BUT SIMPLE.

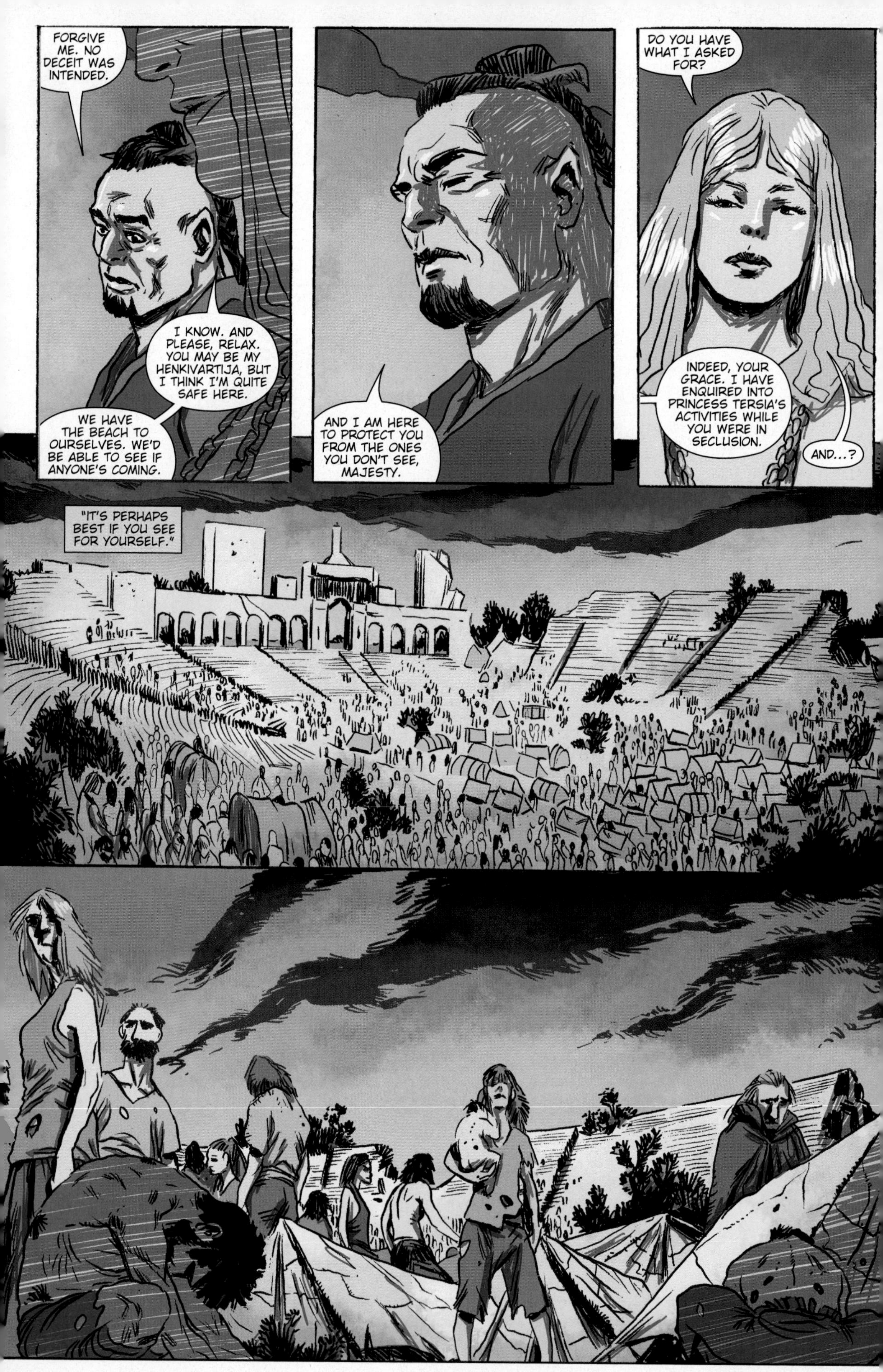
FORGIVE ME. NO DECEIT WAS INTENDED.
I KNOW. AND PLEASE, RELAX. YOU MAY BE MY HENKIVARTIJA, BUT I THINK I'M QUITE SAFE HERE.
WE HAVE THE BEACH TO OURSELVES. WE'D BE ABLE TO SEE IF ANYONE'S COMING.
AND I AM HERE TO PROTECT YOU FROM THE ONES YOU DON'T SEE, MAJESTY.
DO YOU HAVE WHAT I ASKED FOR?
INDEED, YOUR GRACE. I HAVE ENQUIRED INTO PRINCESS TERSIA'S ACTIVITIES WHILE YOU WERE IN SECLUSION.
AND...?
"IT'S PERHAPS BEST IF YOU SEE FOR YOURSELF."

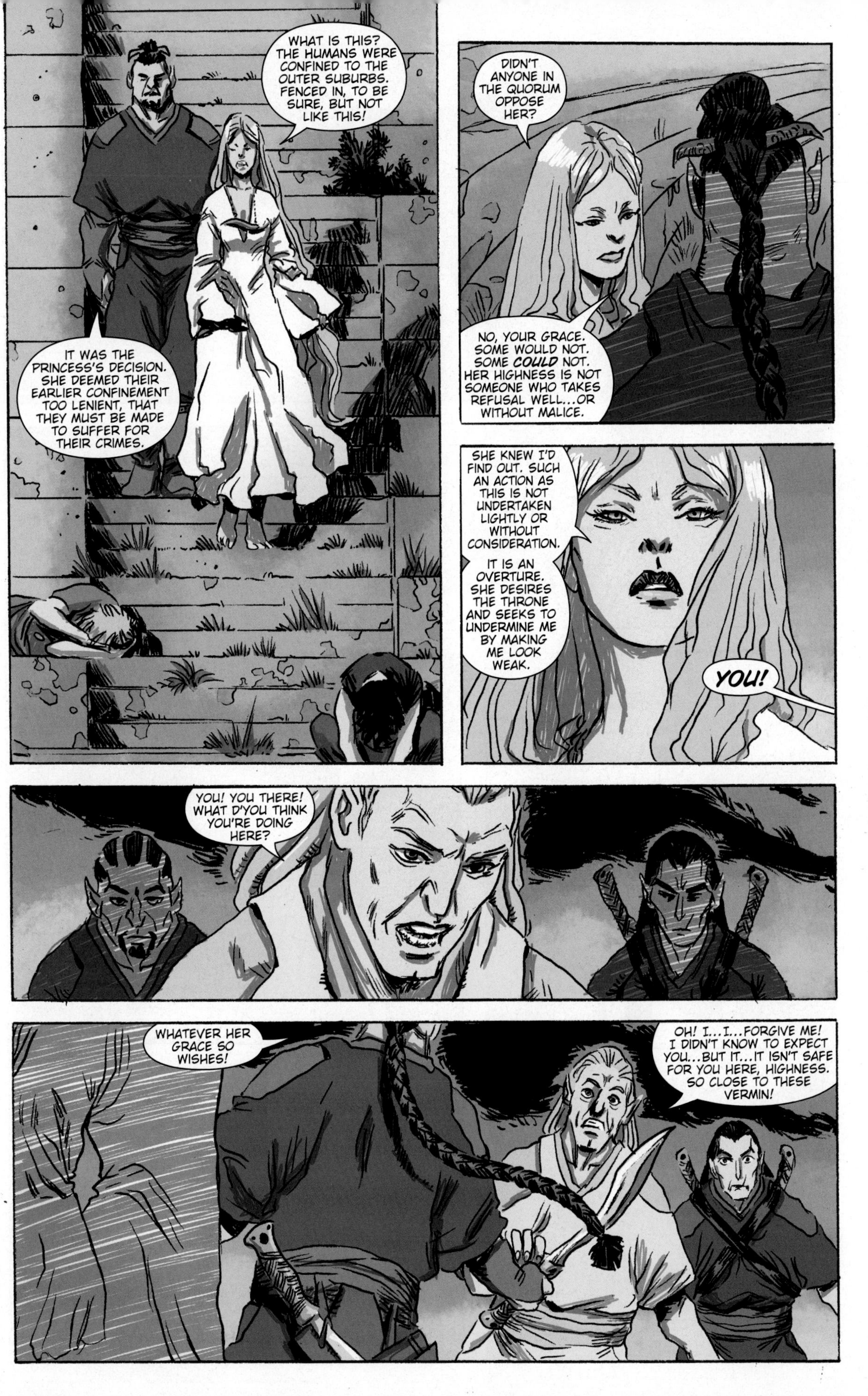
WHAT IS THIS? THE HUMANS WERE CONFINED TO THE OUTER SUBURBS. FENCED IN, TO BE SURE, BUT NOT LIKE THIS!
IT WAS THE PRINCESS'S DECISION. SHE DEEMED THEIR EARLIER CONFINEMENT TOO LENIENT, THAT THEY MUST BE MADE TO SUFFER FOR THEIR CRIMES.
DIDN'T ANYONE IN THE QUORUM OPPOSE HER?
NO, YOUR GRACE. SOME WOULD NOT. SOME COULD NOT. HER HIGHNESS IS NOT SOMEONE WHO TAKES REFUSAL WELL...OR WITHOUT MALICE.
SHE KNEW I'D FIND OUT. SUCH AN ACTION AS THIS IS NOT UNDERTAKEN LIGHTLY OR WITHOUT CONSIDERATION.
IT IS AN OVERTURE. SHE DESIRES THE THRONE AND SEEKS TO UNDERMINE ME BY MAKING ME LOOK WEAK.
YOU!
YOU! YOU THERE! WHAT D'YOU THINK YOU'RE DOING HERE?
WHATEVER HER GRACE SO WISHES!
OH! I...I...FORGIVE ME! I DIDN'T KNOW TO EXPECT YOU...BUT IT...IT ISN'T SAFE FOR YOU HERE, HIGHNESS. SO CLOSE TO THESE VERMIN!

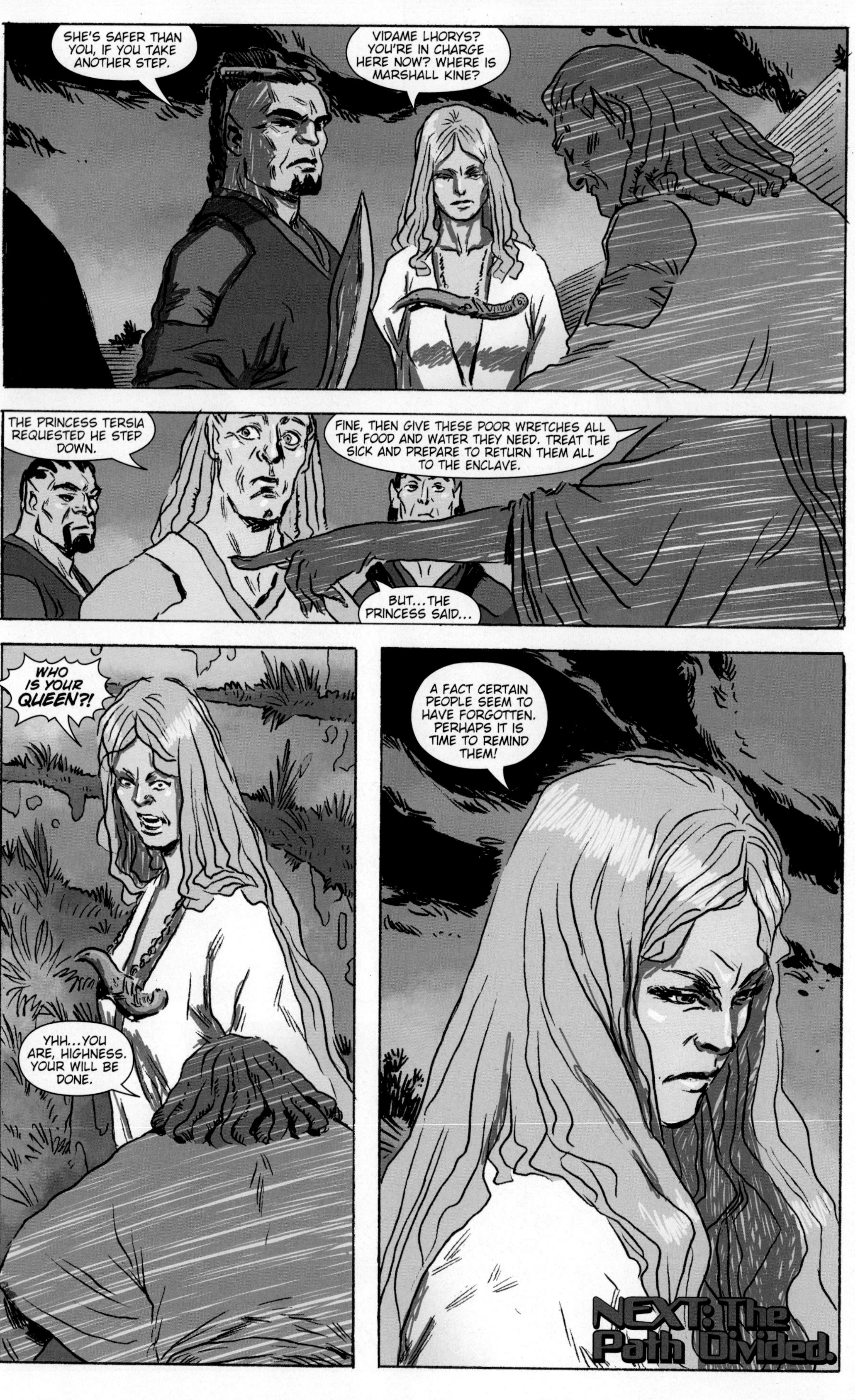
SHE'S SAFER THAN YOU, IF YOU TAKE ANOTHER STEP.
VIDAME LHORYS? YOU'RE IN CHARGE HERE NOW? WHERE IS MARSHALL KINE?
THE PRINCESS TERSIA REQUESTED HE STEP DOWN.
FINE, THEN GIVE THESE POOR WRETCHES ALL THE FOOD AND WATER THEY NEED. TREAT THE SICK AND PREPARE TO RETURN THEM ALL TO THE ENCLAVE.
BUT...THE PRINCESS SAID...
WHO IS YOUR QUEEN?!
YHH...YOU ARE, HIGHNESS. YOUR WILL BE DONE.
A FACT CERTAIN PEOPLE SEEM TO HAVE FORGOTTEN. PERHAPS IT IS TIME TO REMIND THEM!
NEXT: The Path Divided.

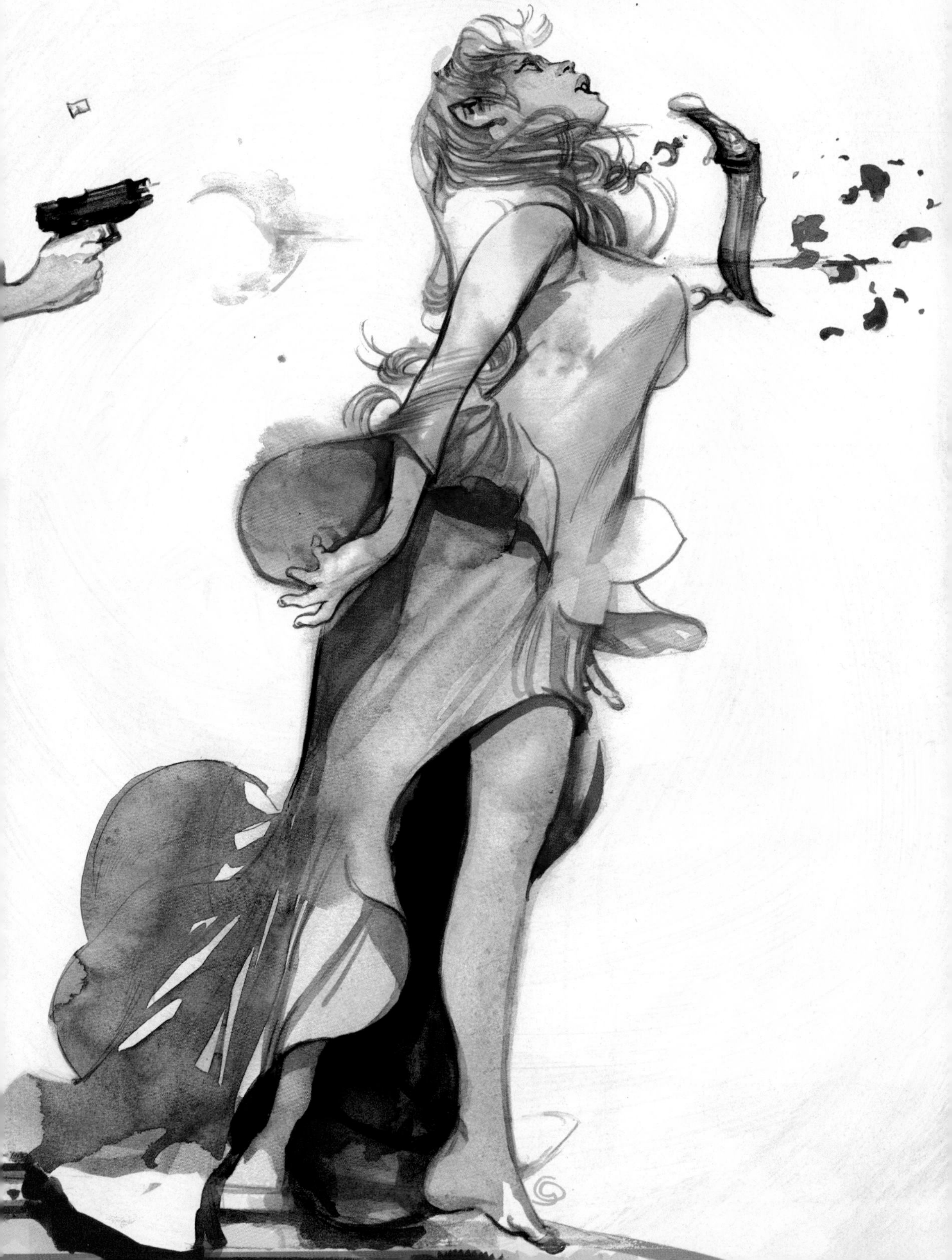

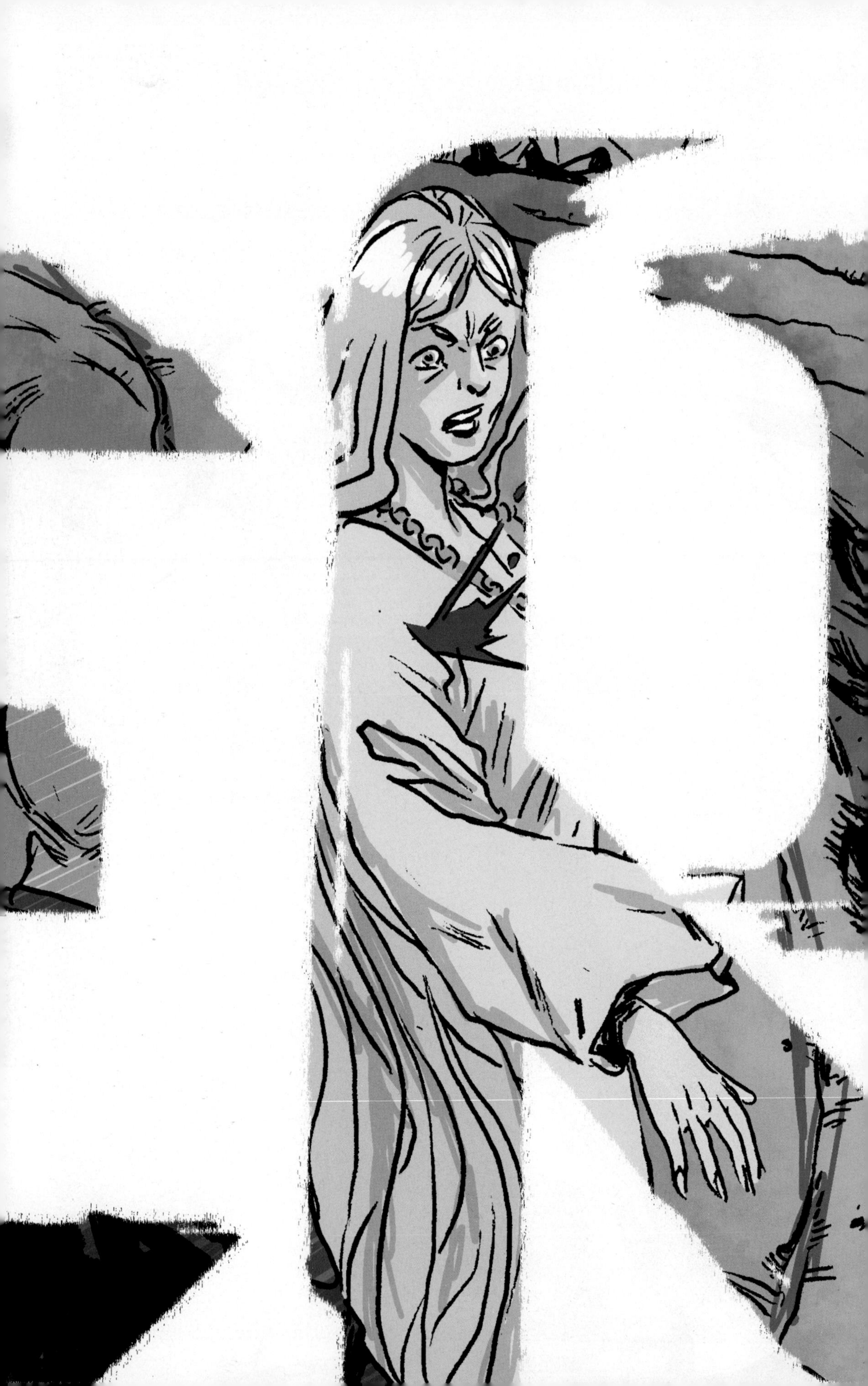

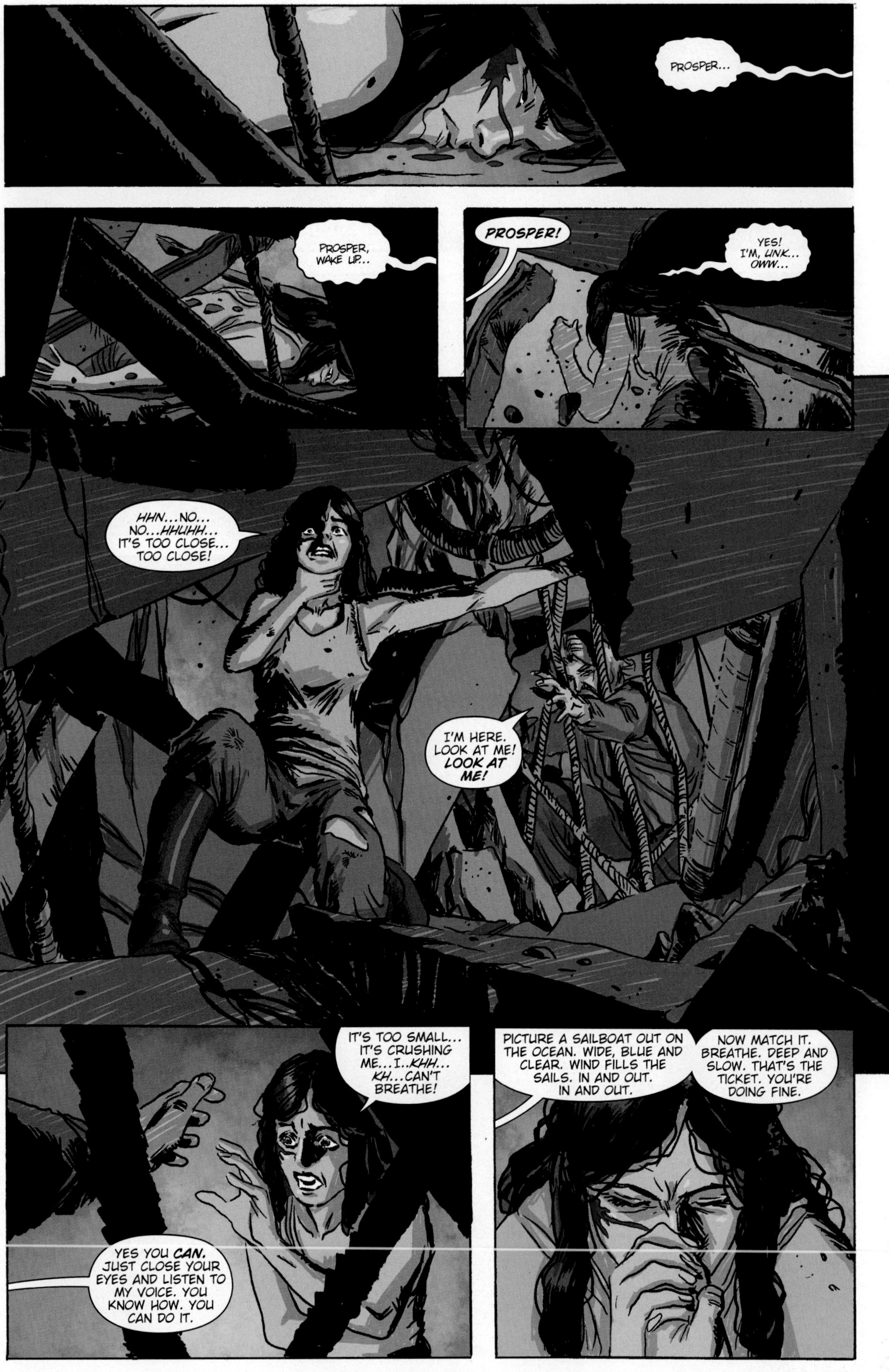
PROSPER...
PROSPER, WAKE UP...
PROSPER!
YES! I'M, LINK... OWW...
HHN...NO... NO...HHUHH... IT'S TOO CLOSE... TOO CLOSE!
I'M HERE. LOOK AT ME! LOOK AT ME!
IT'S TOO SMALL... IT'S CRUSHING ME...I..KHH... KH...CAN'T BREATHE!
YES YOU CAN. JUST CLOSE YOUR EYES AND LISTEN TO MY VOICE. YOU KNOW HOW. YOU CAN DO IT.
PICTURE A SAILBOAT OUT ON THE OCEAN. WIDE, BLUE AND CLEAR. WIND FILLS THE SAILS. IN AND OUT. IN AND OUT.
NOW MATCH IT. BREATHE. DEEP AND SLOW. THAT'S THE TICKET. YOU'RE DOING FINE.

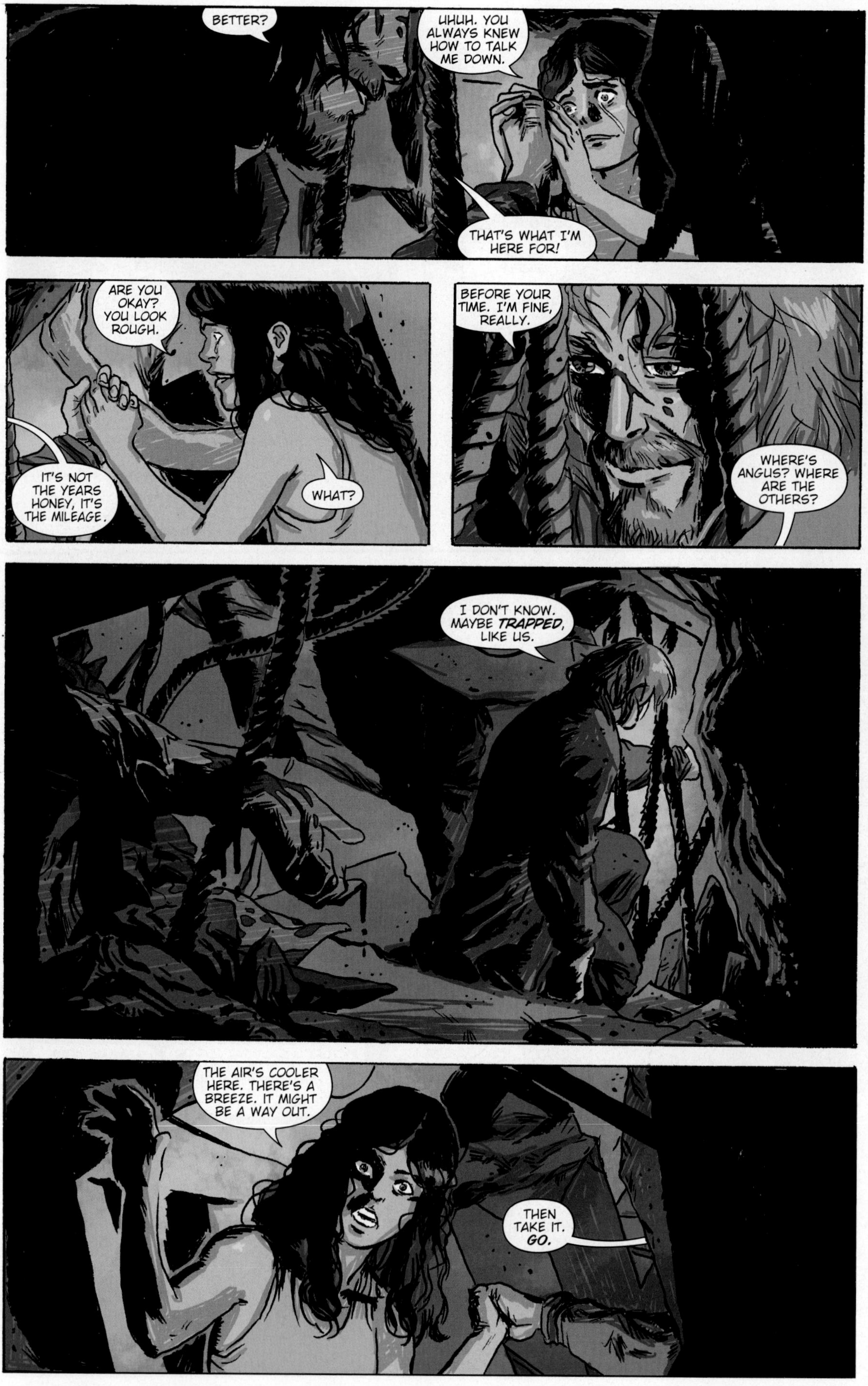
BETTER?
UHUH. YOU ALWAYS KNEW HOW TO TALK ME DOWN.
THAT'S WHAT I'M HERE FOR!
ARE YOU OKAY? YOU LOOK ROUGH.
IT'S NOT THE YEARS HONEY, IT'S THE MILEAGE.
WHAT?
BEFORE YOUR TIME. I'M FINE, REALLY.
WHERE'S ANGUS? WHERE ARE THE OTHERS?
I DON'T KNOW. MAYBE TRAPPED, LIKE US.
THE AIR'S COOLER HERE. THERE'S A BREEZE. IT MIGHT BE A WAY OUT.
THEN TAKE IT. GO.

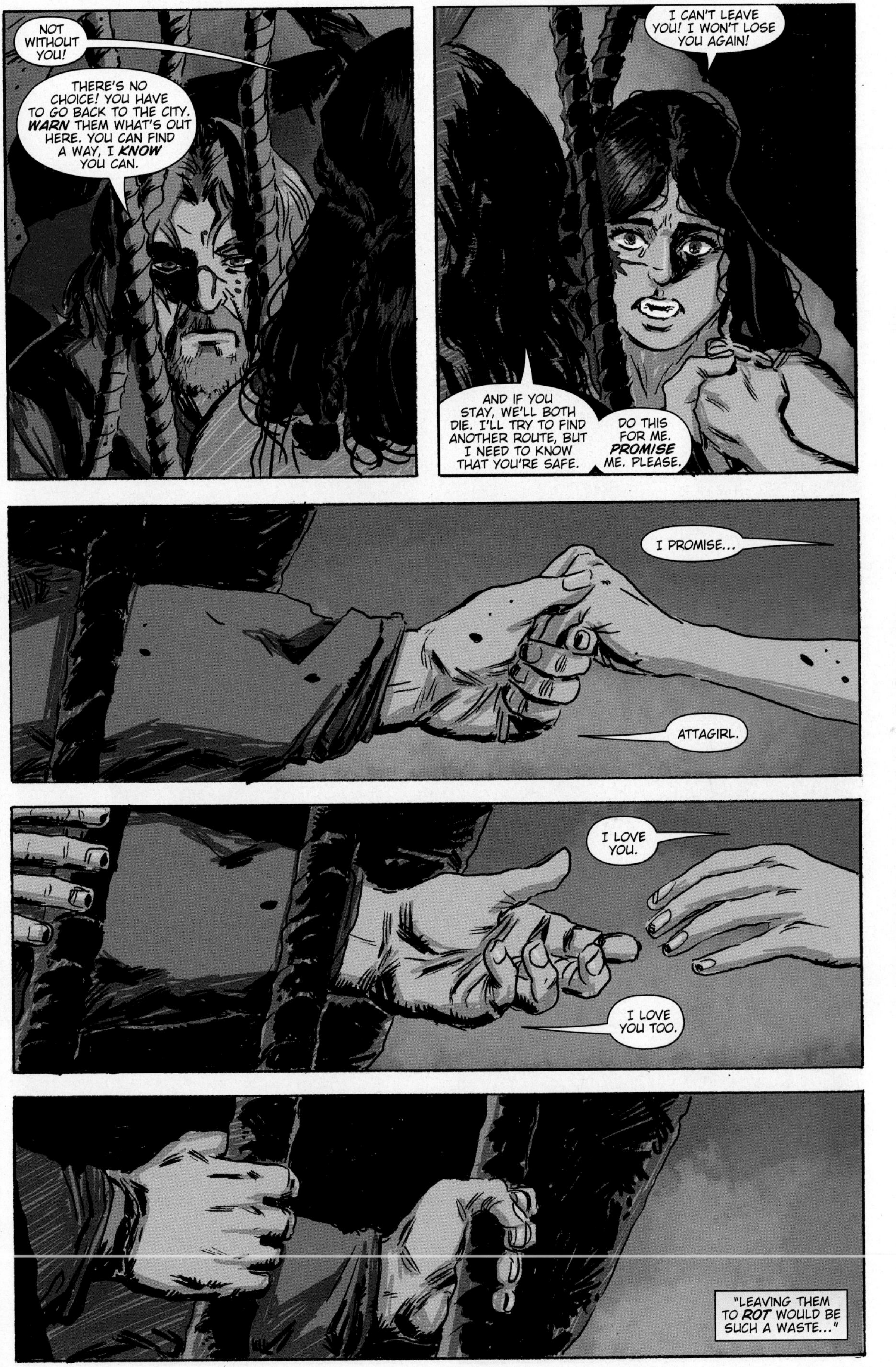
NOT WITHOUT YOU!
THERE'S NO CHOICE! YOU HAVE TO GO BACK TO THE CITY. WARN THEM WHAT'S OUT HERE. YOU CAN FIND A WAY, I KNOW YOU CAN.
I CAN'T LEAVE YOU! I WON'T LOSE YOU AGAIN!
AND IF YOU STAY, WE'LL BOTH DIE. I'LL TRY TO FIND ANOTHER ROUTE, BUT I NEED TO KNOW THAT YOU'RE SAFE.
DO THIS FOR ME. PROMISE ME. PLEASE.
I PROMISE...
ATTAGIRL.
I LOVE YOU.
I LOVE YOU TOO.
"LEAVING THEM TO ROT WOULD BE SUCH A WASTE..."

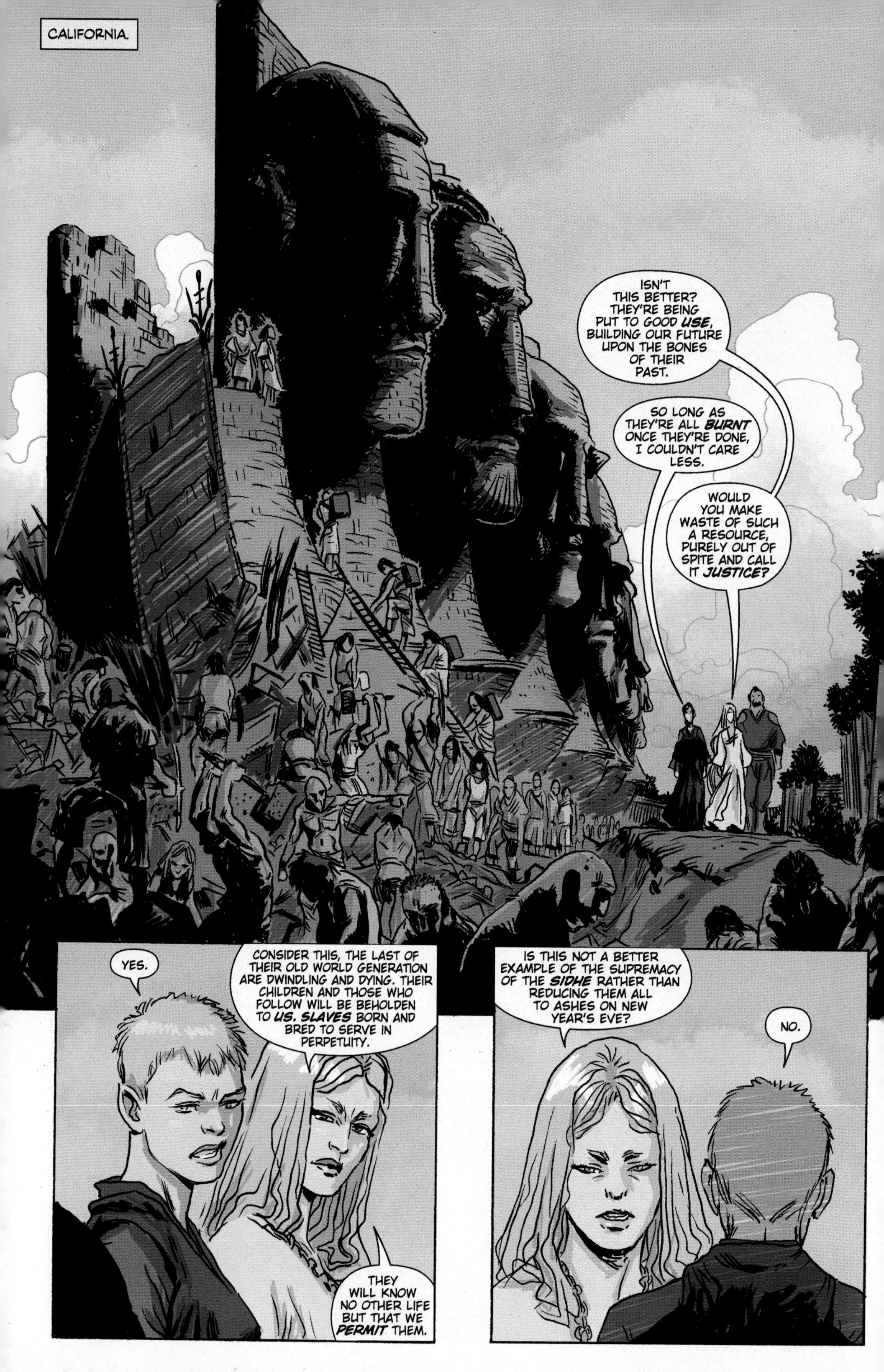
CALIFORNIA.
ISN'T THIS BETTER? THEY'RE BEING PUT TO GOOD USE, BUILDING OUR FUTURE UPON THE BONES OF THEIR PAST.
SO LONG AS THEY'RE ALL BURNT ONCE THEY'RE DONE, I COULDN'T CARE LESS.
WOULD YOU MAKE WASTE OF SUCH A RESOURCE, PURELY OUT OF SPITE AND CALL IT JUSTICE?
YES.
CONSIDER THIS, THE LAST OF THEIR OLD WORLD GENERATION ARE DWINDLING AND DYING. THEIR CHILDREN AND THOSE WHO FOLLOW WILL BE BEHOLDEN TO US. SLAVES BORN AND BRED TO SERVE IN PERPETUITY.
THEY WILL KNOW NO OTHER LIFE BUT THAT WE PERMIT THEM.
IS THIS NOT A BETTER EXAMPLE OF THE SUPREMACY OF THE SIDHE RATHER THAN REDUCING THEM ALL TO ASHES ON NEW YEAR'S EVE?
NO.

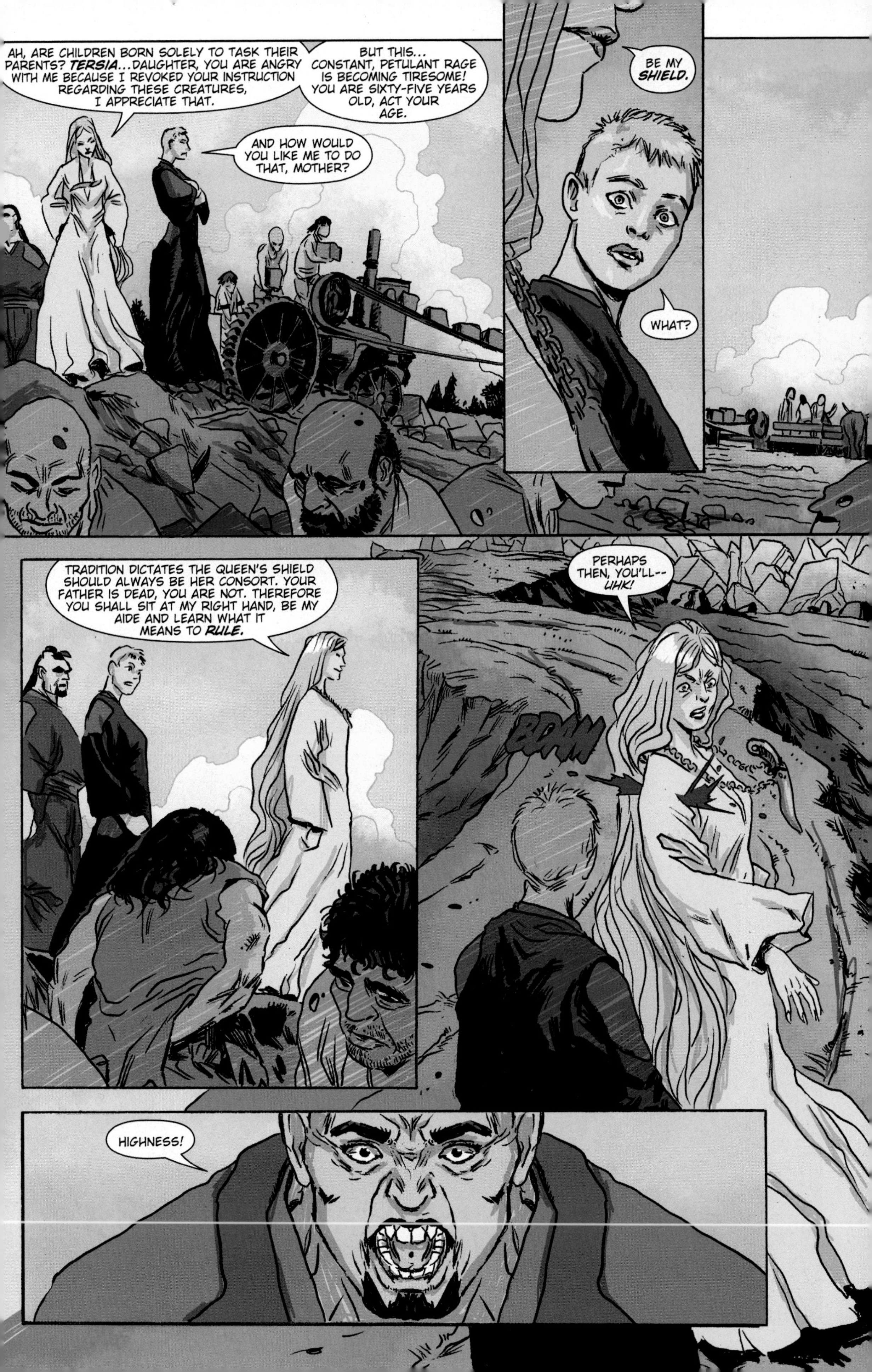
AH, ARE CHILDREN BORN SOLELY TO TASK THEIR PARENTS? *TERSIA*...DAUGHTER, YOU ARE ANGRY WITH ME BECAUSE I REVOKED YOUR INSTRUCTION REGARDING THESE CREATURES, I APPRECIATE THAT.
BUT THIS... CONSTANT, PETULANT RAGE IS BECOMING TIRESOME! YOU ARE SIXTY-FIVE YEARS OLD, ACT YOUR AGE.
AND HOW WOULD YOU LIKE ME TO DO THAT, MOTHER?
BE MY *SHIELD.*
WHAT?
TRADITION DICTATES THE QUEEN'S SHIELD SHOULD ALWAYS BE HER CONSORT. YOUR FATHER IS DEAD, YOU ARE NOT. THEREFORE YOU SHALL SIT AT MY RIGHT HAND, BE MY AIDE AND LEARN WHAT IT MEANS TO *RULE.*
PERHAPS THEN, YOU'LL-- *UHK!*
BLAM
HIGHNESS!

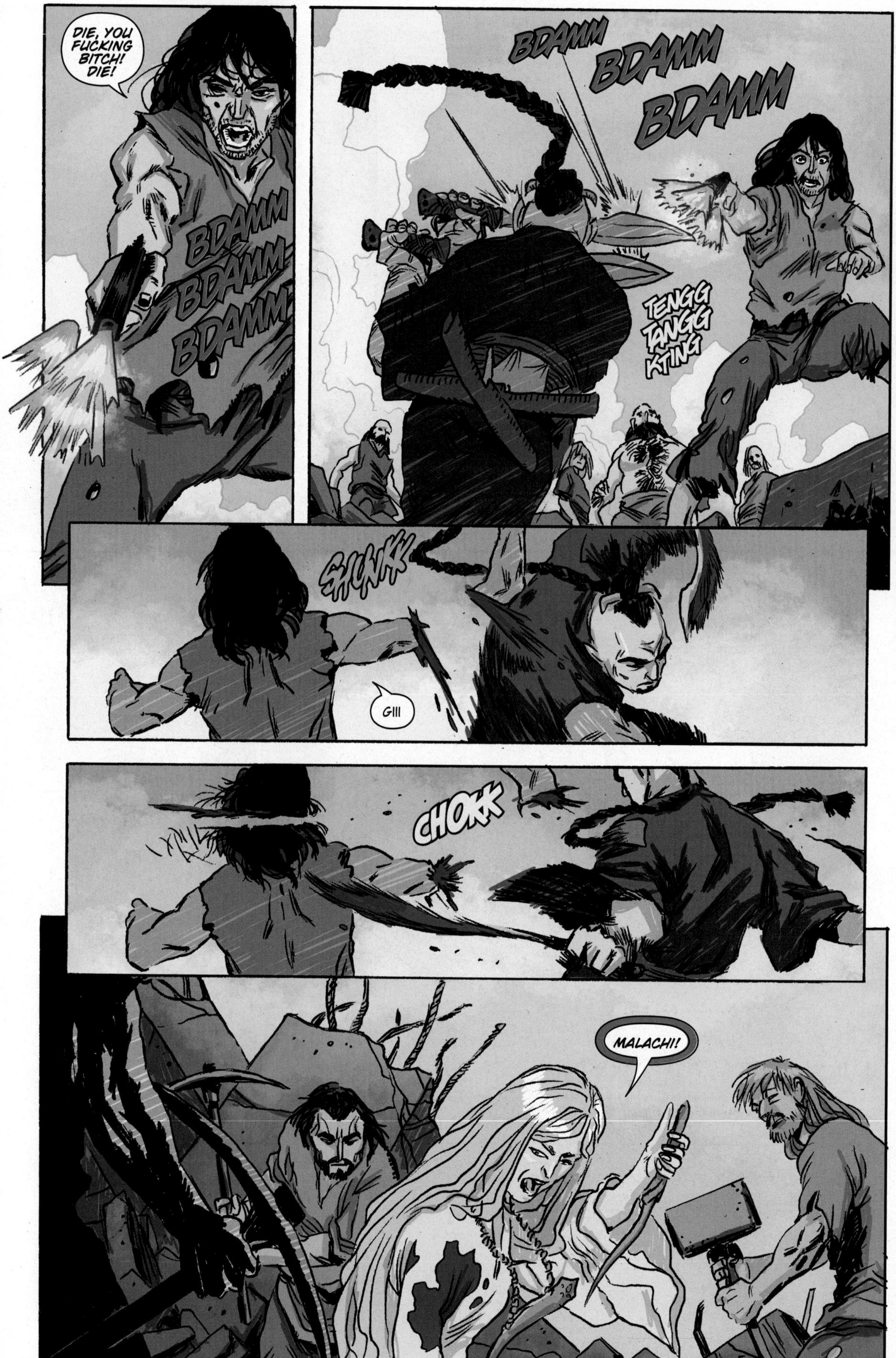
DIE, YOU FUCKING BITCH! DIE!
BDAMM
BDAMM
BDAMM
BDAMM
BDAMM
BDAMM
TENGG
TANGG
KTING
SHUNK
GIII
CHOKK
MALACHI!

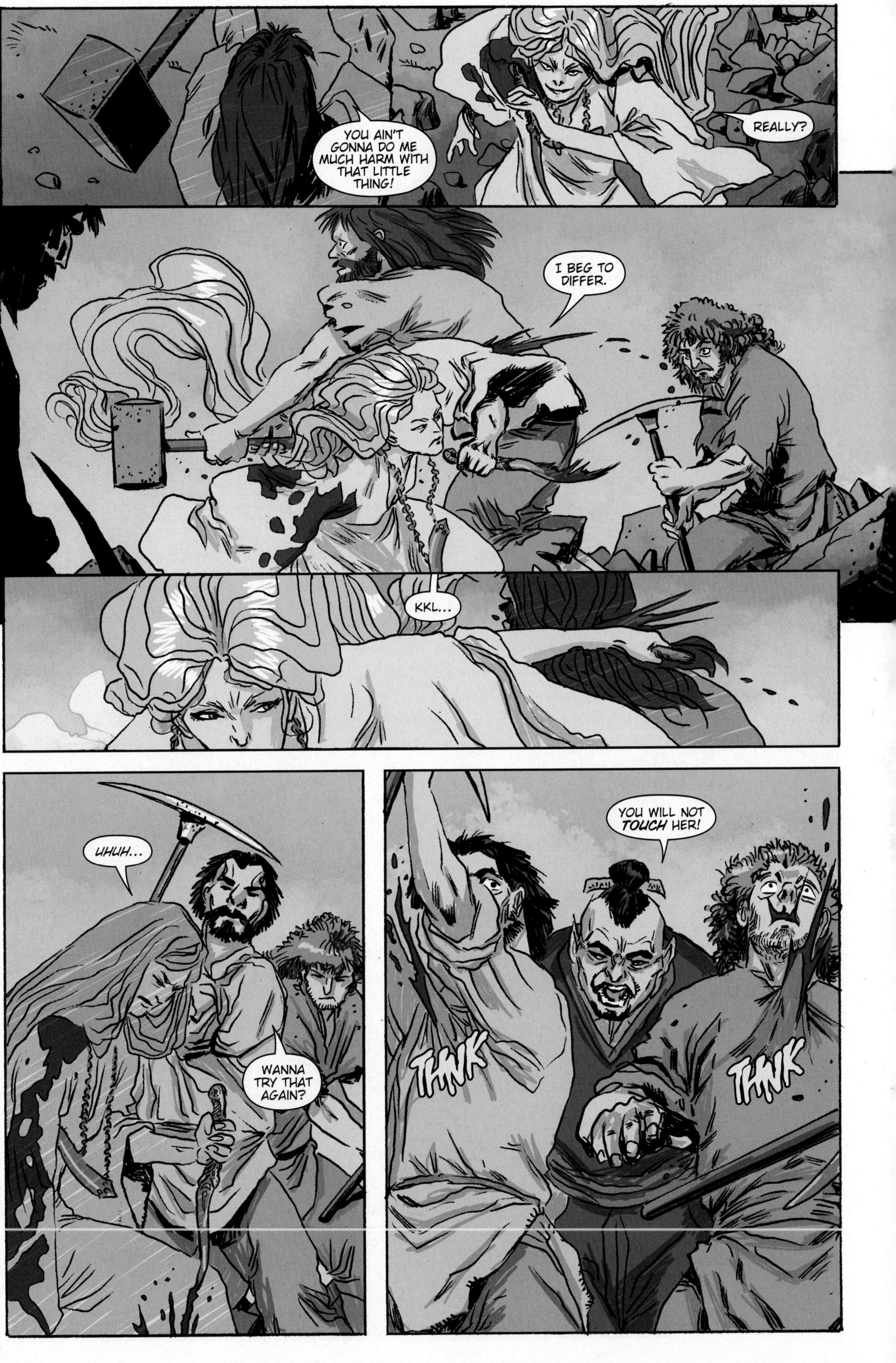
YOU AIN'T GONNA DO ME MUCH HARM WITH THAT LITTLE THING!
REALLY?
I BEG TO DIFFER.
KKL...
UHUH...
WANNA TRY THAT AGAIN?
YOU WILL NOT *TOUCH* HER!
THNK
THNK

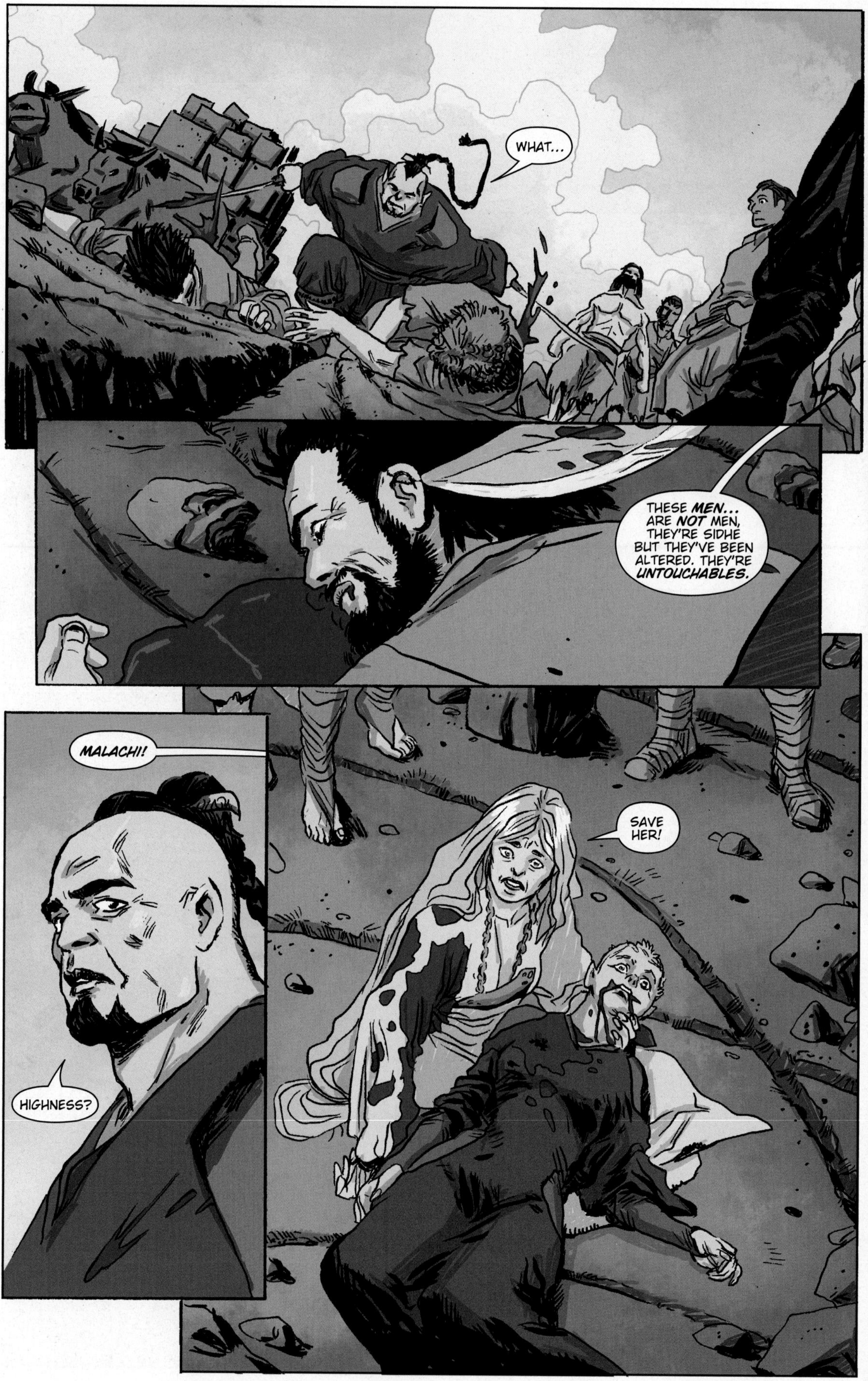
WHAT...
THESE *MEN*... ARE *NOT* MEN, THEY'RE SIDHE BUT THEY'VE BEEN ALTERED. THEY'RE *UNTOUCHABLES.*
MALACHI!
HIGHNESS?
SAVE HER!

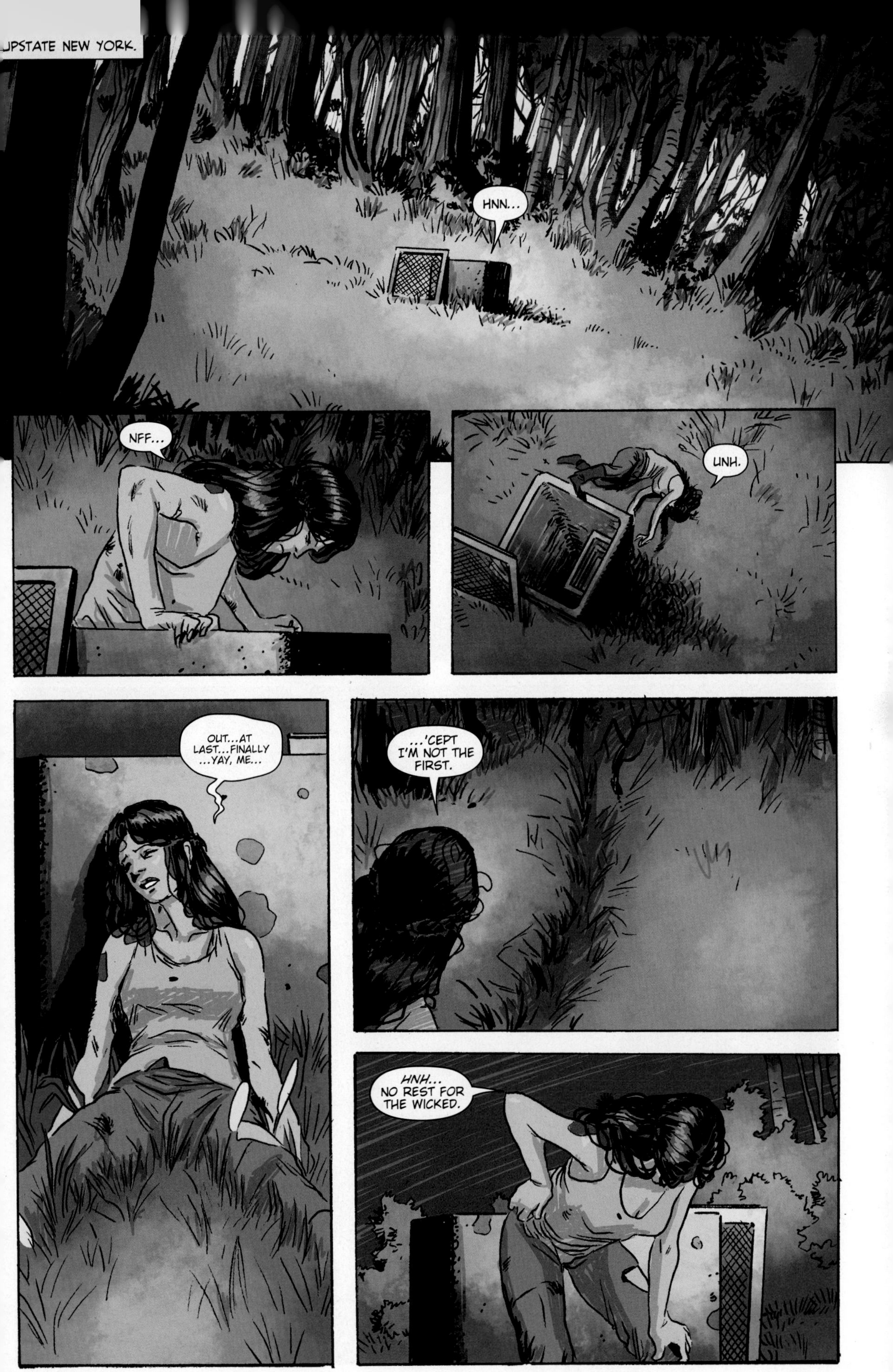
UPSTATE NEW YORK.
HNN...
NFF...
UNH.
OUT...AT LAST...FINALLY ...YAY, ME...
...'CEPT I'M NOT THE FIRST.
HNH... NO REST FOR THE WICKED.

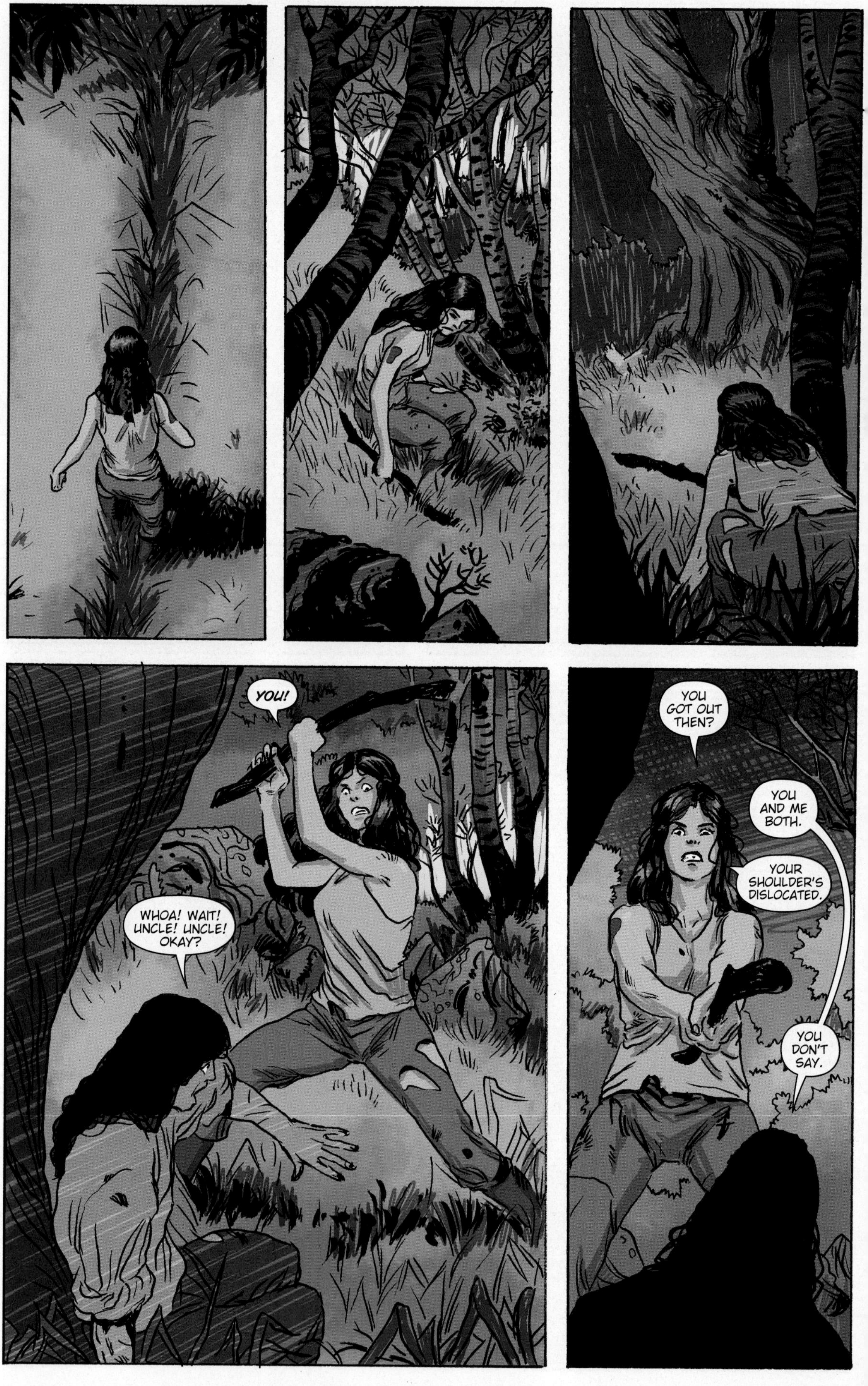
YOU!
WHOA! WAIT! UNCLE! UNCLE! OKAY?
YOU GOT OUT THEN?
YOU AND ME BOTH.
YOUR SHOULDER'S DISLOCATED.
YOU DON'T SAY.

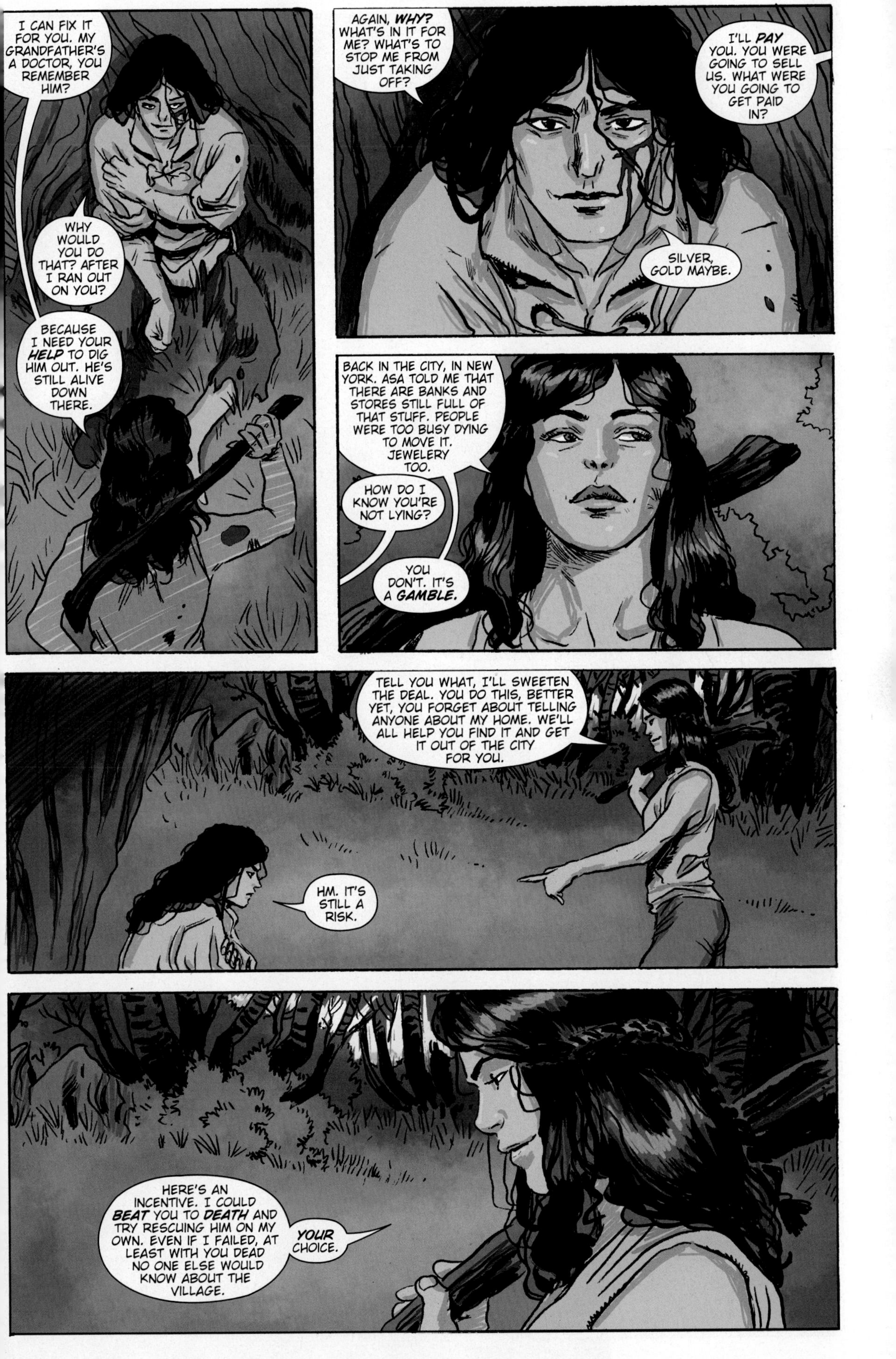
I CAN FIX IT FOR YOU. MY GRANDFATHER'S A DOCTOR, YOU REMEMBER HIM?
WHY WOULD YOU DO THAT? AFTER I RAN OUT ON YOU?
BECAUSE I NEED YOUR HELP TO DIG HIM OUT. HE'S STILL ALIVE DOWN THERE.
AGAIN, WHY? WHAT'S IN IT FOR ME? WHAT'S TO STOP ME FROM JUST TAKING OFF?
I'LL PAY YOU. YOU WERE GOING TO SELL US. WHAT WERE YOU GOING TO GET PAID IN?
SILVER, GOLD MAYBE.
BACK IN THE CITY, IN NEW YORK. ASA TOLD ME THAT THERE ARE BANKS AND STORES STILL FULL OF THAT STUFF. PEOPLE WERE TOO BUSY DYING TO MOVE IT. JEWELERY TOO.
HOW DO I KNOW YOU'RE NOT LYING?
YOU DON'T. IT'S A GAMBLE.
TELL YOU WHAT, I'LL SWEETEN THE DEAL. YOU DO THIS, BETTER YET, YOU FORGET ABOUT TELLING ANYONE ABOUT MY HOME. WE'LL ALL HELP YOU FIND IT AND GET IT OUT OF THE CITY FOR YOU.
HM. IT'S STILL A RISK.
HERE'S AN INCENTIVE. I COULD BEAT YOU TO DEATH AND TRY RESCUING HIM ON MY OWN. EVEN IF I FAILED, AT LEAST WITH YOU DEAD NO ONE ELSE WOULD KNOW ABOUT THE VILLAGE.
YOUR CHOICE.

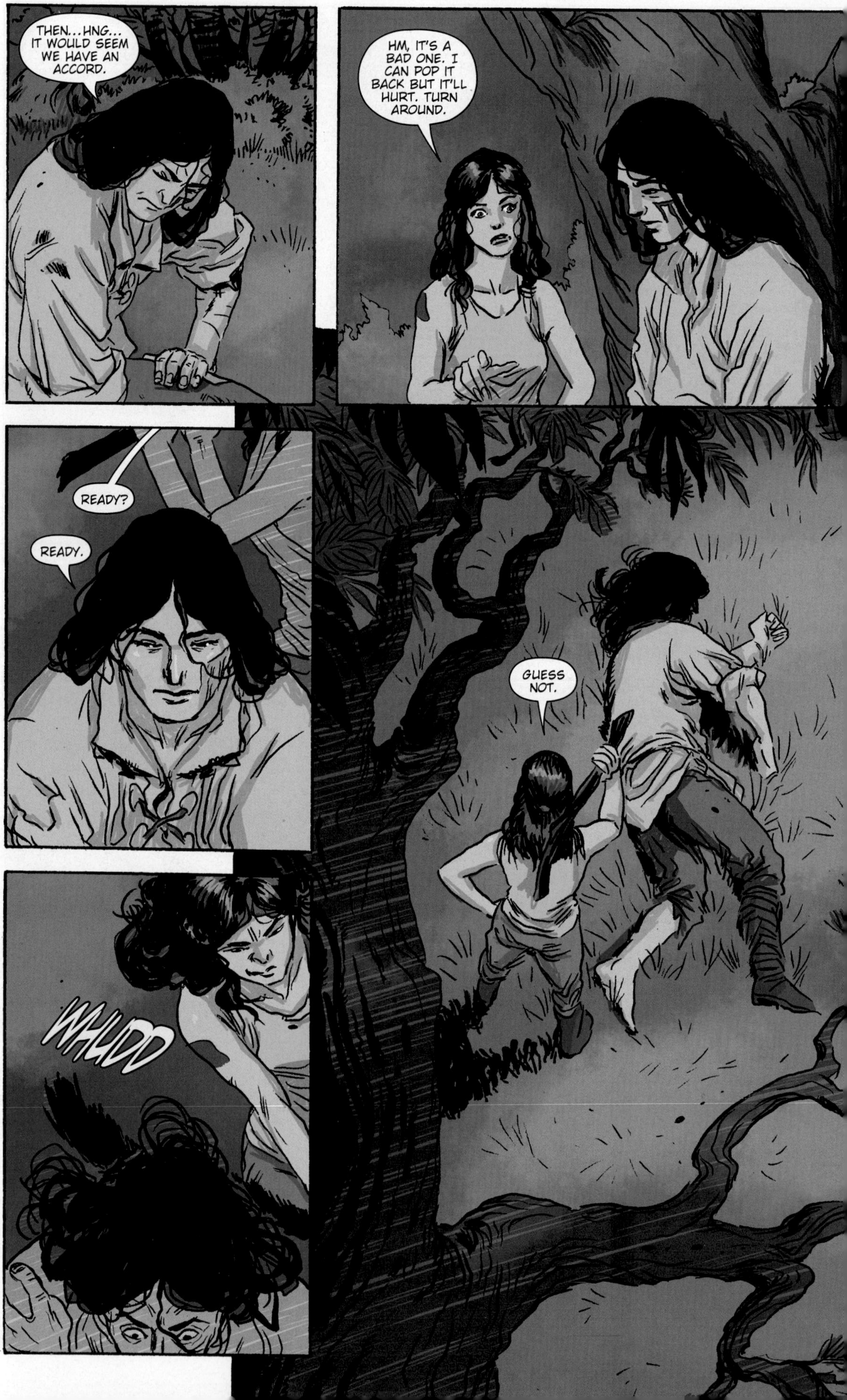
THEN...HNG... IT WOULD SEEM WE HAVE AN ACCORD.
HM, IT'S A BAD ONE. I CAN POP IT BACK BUT IT'LL HURT. TURN AROUND.
READY?
READY.
WHUDD
GUESS NOT.

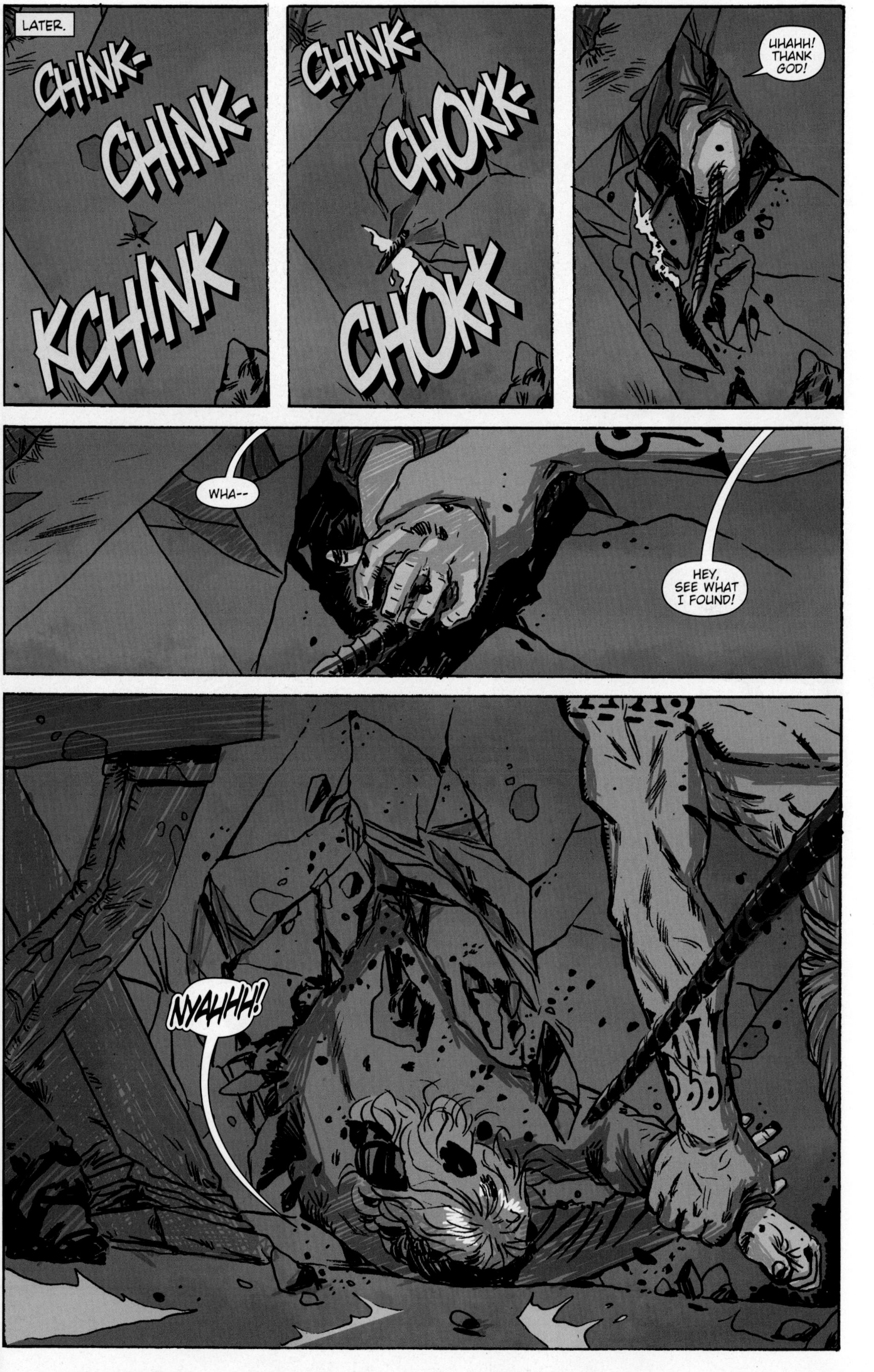
LATER.
CHINK-
CHINK-
KCHINK
CHINK-
CHOKK-
CHOKK
UHAHH! THANK GOD!
WHA--
HEY, SEE WHAT I FOUND!
NYAHHH!

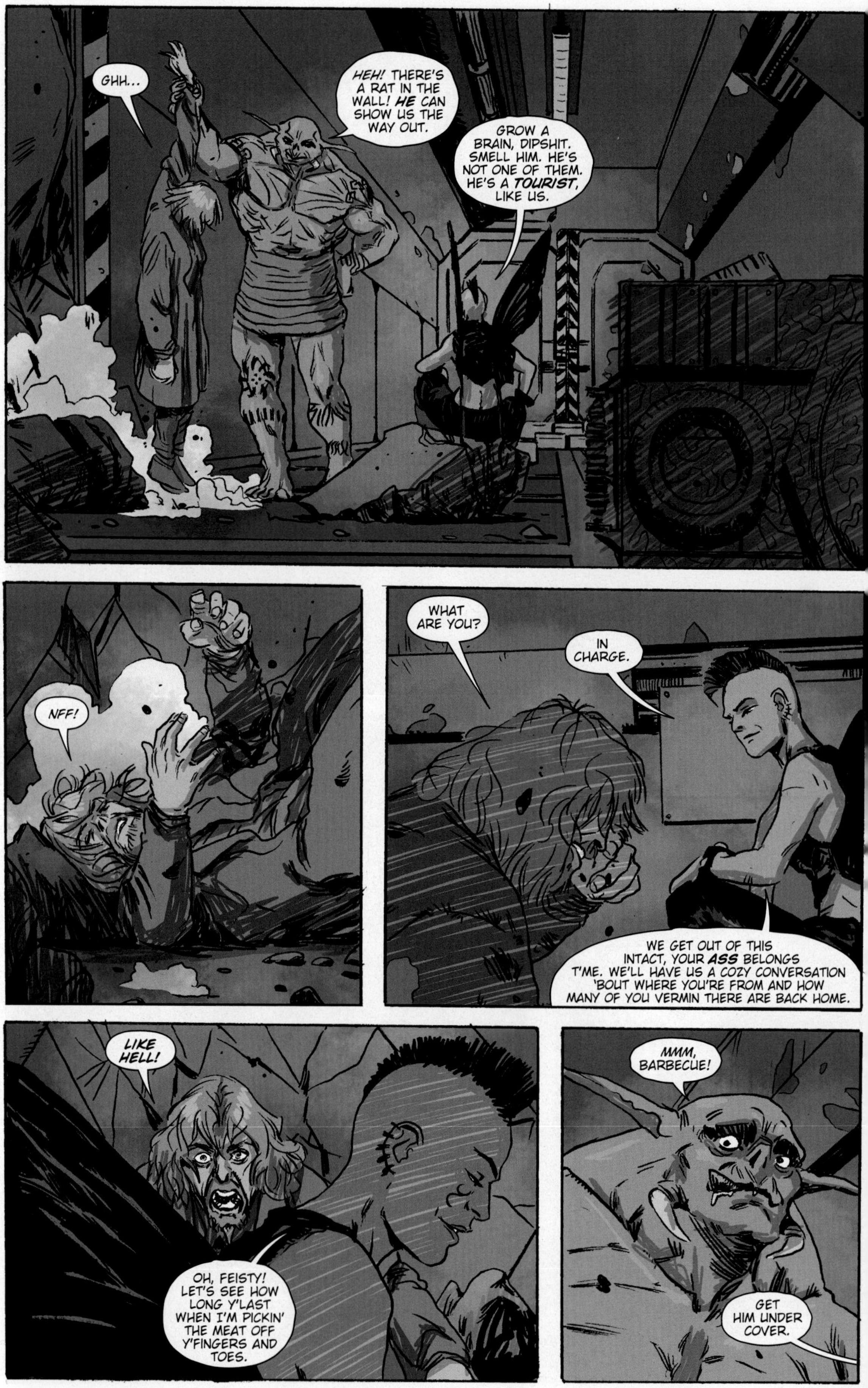
GHH...
HEH! THERE'S A RAT IN THE WALL! HE CAN SHOW US THE WAY OUT.
GROW A BRAIN, DIPSHIT. SMELL HIM. HE'S NOT ONE OF THEM. HE'S A TOURIST, LIKE US.
NFF!
WHAT ARE YOU?
IN CHARGE.
WE GET OUT OF THIS INTACT, YOUR ASS BELONGS T'ME. WE'LL HAVE US A COZY CONVERSATION 'BOUT WHERE YOU'RE FROM AND HOW MANY OF YOU VERMIN THERE ARE BACK HOME.
LIKE HELL!
OH, FEISTY! LET'S SEE HOW LONG Y'LAST WHEN I'M PICKIN' THE MEAT OFF Y'FINGERS AND TOES.
MMM, BARBECUE!
GET HIM UNDER COVER.

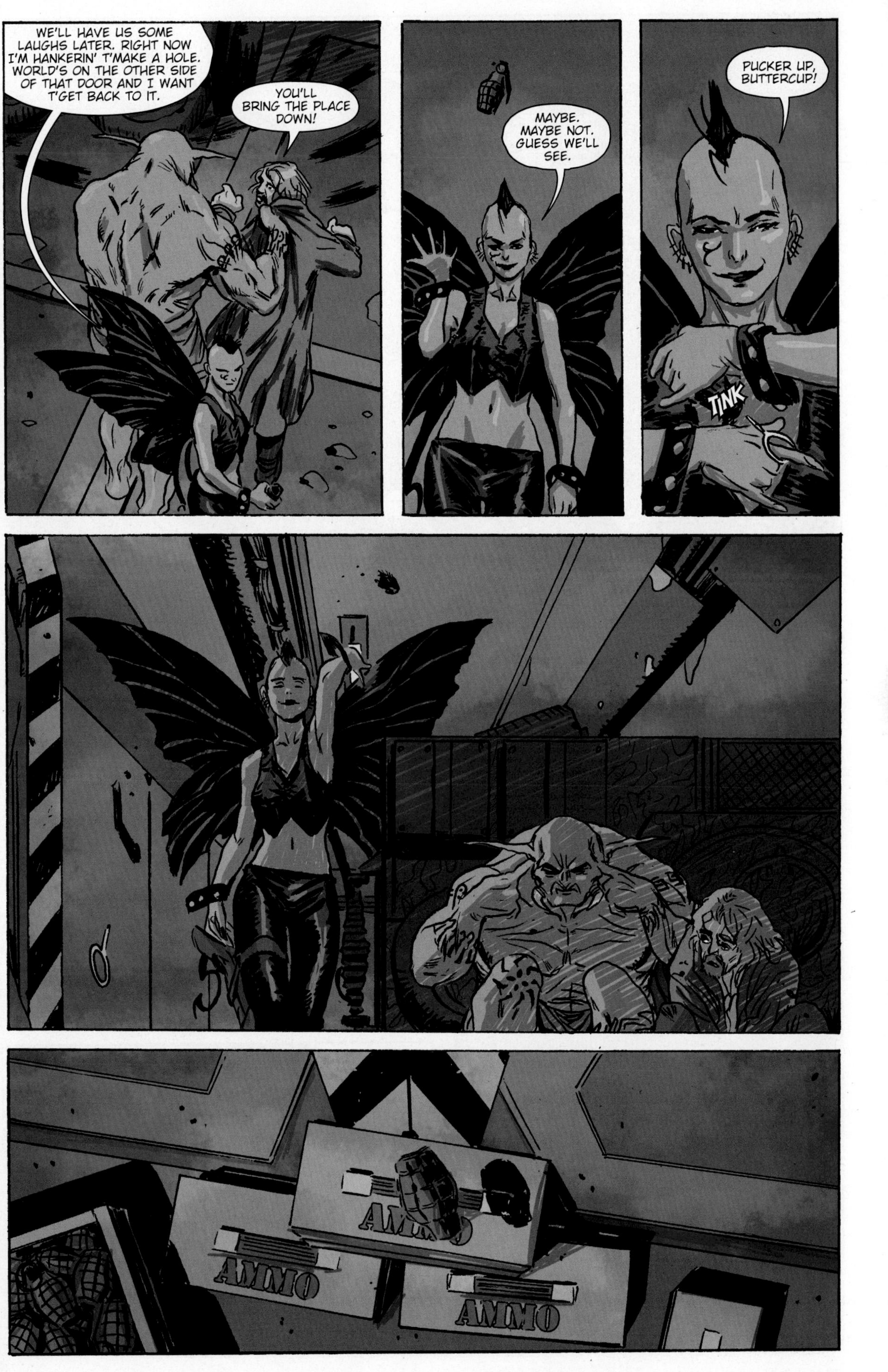
WE'LL HAVE US SOME LAUGHS LATER. RIGHT NOW I'M HANKERIN' T'MAKE A HOLE. WORLD'S ON THE OTHER SIDE OF THAT DOOR AND I WANT T'GET BACK TO IT.
YOU'LL BRING THE PLACE DOWN!
MAYBE. MAYBE NOT. GUESS WE'LL SEE.
PUCKER UP, BUTTERCUP!
TINK
AMMO
AMMO
AMMO

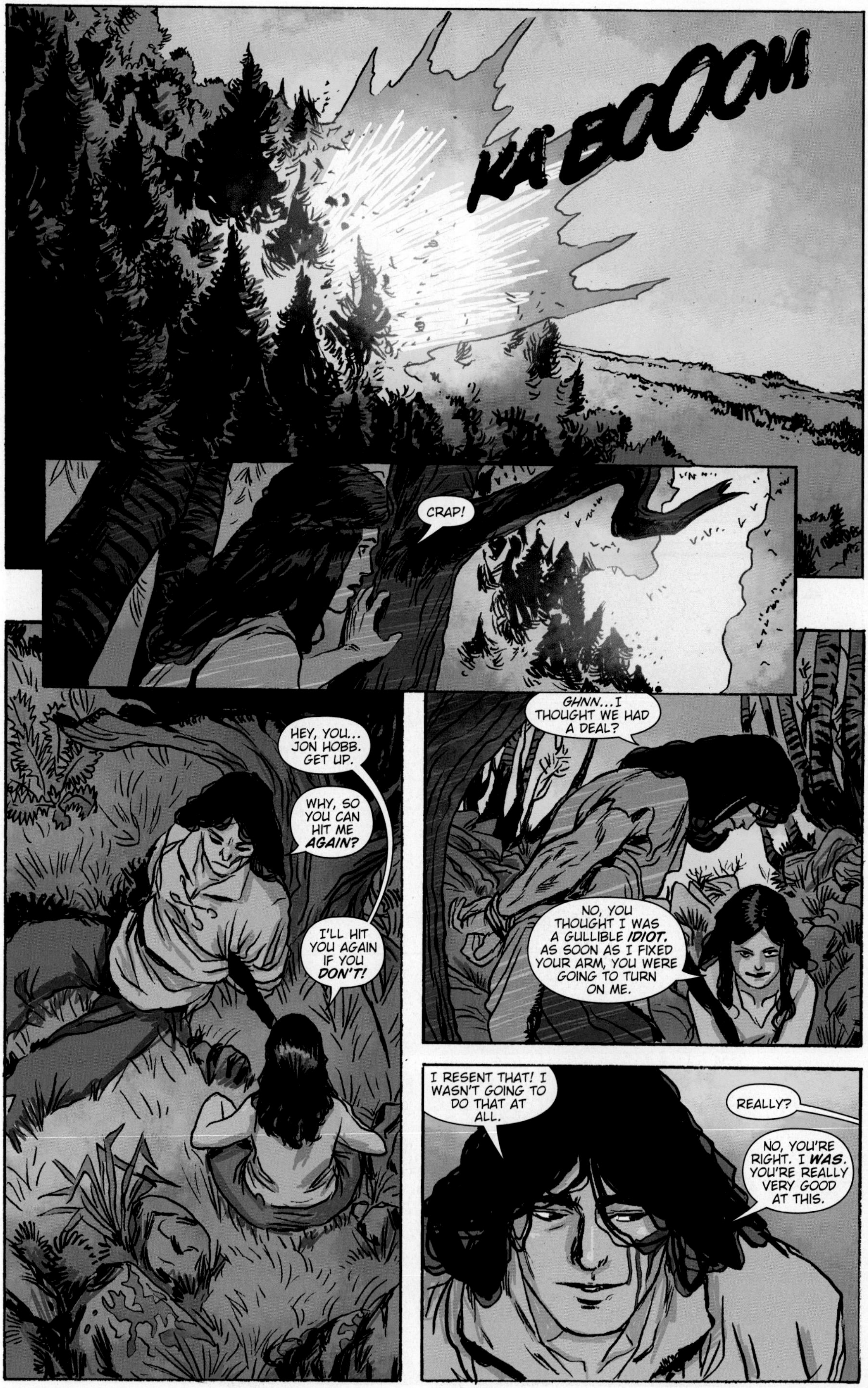
KA'BOOOOM
CRAP!
HEY, YOU... JON HOBB. GET UP.
WHY, SO YOU CAN HIT ME AGAIN?
I'LL HIT YOU AGAIN IF YOU DON'T!
GHNN...I THOUGHT WE HAD A DEAL?
NO, YOU THOUGHT I WAS A GULLIBLE IDIOT. AS SOON AS I FIXED YOUR ARM, YOU WERE GOING TO TURN ON ME.
I RESENT THAT! I WASN'T GOING TO DO THAT AT ALL.
REALLY?
NO, YOU'RE RIGHT. I WAS. YOU'RE REALLY VERY GOOD AT THIS.

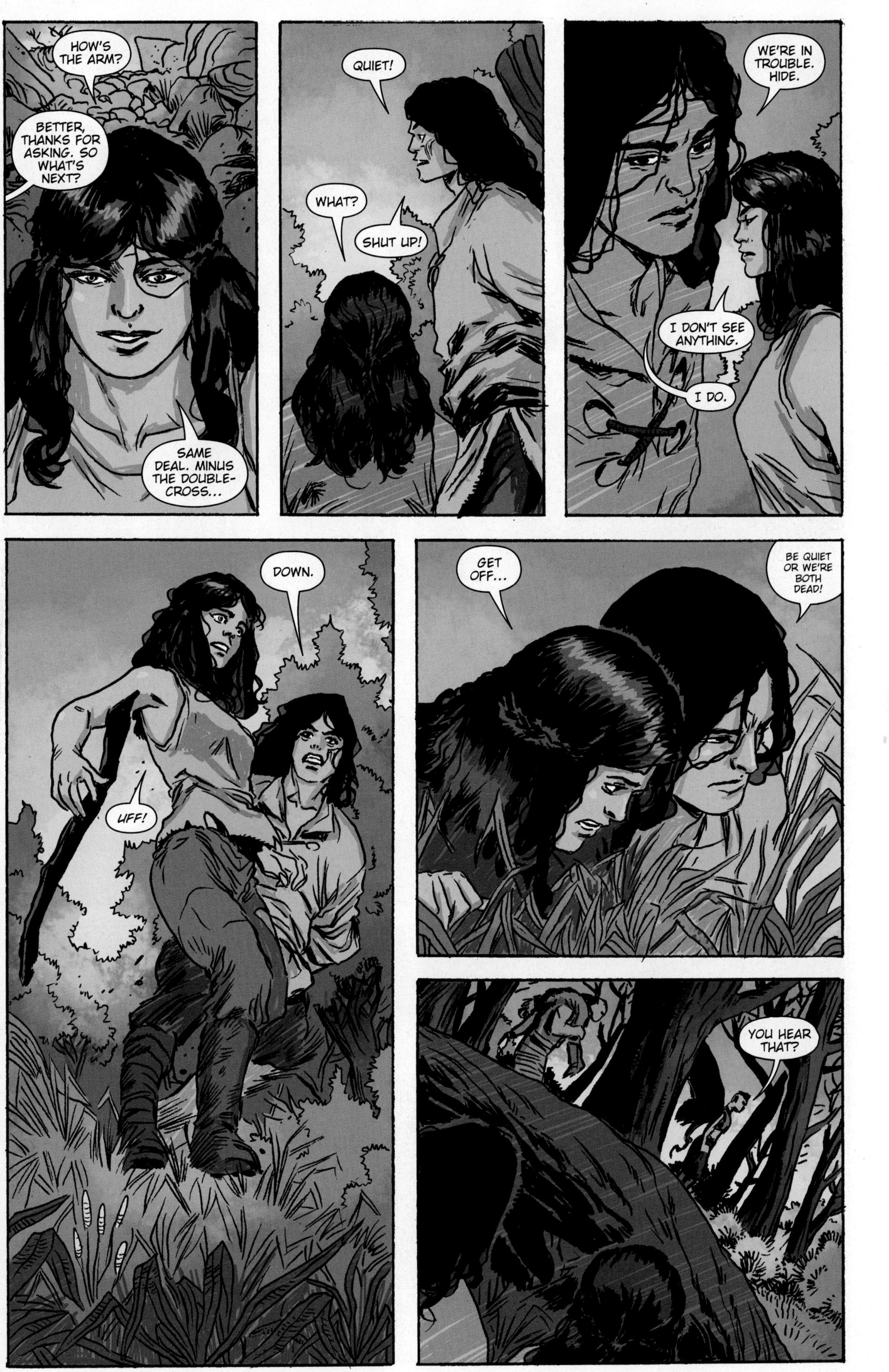
HOW'S THE ARM?
BETTER, THANKS FOR ASKING. SO WHAT'S NEXT?
SAME DEAL. MINUS THE DOUBLE-CROSS...
QUIET!
WHAT?
SHUT UP!
WE'RE IN TROUBLE. HIDE.
I DON'T SEE ANYTHING.
I DO.
DOWN.
UFF!
GET OFF...
BE QUIET OR WE'RE BOTH DEAD!
YOU HEAR THAT?

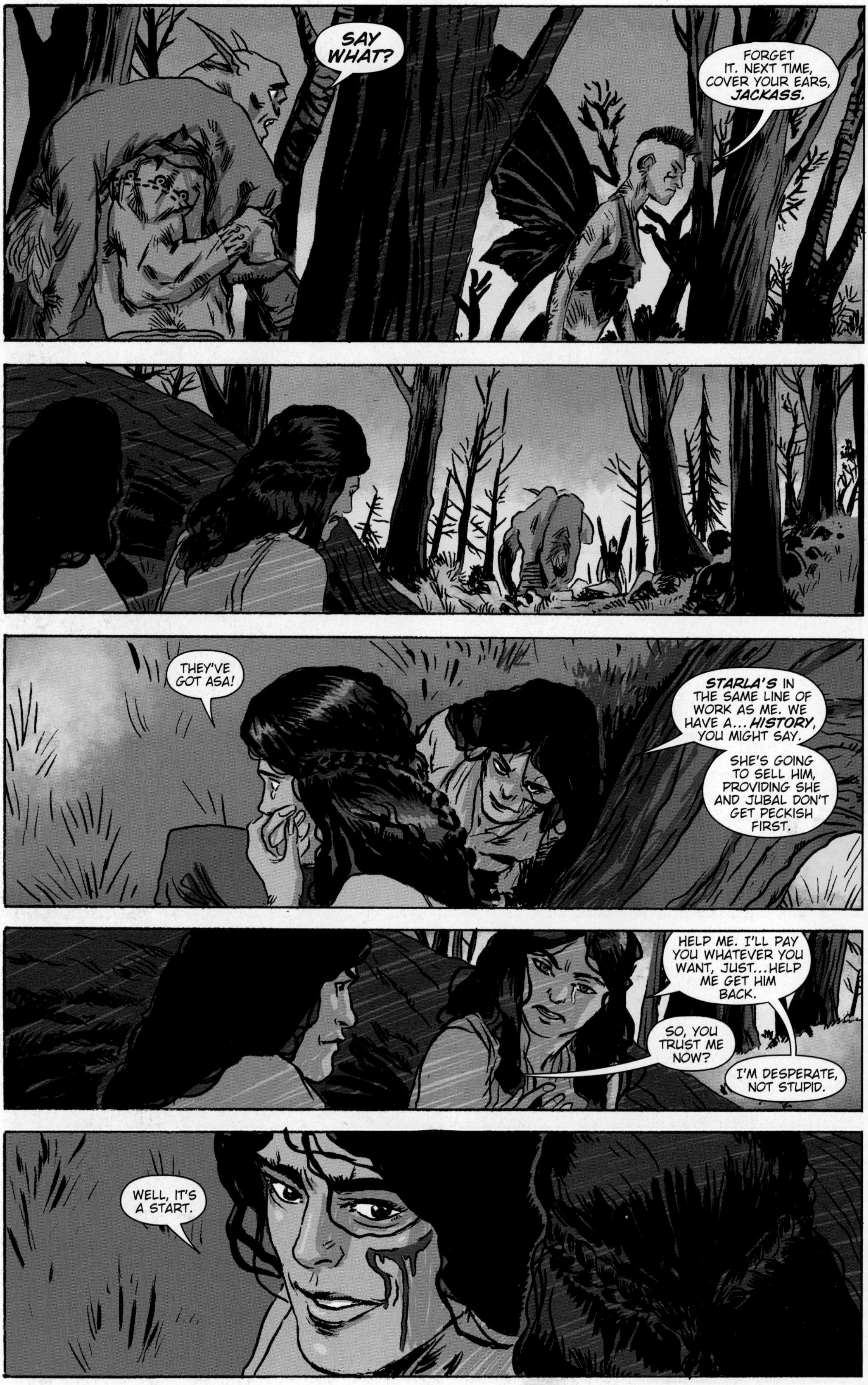
SAY WHAT?
FORGET IT. NEXT TIME, COVER YOUR EARS, JACKASS.
THEY'VE GOT ASA!
STARLA'S IN THE SAME LINE OF WORK AS ME. WE HAVE A...HISTORY, YOU MIGHT SAY.
SHE'S GOING TO SELL HIM, PROVIDING SHE AND JUBAL DON'T GET PECKISH FIRST.
HELP ME. I'LL PAY YOU WHATEVER YOU WANT, JUST...HELP ME GET HIM BACK.
SO, YOU TRUST ME NOW?
I'M DESPERATE, NOT STUPID.
WELL, IT'S A START.

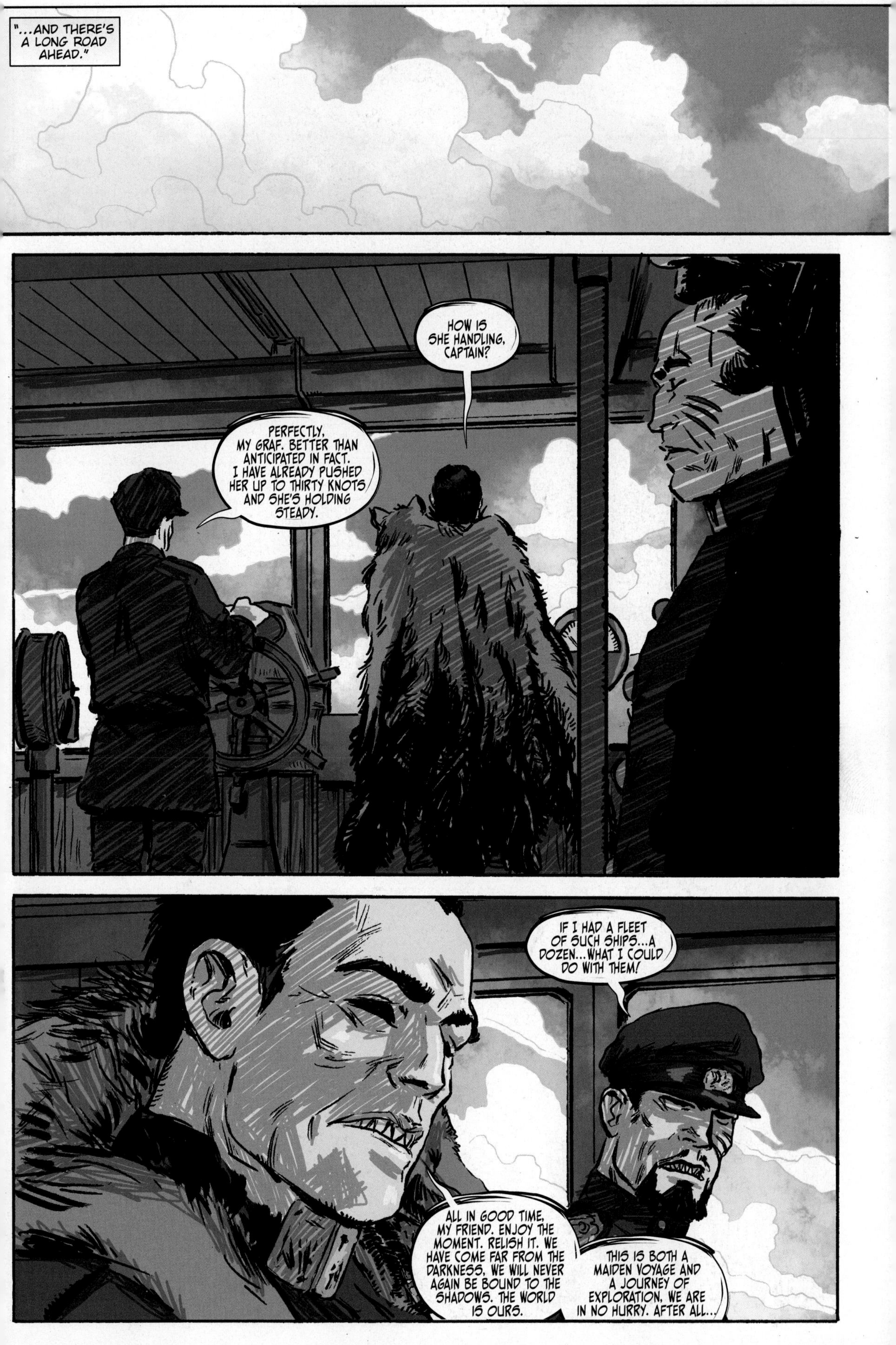
"...AND THERE'S A LONG ROAD AHEAD."
HOW IS SHE HANDLING, CAPTAIN?
PERFECTLY, MY GRAF. BETTER THAN ANTICIPATED IN FACT. I HAVE ALREADY PUSHED HER UP TO THIRTY KNOTS AND SHE'S HOLDING STEADY.
IF I HAD A FLEET OF SUCH SHIPS...A DOZEN...WHAT I COULD DO WITH THEM!
ALL IN GOOD TIME, MY FRIEND. ENJOY THE MOMENT. RELISH IT. WE HAVE COME FAR FROM THE DARKNESS. WE WILL NEVER AGAIN BE BOUND TO THE SHADOWS. THE WORLD IS OURS.
THIS IS BOTH A MAIDEN VOYAGE AND A JOURNEY OF EXPLORATION. WE ARE IN NO HURRY. AFTER ALL...

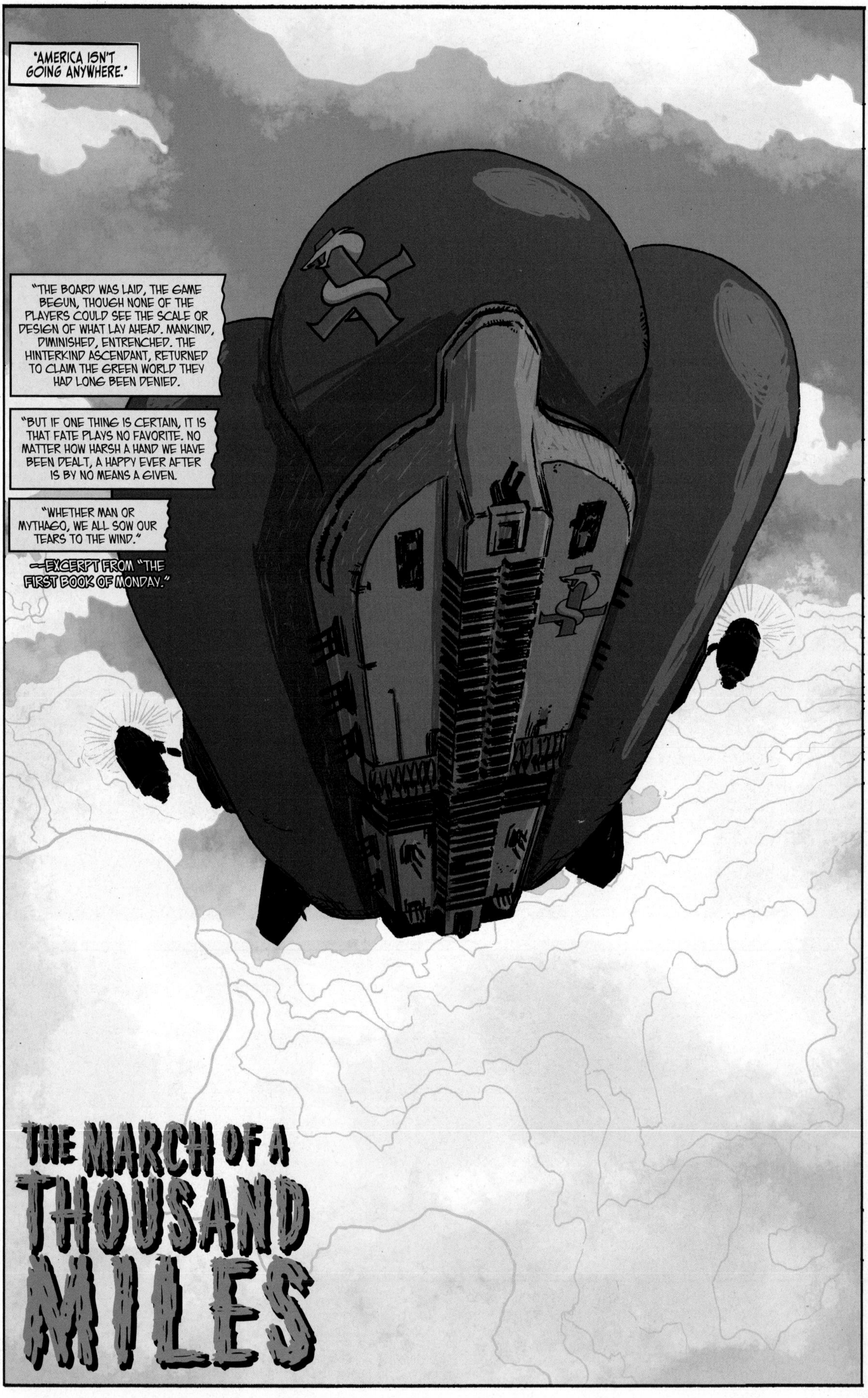
"AMERICA ISN'T GOING ANYWHERE."
"THE BOARD WAS LAID, THE GAME BEGUN, THOUGH NONE OF THE PLAYERS COULD SEE THE SCALE OR DESIGN OF WHAT LAY AHEAD. MANKIND, DIMINISHED, ENTRENCHED. THE HINTERKIND ASCENDANT, RETURNED TO CLAIM THE GREEN WORLD THEY HAD LONG BEEN DENIED.
"BUT IF ONE THING IS CERTAIN, IT IS THAT FATE PLAYS NO FAVORITE. NO MATTER HOW HARSH A HAND WE HAVE BEEN DEALT, A HAPPY EVER AFTER IS BY NO MEANS A GIVEN.
"WHETHER MAN OR MYTHAGO, WE ALL SOW OUR TEARS TO THE WIND."
--EXCERPT FROM "THE FIRST BOOK OF MONDAY."
THE MARCH OF A THOUSAND MILES